FOX NEWS AND AMERICAN POLITICS

D1594588

"Dan Cassino expands our understanding of Fox News' impact on what Americans know about politics and how they respond to political events. Particularly fascinating is the way Prof. Cassino documents Fox's impact on the 2012 Republican nomination; the dramatic changes in the candidates' fortunes over time are much better understood by reading this book. But the bigger picture it paints is important as well: the influence of Fox News on American politics is not easily accounted for by simple media framing perspectives. Instead, as Prof. Cassino shows, Fox News not only sets agendas, but its coverage is also linked to measurable behaviors as the choices of what and how it covers politics seem to be able to move viewers with certain tendencies to action. This book will be a valuable addition to any reader's collection on media and public opinion."

David Redlawsk, *Professor of Political Science, Rutgers University*

In recent years, scholars have argued that the ability of people to choose which channel they want to watch means that television news is just preaching to the choir, and doesn't change any minds. However, this book shows that the media still has an enormous direct impact on American society and politics.

While past research has emphasized the indirect effects of media content on attitudes – through priming or framing, for instance – Dan Cassino argues that past data on both the public opinion and the media sides wasn't detailed enough to uncover it. Using a combination of original national surveys, large-scale content analysis of news coverage along with data sets as disparate as FBI gun background checks and campaign contribution records, Cassino discusses why it's important to treat different media sources separately, estimating levels of ideological bias for television media sources as well as the differences in the topics the various media sources cover. Taking this into account proves that exposure to some media sources can serve to actually make Americans less knowledgeable about current affairs, and more likely to buy into conspiracy theories.

Even in an era of declining viewership, the media – especially Fox News – is shaping our society and our politics. This book documents how this is happening, and shows the consequences for Americans. The quality of journalism is more than an academic question: when coverage focuses on questionable topics, or political bias, there are consequences.

Dan Cassino is Associate Professor of Political Science at Fairleigh Dickinson University and Director of Experimental Research for the PublicMind poll. He conducts research on American politics and political psychology.

Routledge Studies in Political Psychology
Edited by Howard Lavine, University of Minnesota

Advisory Board: Ted Brader, University of Michigan; Eugene Borgida, University of Minnesota; Marc Ross, Bryn Mawr College and Linda Skitka, University of Illinois, Chicago

Routledge Studies in Political Psychology was developed to publish books representing the widest range of theoretical, methodological and epistemological approaches in political psychology. The series is intended to expand awareness of the creative application of psychological theory within the domain of politics and foster deeper appreciation of the psychological roots of political behavior.

FOX NEWS AND AMERICAN POLITICS

How One Channel Shapes
American Politics and Society

Dan Cassino

Routledge
Taylor & Francis Group

NEW YORK AND LONDON

First published 2016
by Routledge
711 Third Avenue, New York, NY 10017

and by Routledge
2 Park Square, Milton Park, Abingdon, Oxon, OX14 4RN

Routledge is an imprint of the Taylor & Francis Group, an informa business

Library of Congress Cataloging in Publication Data
Names: Cassino, Dan, 1980- author.
Title: Fox News and American politics : how one channel shapes
    American politics and society / Dan Cassino.
Description: New York : Routledge, 2016. | Series: Routledge studies
    in political psychology ; 3 | Includes bibliographical references and
    index.
Identifiers: LCCN 2015043058 | ISBN 9781138900103 (hbk) |
    ISBN 9781138900127 (pbk)
Subjects: LCSH: Fox News. | Television and politics—United States. |
    Television broadcasting of news—United States.
Classification: LCC PN4888.T4 C37 2016 | DDC 070.4/30973—dc23
LC record available at http://lccn.loc.gov/2015043058

ISBN: 978-1-138-90010-3 (hbk)
ISBN: 978-1-138-90012-7 (pbk)
ISBN: 978-1-315-70748-8 (ebk)

Typeset in Bembo Std
by Swales & Willis Ltd, Exeter, Devon, UK

Printed and bound in the United States of America by Publishers Graphics,
LLC on sustainably sourced paper.

CONTENTS

ACKNOWLEDGMENTS

This book would not have been possible without the invaluable assistance of Roland Schatz, Ingo Buse, Racheline Maltese, and the rest of the Media Tenor team. Nor would it have been possible without the support of the Director of the PublicMind Poll, Dr. Krista Jenkins, and the support and mentorship of her predecessor in the position, Dr. Peter Woolley.

I would also like to thank the editor of the series, Dr. Howard Lavine, for his enormous help in shaping the manuscript, as well as the teachers who have made this work possible, including Milton Lodge, Charles Taber, Matt Lebo, Kris Kanthak, Henry Kenski, Marc Saab, Jeannie Madden and Jefferson Stensrud.

Finally, this project would not have been possible without the saintly patience and support of my brilliant wife, Dr. Yasemin Besen-Cassino, and our son Julian.

1

THE MOST POWERFUL NAME IN NEWS

Over the course of the last 20 years, the American news media has undergone rapid and entirely transformative change, and it's only now that science can start to describe the effects this change has had on American politics and society. The clearest example of the change in how news is presented and consumed in America comes from Fox News, a channel which has found enormous ratings success while presenting a consistent ideological viewpoint. While there has been a great deal of hand-wringing about what effect Fox News may be having on the American political system – a recent bestseller about the channel notes in the title that Fox has "divided a country" – there has been relatively little scientific analysis of the effects that Fox has had on actual Americans, their attitudes, and their behavior in real elections. This book moves beyond past work, to show how what is said on Fox News directly impacts Presidential elections, the Republican Presidential primary, campaign contributions, the political knowledge of the American public, and the social views and behaviors of Americans.

Unlike most of the books written about Fox News, this is a work of social science. Whether the effects Fox News has on politics and society are good or bad is beyond the scope of this work. Since 1998, Fox News has called itself "the most powerful name in news," and the purpose of this book is to show exactly how this power has played out. As the later chapters show, the effects of Fox coverage on American politics are enormous. One day of positive coverage of the President, for instance, can increase his approval rating by as much as a full percentage point. Fox coverage is also somewhat responsible for the radical swings in support between a large number of candidates in the 2012 Republican primary, and is one of the major factors driving campaign contributions, especially to lower-tier candidates. For these lower-tier candidates, a single positive mention on Fox was worth more than $20,000 in increased contributions over the following few days, with most of it coming from small donors. Media coverage shapes the general election, too: while campaign events such as the debates are often thought to have a huge effect on the race, the results here show that it's not the events that matter, but the coverage of those events in the media that pushes voters to one side or the other. On the individual level, watching Fox leads many viewers to concentrate their attention on a small subset of issues that aren't frequently discussed in other outlets, leading them to do worse in answering political knowledge questions than they would if they weren't watching any news at all. Those viewers are also much more likely to think that President Obama is not a citizen, that the US found weapons of mass destruction (WMD) in Iraq, and that global warming is a hoax. These effects go beyond political attitudes and behaviors as well: discussions of gun control on Fox increase the number of gun sales in the United States, with effect sizes into the hundreds of thousands per month.

The Rise of Ideological Media

Before widespread access to the internet, Americans got their news from newspapers, or evening news broadcasts, or the single cable news channel, or the radio. This was broadcasting: unless you were part of the small minority of Americans listening to a political talk radio show, subscribing to a newsletter or firing up a modem to read and post comments on a message board, you were getting news that was designed to appeal to the widest possible audience. This news was, by and large, non-partisan, and, as Prior (2007) points out, since it was on all of the channels at the same time, anyone who wanted to watch TV during the news had no choice but to watch it. If you lived in a medium-sized city, you might well have had the choice between two newspapers, one with an opinion page that leaned a little left, and one with an opinion page that leaned a little right. Shows like *Crossfire* or Sunday morning talking head programs like *The McLaughlin Report* had plenty of opinions, but they were designed to be balanced between conservatives and liberals, Democrats and Republicans, and even so, they were the subject of intense mockery from *Saturday Night Live* and similar programs for their hyperbolic arguments. News outlets weren't for Republicans, weren't for Democrats, but were trying to capture the widest possible audience, which meant staying above the partisan fray.

But if there's one thing that's true of any American institution of the twentieth century, it's that advances in telecommunication technology changed everything. Newspapers, which had already been struggling, had to start sharing ad revenue with websites, and lost the profits from the exceptionally lucrative classified ad business entirely. To keep up with the times, many, if not most, began giving away their content online for free, in the hopes that ad dollars would follow. There aren't too many American cities with two newspapers any more.

People with any interest in politics could now find news sources that catered directly to their opinions and interests: it's easy to forget that Drudge Report was one of the first breakout websites of the internet. People of any political stripe, from the mainstream to the obscure, could find an online community that reported news from their perspective, and didn't force them to listen to opposing points of view in the way that the political debate shows had. These sites often weren't run by professional journalists, but rather by activists and advocates, who saw their job as being the advancement of a point of view or a cause, rather than the advancement of knowledge. The line between news and opinion, which had previously been sharp and clearly delineated, became a little blurrier (Sunstein 2007).

Perhaps the most important shift, however, came from the huge increase in the number of cable channels available to Americans. According to Nielsen data for 2013, the number of channels available to the average American had risen from 41.1 in 1995 to 189.1 (though the number of channels they actually watched hadn't gone up since 2008, even as the number of channels available increased by more than 50 percent). Nearly every cable package now includes at least three 24-hour cable news channels – CNN, Fox News and MSNBC – and many include several less popular ones such as BBC World News, not counting the financial news channels that generally have little political content.

Just as widespread access to the internet allowed Americans to choose news content that was in line with their predispositions (Sunstein 2007), the rise of multiple news channels allowed Americans to pick the television news that would tell them mostly what they wanted to hear, and politically active Americans have largely taken advantage of the opportunity. It took some time for the channels to achieve their present form: MSNBC began broadcasting in July 1996, with Fox News following a few months later in October, but neither was an ideological force in American politics until later. Fox's political tone was fairly evident from the beginning, but wasn't available in most of the country until after the 2000 Presidential election, when cable providers noted the ratings it had achieved during the coverage of the election and its aftermath. MSNBC was started as a combination of repackaged stories from *Dateline NBC*, delayed re-broadcasts of *The Today Show*, viewer emails and links to stories on the channels' website. There was some opinion commentary, though this was reasonably balanced: conservative firebrand Ann Coulter was one of the hosts on the first day of programming. It wasn't until the channel's *Countdown: Iraq* dropped subtitles and became *Countdown with Keith Olbermann* in 2003 that the liberal tone of the channel started to be established (Sherman 2014).

The rise of these channels is important because of their reach and their audience. While there are plenty of individual websites with strong political viewpoints, the largest of them – TheBlaze, Drudge Report, Newsmax, Infowars – are viewed by about 20 million people per month (the most popular liberally oriented site, Daily Kos, gets about 6.5 million views per month). In contrast, Fox News can expect more than 2 million viewers on a slow news night during primetime, vastly outpacing online conservative sources, and MSNBC gets about 800,000 viewers on a slow news night (Pew Project for Excellence in Journalism 2010). For both, big news events can dramatically increase those numbers: Fox has garnered as many as 11.5 million viewers on a single night (the final Presidential debate of the 2012 election).

Relative to the network evening news broadcasts, these aren't a lot of viewers: the three evening news broadcasts on ABC, NBC and CBS typically get 6–8 million viewers a night each. But while the evening news broadcasts get far more viewers than their cable competitors, their audiences aren't nearly as politically polarized, moderating their political impact. Using data from the 2010 American National Election Study (ANES), it is possible to estimate that ideological composition of forty-four different news sources, across television, radio and print media (full results are in Table 1.1). The most polarized audiences are all for conservative radio shows: the audience for *The Rush Limbaugh Show* is 83 percent conservative, just 4 percent liberal, and he barely makes the top five. The most polarized audiences for television shows are all for programs on Fox – *Hannity*, *Fox & Friends* and *The O'Reilly Factor* – with MSNBC's *Rachel Maddow Show* following with the most polarized liberal audience. The most politically polarized network program isn't even a news show, but *The Tonight Show* (then with Jay Leno), with an audience that leans conservative, mostly because of their age. Of the evening news broadcasts, the most polarized audience is for *CBS Evening News*, coming in at twenty-three out of the forty-four sources, with an audience about as polarized as that of *The Ellen DeGeneres Show*. ABC and NBC's broadcasts are a little less polarized than that, both with audiences that lean a little conservative (again, largely due to age), and the venerable *PBS News Hour* manages to have an audience that isn't polarized at all: exactly 38.1 percent liberal, 38.1 percent conservative, and 23.8 percent moderate in the ANES data (a closer examination of these figures can be found in Chapter 5 and methodology note 5.3).

Even though MSNBC and Fox News don't get nearly the viewership of their network rivals, they're doing a good job of speaking to one particular ideological audience. They're important not just because of the number of viewers they get, but because those viewers are liberal or conservative, giving them the opportunity for outsize influence over the political and social views of those segments of the population.

These changes in the media landscape are often spoken of as unprecedented, but, in reality, America is simply moving back to the old way of presenting news. In the eighteenth and nineteenth centuries, American political parties were closely affiliated with news outlets, and many newspapers and books were produced with either direct or indirect party funding. The debate over the ratification of the Constitution was played out in partisan newspapers, between dueling Federalist and Anti-Federalist opinion pieces, which were never

TABLE 1.1 Ideological Composition of Most Polarized Media Sources, 2010 ANES

Rank	Source	% Liberal	% Conservative	Difference
1	Mark Levin (radio)	0.0	95.4	−95.4
2	Glenn Beck (radio)	4.2	87.5	−83.3
3	Michael Savage/Savage Nation (radio)	6.7	86.7	−80.0
4	Rush Limbaugh	3.9	83.0	−79.1
5	Sean Hannity (radio)	4.2	82.3	−78.1
6	Hannity	8.8	80.0	−71.2
7	Laura Ingraham (radio)	9.1	79.6	−70.5
8	Neal Boortz (radio)	13.0	82.6	−69.6
9	Fox & Friends	9.2	69.5	−60.3
10	O'Reilly Factor	14.9	68.0	−53.1
11	Fox News	15.7	52.8	−37.2
12	Wall Street Journal	27.3	52.7	−25.5
13	Tonight Show	26.4	39.0	−12.6
14	CBS Evening News	27.3	38.0	−10.7
15	Dateline	23.8	34.2	−10.4
16	Face the Nation	32.1	42.2	−10.1
17	Good Morning America	24.9	33.9	−9.0
18	Late Edition with Wolf Blitzer	29.2	37.5	−8.3
19	ABC World News	27.6	35.8	−8.2
20	60 Minutes	27.1	34.5	−7.4
21	The Situation Room	31.3	38.6	−7.2
22	This Week	36.2	42.6	−6.4
23	20/20	28.0	30.6	−2.6
24	NBC Nightly News	29.0	31.5	−2.5
25	Early Show	26.5	28.2	−1.7
26	USA Today	34.4	36.0	−1.6
27	CNN Newsroom	31.7	32.1	−0.4
28	PBS NewsHour	38.1	38.1	0.0
29	Today	28.0	26.0	2.0
30	Meet the Press	35.8	33.6	2.2
31	Piers Morgan Tonight	37.4	31.9	5.5
32	Frontline	38.5	32.3	6.2
33	New York Times	42.6	35.2	7.4

separated out from the "news" portion of the papers, to the extent that objective journalism even existed. When the first political parties in post-Constitution America began to take form, Thomas Jefferson and Alexander Hamilton immediately began funding newspapers to promote their political movements (Leonard 1986). These proved successful enough that the Federalists in control of Congress passed the Alien and Sedition Acts partially to shut down opposition newspapers. The law allowed Federalists to jail writers who were critical of them (it even included a sunset provision, phasing the law out after the next election to ensure that it couldn't be used against them if they lost control of

Congress or the Presidency, as they did), and deport foreign-born writers for doing so (Rosenfeld 1997). These newspapers traded in partisan sensationalism – claims that John Adams wanted to make himself king, that Hamilton was giving bribes to a member of Congress, that Jefferson was having an affair with his dead wife's half-sister who happened to be his slave (though at least some of these claims were true), and the state of journalism didn't get much better over the next century, with the rise of yellow journalism in the nineteenth and early twentieth century (Miller and Dershowitz 1951). It wasn't until the early to mid-twentieth century that journalism started to become professionalized and aspire to objective reporting of facts, clearly separating out opinion from news. This push was embraced by television news broadcasts, both as a matter of ethics and for profit (Muhlmann 2008, Iyengar and Kinder 2010). In an era when three evening news broadcasts were competing for a national audience, none of them could afford to have a political slant that might alienate a large slice of the potential viewing audience. This conformity to a non-political tone was further enforced by the Cold War, and the notion that politics – and, to some extent, debate – stopped at the water's edge. In sum, the recent move back to a fragmented, partisan media without a clear separation between news and opinion is less a historical anomaly than a move back to traditional media practices in the US. The anomaly was the type of news Americans were used to for most of the twentieth century – but this doesn't make the move back any less jarring.

Does Media Matter?

By no means is the question of media influence in America a new one, but most social science of the twentieth century found the effects to be subtle, at best. Some of the earliest work on public opinion and politics began with the question of whether the media really matters. This wasn't an idle question: researchers like the Columbia team led by Bernard Berelson in the 1940s were motivated by the propaganda of Nazi Germany (Lazarsfeld et al. 1948). It was thought that a government with control over the media had effectively brainwashed the population of Germany, leading to a fear that the same could happen in the US. The good news was that Berelson and his colleagues found that the media's influence was almost entirely indirect: it mattered only to the extent that it influenced local opinion leaders, what they called the two-step flow of communication (Katz and Lazarsfeld 1955, Katz 1957).

These findings, and others like them, set the stage for what's been called the minimal effects model. To simplify, the minimal effects model holds that the media doesn't actually change minds. The media may set the agenda, it may change the issues on which people assess candidates, it may even give people ammunition to defend their opinions – but it doesn't actually change how they feel about a politician or an issue (Finkel 1993, Bennett and Iyengar 2008). The strongest effects of the media were found to be in the area of framing: in a classic experiment, researchers at Ohio State and Purdue showed volunteers one of two news clips about a Ku Klux Klan (KKK) rally in a small Midwestern city. They used the same footage of the rally and counterdemonstrations, and reported the same facts: but half of the group saw a version in which the rally was discussed as a freedom of speech issue, and the other half saw it discussed as an issue of public order. Those that saw the right of the KKK to rally as a free speech issue subsequently expressed much greater support for the rally than those that saw it as an issue of public order. The idea is that the media wasn't going to change anyone's mind about free speech or civil disorder or the KKK – but it could change how the concepts were related in the minds of the volunteers (Nelson et al. 1997). This concept of indirect effects has taken hold throughout the study of politics and the media. For instance, the consensus in political science isn't that campaign attack ads make people dislike the candidate they're directed at: instead, the debate in political science is about whether or not voters find the ads so distasteful that they decide to just not vote at all (Ansolabehere et al. 1994, Ansolabehere and Iyengar 1995, Ansolabehere et al. 1999).

Some researchers were able to uncover direct effects of media – actual attitude changes, based on the information that had been presented – but these findings were mostly limited to lab studies, and have come under a great deal of criticism. For one, lab studies often make use of student sample, and the students who are recruited into these studies are different from the general public in important ways: they're whiter, richer, have more education and are much younger than most Americans. Maybe campaign ads and news coverage impacted the participants in these studies in ways that they wouldn't impact others. Similarly, lab studies generally force their participants to watch the political content, or at least other shows into which the political content is embedded, and that's not quite realistic either. These participants might normally have skipped over political ads with a digital video recorder, or not watched the sorts of programming in which political content normally comes up. Even if political information can potentially have an impact on these groups, it doesn't really matter if members of that group are never actually exposed to it. Indeed, as media choice has increased, those individuals who are most likely to opt in to political content are those who have the strongest attitudes to begin with (Prior 2007, Sunstein 2007).

The best lab-based research on the effect of the media on political attitudes comes from researchers at Temple and University of California, Riverside (Arceneaux and Johnson 2013, Arceneaux et al. 2012). In many of their studies, participants were given a choice of what channels to watch, allowing the researchers to avoid the forced exposure issues that have been problematic in other studies. They find that individuals with strong initial political beliefs choose media that matches those beliefs, and when they do happen upon media that goes against their predispositions, their beliefs only become hardened. This leads Arceneaux and Johnson (2013) back to something close to minimal effects: ideological media isn't changing the direction of attitudes, though it may be changing their magnitude. These sorts of experiments can reveal a great deal about the cognitive processes underlying attitude formation about candidates and issues, but, like all experiments, they face problems of external validity. Even the best experiments make use of a relatively small and non-representative sample of the American public, who may or may not act differently because they know that they're part of an experiment. In addition, the relatively small sample size of experiments (even the best have sample sizes in the hundreds) means that they may be unable to pick up small shifts in opinion, especially small shifts among subgroups of the population, that may be evident from large-scale samples.

Researchers who have looked for large-scale effects of media content on voting outcomes and polls have generally come up empty-handed (Bartels 1993, Finkel and Geer 1998, Wattenberg and Brians 1999); the conventional wisdom is that while direct effects of the media are theoretically possible, they just don't happen in the real world very much. Studies carried out in the lab show researchers that *if* people were randomly assigned to watch various political messages, *and then* were asked to choose between candidates, those messages could make a difference. But since that doesn't really happen outside of social science laboratories (or field experiments assigning individuals to receive certain media sources, as in Gerber et al. 2009), what's left is indirect media effects (Miller and Krosnick 2000). Political scientists have even provided a theoretical framework to understand why these effects are so limited in the real world, a model called motivated reasoning (Kunda 1990, Lodge and Taber 2000, Redlawsk 2002, Taber and Lodge 2006, Lebo and Cassino 2007).

In essence, motivated reasoning holds that when people who care about politics process information about issues or candidates, they're not trying to reach a certain conclusion, which may or not actually be the correct one. If supporters of a candidate receive information that might cause them to question that support, they tend to find ways to avoid changing their minds. They might find reasons to disbelieve the source, downplay the relevance of the information, counter-argue the information, or even just forget that they ever heard it. Political views can be an important part of people's identities, so it makes sense that they'd be prone to defending those views. This doesn't mean that people with strong political views never change their minds, but it does mean that they don't do it easily, and given a choice, they'll avoid information that might make them do so. In the current media environment, they'll opt in to media sources that tend to agree with what they already believe, and they seem to do a pretty good job: politically conservative TV and radio shows have overwhelmingly conservative audiences, and liberal TV programs have largely liberal audiences, even if the polarization isn't quite as great for them. It seems safe to say that even if political information can make people with strong political views change their minds, a diet of news sources that agree with those views isn't likely to do so.

This sort of motivated reasoning, though, is only gone to happen when people are *motivated*. For people who care less about politics, there's less incentive to expend the mental effort necessary to maintain beliefs in the face of contradictory evidence. Just as laboratory studies have shown fairly strong media effects resulting from essentially forcing people to consume political content, people who don't follow politics as closely should be prone to changing their minds in the face of new information. But if this is the case, why haven't researchers looking for these sorts of large-scale direct effects found them? The reason seems to be the availability of data. When researchers are looking in the aggregate, the effects of an individual media source are expected to be fairly small, especially given the many other sources of political information that people use. There are, quite simply, a lot of other things that are likely to be pushing around people's opinions about a politician or an election: the views of opinion leaders, or friends, of spouses, campaign signs on a neighbor's lawn, a certain comment or anecdote that just happens to rub them the wrong way. All of these other effects are really unmeasurable in the aggregate and amount to a lot of noise in analyses of media effects, and without an enormous amount of data, the effects will just be hidden in all that randomness.

Understanding how these effects work in the real world – rather than in a social science laboratory – is an important part of what makes this book different from other studies of the effects of ideological media in general, and Fox in particular. Past studies of the effects of media have shown very different results in the lab and in the real world, and there's no reason why the effects of ideological media should be different. Even in the best experimental studies, external validity – the degree to which the effects isolated in the study correspond to what's happening in the real world – can be problematic. The use here of large-scale aggregate data means that external validity is assured, because all of the data comes from the real world, and from people who don't know that they're being studied. In essence, many other studies pose a hypothetical – *if* the outside world is like this, *then* the effects of media would be this – while the studies here are based in the outside world, so the effects identified aren't hypothetical.

Bias in the Media

For the most part, it's assumed that media coverage on ideological media sources is biased in some way: that Fox News favors conservatives, that MSNBC favors liberals, and that the various evening news broadcasts favor one side or the other to some extent. However, such bias, if it exists, could take several forms. Bias could arise from Fox News presenting more positive statements about Republicans, and more negative statements about Democrats, or from Fox News focusing on a different set of issues than other news sources. While both are likely occurring – in 2013, potential scandals centered around the attack on the US Consulate in Benghazi and the distribution of firearms to Mexican drug cartels by the ATF were both mentioned much more frequently on Fox News programming than in other sources (Benghazi was mentioned on 2,613 Fox

News programs between February 2011 and the end of 2014; this is more than the combined coverage on MSNBC and all three broadcast news networks; the "Fast and Furious" Bureau of Alcohol, Tobacco, Firearms and Explosives (ATF) scandal was mentioned on 908 Fox News programs in the same period, about twice as much as on MSNBC and the networks combined) – the analyses here are much more concerned with differences in the tone of the information presented, as this is where direct effects are most likely to occur. A statement in the news linking President Obama to the ATF "Fast and Furious" scandal impacts attitudes about Obama to the extent that viewers accept that link, have existing attitudes about "Fast and Furious," and come to apply those attitudes about "Fast and Furious" to their attitudes about Obama. Some of the coverage studied, especially on Fox, makes these sorts of links explicit: as an hour-long discussion of the ATF scandal on Fox News broadcast on October 7, 2011 put it: "In the scope of American politics, though, the 'Fast and Furious' scandal may actually bear the most resemblance to Watergate. What did the President know, and when did he know it?" Statements like this are an invitation to apply attitudes about one area – "Fast and Furious" – to another – Obama. Framing effects like these are well studied, and almost certainly happen, but they aren't really a direct effect of the media (Bennett and Iyengar 2008, Iyengar and Kinder 2010, Iyengar 2014). In cases like this, media content is having an impact because it makes certain issues more or less relevant to evaluations of a political figure, not because any attitudes were actually changed. Direct effects would arise from positive or negative statement about a political figure: President Obama is lying about the ATF scandal, or didn't take proper steps to monitor ATF activities. If the media is having direct effects, the positivity or negativity of the coverage, regardless of the issue being discussed, should have an impact on how viewers evaluate the figure.

Importantly, these two types of bias don't necessarily go together. There are many news sources that focus a great deal on certain issues because people working there think those issues are important. The fact that the *Wall Street Journal* reports on financial issues, which may prime readers to evaluate political figures on the basis of those issues, doesn't mean that they'll be more positive or more negative towards a particular figure. Such a focus would only represent bias to the extent that the issues were selected in order to paint a particular figure or group in a bad light – and there's no way for outsiders to know the motivations of the people making the decisions on these points. What can be evaluated, however, is how positively or negatively a figure is treated in one media source relative to other media sources. If the *Wall Street Journal* is covering financial issues more, or Fox News is covering the attack on Benghazi more, that's not necessarily bias: it's possible that this coverage would be just as balanced as any other news source. If the coverage of a particular figure winds up being much more negative or positive than coverage of the same figure in another source, however, that would be considered bias.

Before actually looking at the data, it's important to note that bias, for the purposes of these analyses, is entirely relative. There's no absolute threshold for bias, mostly because there's no correct amount of positivity or negativity with which to report on a political figure. It would be silly to ask that all media sources have exactly equal positive and negative coverage of a political figure: when the mayor of Newark, New Jersey, Cory Booker (now US Senator for New Jersey), ran into a burning building to save a constituent, the coverage was going to be pretty positive; when then US Senator Larry Craig was arrested in an airport men's room for lewd behavior, the coverage was going to be negative (though, it should be noted, there was a great deal of neutral coverage of the topic as well). The key here is that since the agreed-upon facts are generally positive or negative, the coverage on all of the media sources should be about equally positive or negative: bias wouldn't be covering Booker positively, or Craig negatively, but covering either one of them much more positively or negatively than other media sources. Since there's no objectively correct amount of positivity or negativity, bias is in the eye of the beholder. The most famous example of this in political science comes from a 1985 study (Vallone et al. 1985), in which researchers prepared news stories about the Palestinian–Israeli conflict, and asked Palestinians and Israelis to rate the bias in the coverage. When faced with a balanced account, both sides tended to see it as biased – Palestinians saw it as overly positive towards the Israelis, and the Israelis saw it as overly positive towards the Palestinians. Similarly, if someone believes that Republicans are intent on destroying the Republic, or that Hillary Clinton is a murderer, it's hard to imagine a level of negativity that they would not perceive as overly biased towards the other side.

Using this subjective standard for bias, there are clear differences between media sources in how they cover certain figures. Since his inauguration, the general tone of coverage on Fox's non-opinion evening news coverage (see methodology note 1.1 for how this was calculated) about Barack Obama has been strongly negative: the mean tone is –0.26, meaning that there have been, on average, about 26 percent more negative statements about him than positive ones, and there are more negative statements about him than positive ones on about 95 percent of the days of his presidency. In comparison, ABC, NBC and CBS are still more negative than positive, but not by nearly the same margin: mean tones for ABC and NBC are –0.13 (political coverage on NBC and ABC is so similar that they're collapsed in later analyses), while CBS is a little more positive, with a mean value of –0.11. In all of the evening news broadcasts, coverage of Obama is, on the whole, positive about 20 percent of the time. This doesn't mean that Fox is biased against Obama, but it does mean that coverage on Fox is biased against Obama relative to coverage on the mainstream evening news broadcasts, just as coverage on CBS is slightly biased towards Obama relative to ABC and NBC, and very biased towards Obama relative to Fox. None of this is surprising, but it would be wrong to just assume that all coverage on

Fox is biased against Democrats. For instance, for the 2011–2014 period, Fox's equivalent of an evening news report – *Special Report with Bret Baier* – covered Hillary Clinton rather more than the evening news broadcasts, but in 2011, 2012 and 2013, that coverage wasn't any more positive or negative towards her than coverage on other networks. There were, by quantity, more statements about Clinton (and more than would simply be expected because the Fox broadcast is twice as long as the network evening news broadcasts) on Fox, and more negative statements, but the proportion of negative to total statements was about the same across the networks. Fox was about 4 percent more negative than NBC in 2011, 2012 and 2013, and about 7 percent more negative than CBS. This all changed in 2014, though: in the first half of the year, coverage on Fox was 51 percent negative, compared to 25 percent negative on NBC and 8 percent negative on CBS. Suddenly, Fox's coverage went from being broadly in line with the other networks to more than twice as negative. These coverage patterns are presented in Figure 1.1.

As interesting as it may be to look at differences in how various networks report on political figures, it's necessary to look at a larger number of individuals in order to get a good sense of the relative bias in each network. To do this, the coverage of a number of figures, well-known Republicans and Democrats, from 2011 to 2013 (Joe Biden, John Boehner, George W. Bush, Chris Christie, Bill Clinton, Hillary Clinton, John Kerry, Barack Obama, Rand Paul, Ronald Reagan,

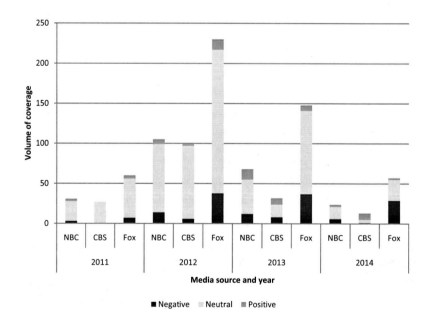

FIGURE 1.1   Coverage of Hillary Clinton on Fox, NBC and CBS, by Year, 2011–14

Mitt Romney and Marco Rubio) are aggregated by network and year. The results show how much of an outlier Fox coverage generally is. Largely because of coverage of the President (which is generally negative – and not just for Obama; past research has shown that Presidential coverage tends to lean negative in general), all of the networks (including the *Wall Street Journal*, for comparison) tend to lean towards Republicans, but the extent to which they do so varies widely. As of 2013, CBS has the most positive coverage of Democrats and negative coverage of Republicans, but it isn't too different from ABC, NBC and the *Wall Street Journal*, all of which score between 0.07 and 0.09 (on a scale in which 1 would be the most possible positive coverage of Republicans and −1 would be the most possible positive coverage of Democrats). Fox, on the other hand, scores at 0.23 (note that these bias calculations are different from the tone calculations made for individual figures above). These numbers do tend to vary by year (as seen in Table 1.2), but while all of the broadcast networks have been growing more positive towards Democrats over the years (including Fox), Fox's coverage started out so far in favor of Republican figures that even with this movement, it's far more biased towards Republicans than the other outlets (details of this analysis can be found in methodology note 1.2).

However, even when Obama is removed from the calculations, the general pattern remains, as seen in Table 1.3. CBS is rather more positive towards Democrats than the other media outlets, Fox is a bit more positive towards Republicans, and the other channels fall in the middle. It also should be noted that much of the perceived bias on Fox isn't against Democrats in general, but against Obama specifically. While coverage on all of the networks is more negative than positive towards Obama, Fox's coverage is far more so. In 2013, Fox's coverage of major Democratic figures other than Obama was about 16 percent negative and 3 percent positive; coverage of major Republicans was 13 percent negative and 4 percent positive. This coverage isn't quite balanced, but it isn't too different from ABC's coverage. Fox's coverage of Obama in the same year was 40 percent negative and just 2 percent positive.

TABLE 1.2 Media Bias Ratings for Major Political Figures, 2011–13, Selected Media Sources

Source	Year			
	2011	2012	2013	2014
ABC	0.26	0.05	0.09	
CBS	0.27	0.09	0.00	−0.36
FOX	0.47	0.29	0.23	0.34
NBC	0.38	0.30	0.09	−0.62
Wall Street Journal	0.00	0.05	0.07	0.11

TABLE 1.3 Bias Calculations for Obama and Non-Obama Figures, 2011–13, Selected Media Sources

Source	Obama			All figures other than Obama		
	Year			Year		
	2011	2012	2013	2011	2012	2013
ABC	0.20	0.05	0.02	−0.05	0.04	0.02
CBS	0.16	0.08	0.18	0.11	0.02	−0.13
FOX	0.45	0.38	0.38	0.19	0.06	0.05
NBC	0.26	0.15	0.23	0.08	0.00	−0.06
WSJ	0.00	0.06	0.16	0.00	0.03	0.05

Why is there so much between-year variation? Much of it has to do with coverage of the President, but it's also driven by the topics that are covered. Statements about the economy in 2011 and 2012 tended to be strongly negative, and many of these were linked to the President. Similarly, there was a great deal of coverage of Mitt Romney in 2012, and much of it was reporting on his victories in the Republican primary – coverage that was fairly positive.

Establishing that there are real differences between the networks, and that these differences aren't as simple as it might seem, is important because of the way in which it informs the analyses carried on throughout the book. Because there are real differences in the tone of the coverage between channels, it's not enough to aggregate coverage among all media sources. The overall tone of coverage of Hillary Clinton turned rather negative in the first half of 2014, but that's mostly a function of the increased negative coverage on Fox, while coverage of Chris Christie turned negative at about the same time, but because of increased negative coverage across the board. Since coverage on Fox is so different than coverage on the other broadcasts coded, it's necessary to separate out Fox's coverage when looking for direct effects of the media. Once Fox is separated out, though, coverage on the other networks is similar enough that it makes sense to aggregate the non-Fox networks. Most of the analyses are looking for the independent effects of media coverage on different sources, and since coverage on ABC, NBC and CBS is so similar, there's not really enough variance between them to isolate any independent effects. They all look about the same, so there's no way to tell which is moving public opinion and behavior. As a result, the analyses are better off using one measure for coverage on Fox, and another for coverage on the other networks.

Data

So what makes the analyses of media effects here different? Two things. The first is the greater availability of public opinion data. As recently as the 2000

Presidential election, national polls of the public were released on about a weekly basis, with fewer polls at the start of the campaign and more towards the end. It wasn't until the 2008 Presidential election that multiple national polls were being released per week throughout the campaign, and not until 2012 that there were reliably multiple daily releases, allowing poll aggregation sites like Pollster and RealClearPolitics to estimate the change in a candidate's standing in the polls on a daily basis without being overly driven by individual data releases. There is, after all, some randomness built into public opinion polls, so reliable estimation of small changes requires multiple polls. During the 2012 Presidential election, there were as many as five national polls released per day, the sort of number that allows researchers to start taking small changes in the poll numbers seriously. Essentially, to see how today's media content impacts changes in the polls tomorrow, or the day after, there simply wasn't enough aggregate-level poll data to see those changes in any election before 2012.

The second thing that makes the analyses here different is the type of media data that's being used. In general, analyses of media effects rely on one of two types of data. The first approach is broad, but shallow. Using transcripts of the programs provided by databases like LexisNexis, researchers can easily find the frequency with which a given term ("Obama" or "Benghazi") is mentioned by various news sources – an approach used occasionally in later chapters. They can even run these transcripts through a key word in context (KWIC) program, which can look at the words surrounding the key term and, using a pre-defined dictionary, determine whether the context is generally positive or generally negative. Because the process is entirely automated, it's fairly quick and cheap to carry out, but it's far from perfect. The first problem is that these programs have trouble with things like pronouns, not knowing when a "he" or an "it" is referring to the concept that's supposed to be looked at. They're also not great at determining whether a statement is actually positive or negative. This isn't entirely the fault of the computer program: as anyone who writes a lot of email can tell you, emotional content is frequently lost when a conversation is put into text. Even if that emotional content were in the text, even the best text analysis software has trouble picking up on it. For instance, in a 2014 broadcast, Fox News host Bill O'Reilly said: "Just 642 days after the attack on the US consulate in Benghazi, the Obama administration has caught the man they say is behind the attack."

A content analysis program looking at that statement would likely pick up that the major actors here are President Obama and/or the White House, and the alleged mastermind of the attack. It might even be able to find other data telling it that the mastermind is Ahmed Abu Khatallah, and link it to other statements about Khatallah. What it likely wouldn't have picked up on is that the statement is a criticism of Obama, based on the preface of "just 642 days," and the implication that it took the administration far too long. This sort of statement is common in the ideological media – if less so on evening news broadcasts – and computers just aren't good at picking up on this sort of implication. So, while these sorts of analyses are good at certain things – like picking up on the frequency of words and terms – they're not so good at other things, like tone. For many sorts of analyses, these types of data might work well, but not for the sort that are of interest here. If the goal were to measure which topics were most important in the public discourse, or the relative frequency with which different sources mention different topics, they would be fine. To understand the impact of media content on how viewers perceive politicians and candidates, knowing the tone of the statements is vitally important. That same report about the capture of Khatallah could easily be positive – "The Obama administration successfully caught . . ." – or neutral – "The alleged mastermind was apprehended." This isn't to say that a sufficiently sophisticated computer coding system, one with the ability to contextualize information and bring outside facts to bear on a statement in order to determine the intent of the speaker, couldn't carry out these sorts of analyses correctly, only that current systems don't.

When a computerized content analysis system misses thinly veiled criticisms like the one O'Reilly is leveling at Obama in that example, it might be possible to get around the problem through aggregation. It's reasonable to assume that the program will miss about as many positive statements as negative, so if enough statements are made, it's fair to assume that the errors will simply cancel each other out. In addition, it seems plausible that the amount of criticism or praise that's missed by the program isn't much different than the amount of praise or criticism picked up by it. Making these sorts of assumptions would allow researchers to determine the average tone of statements about a topic or individual, but that comes at a cost. Looking only at the average tone of statements means not disaggregating the number of positive and negative statements, or accounting for the total number of statements made. Suppose one broadcast makes five negative and five positive statements about Obama; a second makes ten neutral statements, and a third makes two positive and two negative statements. For all of them, the tone is, on average, neutral, but there's reason to believe that they would have very different effects on viewers. If viewers are motivated reasoners who give greater weight to positive or to negative statements, it's not enough to know what the balance of statements is: rather, it's necessary to know how many statements were given on either side.

None of this is to say that techniques relying on word counts, or on KWIC analyses, can't be enormously useful. They have their uses, and may be better than the techniques used here for some purposes, but they simply can't do what the analyses here need them to do, at least given the constraints of current technology. In some chapters of this book, when the goal is simply to look at the amount of coverage of a certain topics, or the number of times a phrase is used, KWIC analysis is applied, but it's simply not the best approach to deal with all research questions.

The content analysis used in this book comes instead from a human coded content analysis set provided by Media Tenor, a Swiss-based firm which carries out daily analysis of major media sources around the world. The coders read through newspapers line by line, and watch television news programs, coding each individual statement as to the actor in the statement, the source of the statement and the tone of the statement, with separate measures for the explicit tone of the statement and the implicit tone of the statement (the O'Reilly statement about Benghazi above would be coded as explicitly neutral, but implicitly negative, for example). Frequent cross-checking and retraining has pushed the overall Cronbach's alpha of their content analysis to 0.82, making it a highly reliable and very detailed data source.

By combining these features – frequent measurement of public opinion and detailed, sentence-by-sentence coding of media content – it becomes possible to determine what effects statements made in the media are having on public opinion. The analysis is further aided by the fact that there's no attempt to measure attitude change on the individual level. Studies that have attempted to show changes in attitudes as a result of media exposure have illustrated some differences, but few that can't be explained as error in the attitude measurement. While political views are a matter of great concern for a portion of the population, they're not terribly important to most Americans, so the answers they give in response to questions about political views tend to shift around a little bit, without any observable cause at all. The political affiliation of a respondent might "lean" towards the Republican Party one day, and be an independent or a "not-so-strong" Republican the next (Franklin 1992, Green and Palmquist 1994). If this sort of measurement and reporting error occurs with an indicator as central as party identification, it seems certain to occur with attitudes that are more subject to change. As such, an observed change in party identification, approval or any other political indicator might be the result of media exposure, or might be a random shift, and the effects of media exposure are generally thought to be small enough that it's impossible to reliably distinguish between real changes and the random shifts. However, these very small changes are magnified when they're aggregated over a large sample. If exposure to a media source decreases the likelihood of supporting a candidate in an election by a few percentage points, the effects might not be observable in a sample of a few dozen, or even a few hundred (as in the lab studies mentioned earlier). In a sample of thousands of people, though, it would be expected that the candidate's support would drop in a measurable way (especially when there are several other polls, released on that day, or the day before, or the day after, showing a similar drop).

A common objection to this sort of analysis, using change in public opinion polls as an outcome measure, is that these polls aren't perfect. In addition to biases resulting from question order or wording, problems with getting certain populations to participate in surveys, and other unmeasured sources of error, every reputable poll has a margin of error attached to it. Simply because polls rely on samples, rather than asking everyone in the country to register their choice, there's some degree of error built in: generally ±3.5 percentage points or so. Anyone familiar with the math underlying this calculation knows that it doesn't really mean that the poll could be 3.5 points higher or lower, but the general criticism still stands. If the polls aren't accurate to within half a point, or a tenth of a point, how is it possible to say that reports in the media increased or reduced that poll result by such a small figure. This is where the length of the election season is an asset. Even if it's impossible to demonstrate that media had a small effect on the poll results of any particular day, if there are enough days, it's possible to show that polls tended to reliably increase or decrease on days following a particular pattern of statements in the media. If this were to happen only once a few times, it could be chance. But if it happens regularly enough, and the size of the effect is large enough, it can be concluded that the media coverage is pushing the poll numbers up or down, even if that push is small.

The final aspect of most of the analyses in this book is that they're better able to determine causality than most studies of media effects. Causality – the determination of what's the cause and what's the effect in a statistical relationship – is one of the most fraught issues in social science, mostly because it can't be established simply by using more advanced statistical procedures. In general, social science relies on correlational studies, which show that two things tend to go together. Correlational analyses can show the extent to which they go together, and how reliable the relationship is, but they can't tell which is the cause and which the effect – or even whether something else is driving them both. For the most part, that determination of causality comes from the theory underlying the research: if the theory says that one thing should cause another, and it turns out that they tend to go together, it's assumed that the causal relationship laid out in the theory is what's driving the relationship.

In most circumstances, this sort of theory-based correlational research works just fine, especially since statistical procedures allow researchers to rule out the most plausible alternative explanations for their findings. For instance, in Chapter 5, it's shown that some people who watch Fox or MSNBC are less able to answer questions about current events in politics than people who don't. It could be argued that these effects are driven by the education of the audience, or their age, or racial composition, or political views – but statistical analysis can rule out these alternate explanations, leading to the conclusion that the media is really having an effect. At the end of the day, though, such explanations are relying on theory, and direct effects of the media are a contentious enough topic that more evidence is desirable. It's possible to get extra leverage on showing causality by introducing the element of time into the analysis. In looking for direct effects of the media on public opinion or campaign contributions, it's not enough to say that changes in coverage are related to changes in public opinion. Rather, it's possible to show that a change in media coverage on Monday is related to changes in public opinion and campaign contribution behavior on Tuesday, Wednesday and Thursday. Having this element of time allows the analyses to establish what's called Granger causality (Granger 1980,

1988a, 1988b). It's still possible that some third factor is leading to both a change in media coverage on one day and a change in public opinion a few days later, but it's hard to think of what that could be. Perhaps more importantly, in the absence of a time machine, the changes in the polls on Tuesday, Wednesday and Thursday couldn't be causing the media coverage on Monday. In normal correlational analyses, the direction of causality could go either way, but once time is introduced into the equation (literally), there's only one way it could be going.

Importantly, this sort of analysis also allows for a distinction between the effects of actual events, and the effects of coverage of those events. A political event – the killing of Osama bin Laden, for instance – may have a direct effect on poll numbers, but it may also have an indirect effect from media coverage of the event. To sort this out, it's possible to look at the size of the shift in the poll numbers, and compare that with the size of the effect that would be expected from the media coverage alone. If the event corresponds with a shift in the polls that's entirely explained by the shift in coverage, it's fair to say that the event itself didn't have a significant direct effect on the polls. This isn't to say that it didn't have any effect – without the event, media coverage would have been different, and the polls would have been as well. However, it's not the event that's having the effect: it's how that event is reported in the media that's doing it.

Finally, some of the analyses, like the discussion of the effects of news consumption on political knowledge, draw on cross-sectional survey data, mostly from Fairleigh Dickinson University's PublicMind poll. As Director of Experimental Research for the PublicMind poll (and a professor of Political Science at Fairleigh Dickinson), I've had the opportunity to add questions about media use and related topics to a number of national and statewide surveys since 2011. While the specifics of these polls vary (and are discussed when the data from each poll is used), all of the surveys were carried out by professional interviewers using a computer-assisted telephone interviewing (CATI) system, on a mixed sample of landlines and cell phones (with the number of cell phones in the sample increasing over time). All of these items were embedded in longer surveys including a number of other topics, and versions of many of the results discussed here were released in the press at the time they were carried out. While these telephone polls cannot provide the strong causal inferences that the time series studies do, carefully constructed cross-sectional polls can provide a wealth of information about how traits go together, and, in conjunction with outside data and findings, can reveal a great deal about the effects of media exposure.

What's Not Being Tested

While aggregate-level analysis may be the most effective way to isolate the direct effects of the media on political behaviors, there are certain things that it can't test. Most importantly, since the analysis is carried out on the aggregate level, it must remain agnostic about the individual-level behaviors that are leading to the results. This isn't to say that that researchers don't have some idea of what's happening on the individual level – lab experiments have given researchers a very good idea of how people process information that's being presented to them in the media – but that there's no way to use this sort of aggregate-level data to differentiate between different models. For instance, there's a heated debate about the extent to which individual voters can be seen as rational (often called "Bayesian") updaters. An individual who acts this way takes the full weight of the knowledge that he or she has about a candidate, then changes that opinion based on new information that comes in. However, for individuals who have very strong existing views, this new information is unlikely to make much of a difference, though, in principle, enough new information could. Other researchers have shown strong evidence that for people with strong views, information that goes against these views isn't incorporated at all. This is an important debate, as it reveals the extent to which people really are looking at the evidence in front of them before casting a ballot, but it's outside the scope of what can be settled using aggregate data. It's possible to show that the media is having an effect, but how it's doing so is largely outside of the scope of the analysis.

In addition, this sort of aggregate analysis can't reveal the mechanisms by which the media is having an effect. While media content having a direct impact on the preferences and behaviors of viewers seems like the most plausible explanation, it's also entirely possible that the media content being measured is being repeated by opinion leaders, or impacting other information sources, which, in turn, impact the preferences of individuals. Since there's no individual-level measurement, and no systematic way to measure all of the ways by which individuals receive political information, the possibility of other sources mediating the effects of the media being measured cannot be easily dismissed. That said, in the individual-level analyses, it certainly seems that actual exposure to the media is what's moving knowledge and opinions, and it's difficult to see how this sort of indirect process could work on the sort of short time frames (1–3 days) at issue in most of the analyses, but it's impossible to completely rule out. Most likely, these indirect effects matter, and are occurring – it's just that the aggregate analysis isn't measuring them.

Nor do the studies discussed here in any way invalidate the strong previous findings of indirect media effects. Priming and framing of issues are very real things, and they are certainly among the ways in which the media has an effect on the political and social views of Americans. However, any such indirect effects are likely to be in addition to the direct effects seen here. The media is likely influential for a lot of reasons: the goal here is to show that the direct effects at issue here are one of those ways.

Finally, the Media Tenor data on the detailed content of the Fox and evening news broadcasts is limited to particular programs. Part of this is for monetary reasons – coding all of the statements on a program is very expensive – but part is also because of issues of comparability. While the most-watched programs on Fox News are personality and opinion-based (*The O'Reilly Factor, Hannity* and so on), these programs aren't at all comparable to the more widely viewed evening news broadcasts on the networks. The format is entirely different, and there's no claim that they're offering objective news or analysis. It would be unfair to judge the overall content of Fox News based on the content of such programs, just as it would be unfair to judge the content of a newspaper based on what's presented in an individual opinion column in a newspaper. As such, when the analyses here look at the content of Fox News, they're limited to the content of the most-watched non-opinion programming on Fox: the hour-long *Special Report with Bret Baier* (hosted by Brit Hume until 2008), on weekday evenings at 6 o'clock (an approach shared by other researchers working in the area: see Groeling 2008). Unlike the opinion-based shows that follow it, *Special Report* follows the same format as a traditional evening news broadcast, and presents itself as a unbiased round-up of the news. The use of this program allows for more direct comparability, and it also means that that the number of statements about politics made is about the same for the major comparison in most of the analyses: Fox versus the network broadcasts. If either one had substantially more or fewer statements about the candidates, it might look as though the effects were artificially larger or smaller. The network evening news broadcasts, combined, are longer than *Special Report*, but they have a bit less political content per minute, so the overall amounts of political coverage on Fox and the aggregated non-Fox outlets wind up being about the same.

The biggest potential problem arising from the use of *Special Report* as a proxy for Fox coverage is that it might lead to an underestimation of the overall effects Fox is having on viewers. The primetime opinion-based programs on Fox News have larger audiences than *Special Report* does, but this isn't a huge concern, for two reasons. The first is that the tone and content of the coverage in *Special Report* and the opinion programs that follow it are roughly the same: in the analyses that have been done, the opinion broadcasts focus on a smaller range of issues, but they tend to be the same issues that are discussed on the non-opinion broadcasts. Similarly, the tone of coverage on the opinion broadcasts isn't much different than the tone on the non-opinion broadcasts. If it were the case that different programs on Fox News were presenting very different views of political figures, and focusing on very different issues, the differences might well prove to be important. Since the content and tone of the programs being measured and those not being measured are very similar, *Special Report* works as a reasonable proxy for coverage on Fox News in general. Moreover, to the extent that this introduces bias into the analyses, that bias would be towards understating the effects of Fox News on viewers. Suppose that *The O'Reilly Factor* or *Hannity* are enormously influential: by not measuring their content, some of the influence that Fox is having may be lost. All that means is that any effects that are found will tend to understate the actual effect, rather than overstate it.

Challenges of Understanding the Effects of the Media

Of course, there are pitfalls associated with trying to isolate the effects of the media on American politics and society. First, and most important, there is the recurring challenge of determining causality. Much of modern social science is carried out cross-sectionally, meaning that the theorized cause and the theorized effect in the research are measured at the same time. In many cases, this isn't much of a problem: for instance, if it's found that older Americans are less supportive of gay rights, it's clear that age is a cause (though the factors that lead to it having an effect may be in question), and attitudes about homosexuality are an effect. The alternative would mean that attitudes about homosexuality make people older or younger, which seems unlikely. With fixed characteristics like gender, race or age, it's possible to assume that the factor which came first can't be an effect.

This gets trickier when researchers look at multiple characteristics that don't have a clear temporal order, like fixed characteristics do. So, if it's found that Republicans are more likely to watch Fox News, it isn't clear if it's because Republicans prefer Fox, or if watching Fox makes people more Republican, or perhaps both at the same time. In most cases, social scientists work around this issue through a reliance on theory: the theoretical framework specifies an expected causal relationship, and if the variables tend to go together, it's taken as an instance of that theory in action. This is the approach taken later in this book in the discussion of the effects of news consumption on political knowledge, and when it's combined with other approaches looking at the same problem in a different way, it can lead to powerful results. However, sometimes the factors in question are so closely related that causality is an issue regardless.

This could be resolved by taking multiple measurements – seeing if Fox viewers do indeed become more Republican – or through an experiment in which respondents were assigned to watch Fox News. Such approaches can give researchers a much better handle on causality – which is one of the reasons why randomized experiments are the gold standard of social science research – but they lead to other problems, mostly with external validity. Once people know that they're being studied, or are put into an artificial situation, their responses are likely to be different than they would be otherwise.

As mentioned earlier in the chapter, most of the analysis in this book adopts a third approach to causality, one that takes advantage of temporal relationships. A (mostly) fixed characteristic like race, age or gender cannot be an effect in most social science because it happens first, and in the absence of a time machine, things that come first cannot be caused by things that happened later. In the same way, if it can be shown that coverage of a candidate on Fox corresponds with changes in that candidate's support in the electorate 2–3 days later, there's no way that the changes in support could be leading to the changes in coverage. This is not the same thing as saying that the change in coverage of the candidate is the cause, but the fact that it can't be the effect is proof of what's called Granger causality. This sort of causality isn't as powerful as the causality established by experimental designs, but has the advantage of not requiring multiple measures of the same people, or placing people into an artificial situation. The statistical analysis required to determine this sort of causality can be complicated – readers who are interested can find the details in the Methodology Notes (Chapter 9) – but they're well in line with the sophistication of modern social science statistical methods.

A second major issue in looking at the effects of media coverage is differentiating between the direct effects of the media and indirect effects caused by phenomena like framing. The difference here is subtle, but important. A direct effect of the media would mean that the coverage is causing people to change their views of politicians or issues; they like the candidate more or less. A framing effect would mean that the media coverage doesn't lead viewers to change their minds about the candidate, but simply leads them to evaluate the candidate in a different way. So, as discussed in Chapter 2, media coverage of President Obama talking about social and economic (though not racial) inequality leads to an increase in his support among poorer Americans. This could be because his statements about inequality lead them to like Obama more, or it could be because these poorer Americans have existing strong attitudes about inequality, and when Obama links himself to the issue, the attitudes about inequality are brought to bear in the evaluation of Obama. In this case, the overall evaluation of Obama hasn't changed, it's just the way in which he's being evaluated – in the light of his link to the issue of inequality – that's different.

This distinction between direct effects and framing effects has been the topic of an enormous amount of social science research over the past 30 years, and it's often very difficult to distinguish between them. The best studies have been carried out in the laboratory, and without the laboratory, we can only look at the question indirectly. However, the evidence presented in later chapters strongly suggests that the media is having a direct effect in addition to any priming effects. For academics in the field, this may be of great interest. For others, it may be enough to say that the content of the media coverage is having substantial effects on the political views and behaviors of the American public, however those effects are being realized.

Fox News

Finally, while this book focuses on the direct effects of Fox News on politics in America, this is not because of any belief that Fox is any better, or any worse, than competing ideological media sources such as MSNBC. Indeed, as seen in Chapter 5, Fox and MSNBC have very similar effects on the political knowledge of viewers, including strongly negative effects among some viewers. The difference between them seems to be a difference of magnitude, rather than one of type, with Fox currently having a larger influence on politics than MSNBC.

However, this is likely the result of two factors: the audience and the party in power. As noted previously, Fox News's audience is rather smaller than the audiences of the network evening news broadcasts, but it remains far larger than the audiences for other cable outlets, getting two to four times the audience in primetime on a normal day (the ratios for daytime programming are smaller overall, though with small overall viewership). Simply put, Fox News has a greater influence on the American public because so many more people are tuning in to watch it. The direct effects of MSNBC will certainly be smaller, because the audience is so much smaller. Perhaps because of its size, Fox's audience also contains much greater political diversity than MSNBC's audience. As discussed in later chapters, there are sizeable numbers of people who self-identify as liberals or moderates who also say that they get at least some of their news from Fox. While MSNBC's audience isn't monolithically liberal, it's not nearly as diverse. As a result, the groups that might be most likely to have their attitudes and behaviors changed by the news coverage – moderates, independents, ideologues who might potentially cross over to support the other party – just aren't watching MSNBC in the numbers that they're watching Fox, further increasing the potential influence Fox News has on American elections. CNN, similarly, has a much smaller audience than Fox News, one that's much less ideologically consistent and doesn't focus nearly as much on politics. While the highest ratings in recent years for both Fox News and MSNBC have come during Presidential election coverage, CNN's ratings spikes have corresponded with natural disasters, fires on cruise ships and plane crashes. In some of the analyses – mostly the effects of consumption on political knowledge – CNN and MSNBC are included, but they're left out of the discussion of the effects of the media on campaign fundraising and national public opinion. Part of this is because the analysis centers on the 2012 election, and while there was a fierce fight for the Republican nomination, President Obama was basically unopposed running for the Democratic nomination. As a result, even if MSNBC had an enormous effect on the views of Democrats, there'd be no way to measure it. In elections with a contested Democratic primary, it would be a good idea to look at the effects of MSNBC – but that's just not the case here. In addition, there is enormous public and scholarly interest in the effects of Fox News, and, therefore a need to sort out what effects the channel is really having. Put another way, no one thinks that MSNBC and CNN are destroying America, but Fox News alarmism is alive and well.

It seems likely that these factors are exacerbated by the fact that the analyses here focus on a period in which a Democratic President was in power. While there is some evidence (as seen in Chapter 2) that Fox News was also very influential during the Bush administration, its importance may well be magnified by the presence of a Democratic President. Under such circumstances, Fox's role as a trusted source of news among Republicans means that it can serve a real purpose, framing the important issues of the day for the opposition, disciplining party members who step out of line, and the like. Without a single central figure for Republicans to rally behind, Fox may take on an organizational function that's simply not needed among Democrats, who can turn to the President to find out which issues are most important. This would imply that MSNBC would have had greater influence over the American political system during the days of the Bush administration – but in the absence of sufficiently detailed survey data from that period, it's difficult to empirically test this. Most likely, it's a topic that will have to be revisited once a Republican President takes office.

In sum, Fox isn't better or worse than any of the other media outlets discussed here, and it's not the purpose of this book to make a case that Fox News, in particular, is good or bad. Fox is singled out because of the size of its influence, which is a result of canny marketing on its part, a loyal audience, and, to some extent, an accident of history, in which it developed a successful business model that others have, thus far, been unable to completely replicate. What this book is about is the direct, significant impact that television coverage has on the views, behaviors, knowledge and beliefs of Americans. Many of these effects runs contrary to notions about what the media should be doing, and while this isn't prescriptive – there are no obvious steps that should be taken to correct them, even if there were agreement that our society should do so – it's vital to understand the size of the influence so that scholars and the public can enter into any debate with clear eyes.

The Structure of the Book

Each of the seven chapters that follow analyzes the effects of Fox News on a different area. Chapter 2 looks at Presidential approval ratings for both George W. Bush and Barack Obama. These approval ratings are often used as a scorecard for the President, and reveal a great deal about the leverage a President has in pursuing his agenda. This chapter shows the extent to which the content of coverage on Fox impacts these national approval ratings, relative to the influence of the broadcast networks.

Next, the analyses turn to the 2012 Republican primary. Chapter 3 looks at the effects of Fox coverage on the standing of candidates in the tumultuous 2012 primary fight, and their ability to raise money. The results show that Fox's coverage greatly increased the volatility of an already volatile race, and was enormously influential in determining which candidates got contributions, especially from small donors. For many of the candidates, coverage on Fox was the difference between staying in the race and dropping out for lack of funding. The results for the frontrunner, Mitt Romney, show the extent to which establishment Republican donors seemed to be fighting against the currents of Fox coverage.

In Chapter 4, the analysis turns to the 2012 Presidential general election between Obama and Romney. While not as influential as it is during a Republican primary, coverage on Fox still has a large impact on the dynamics of the general election, though coverage on the networks matters as well.

Chapter 5 turns to what has been the most contentious finding of this research program, the effects of exposure to Fox News on political knowledge. The results show that political moderates and liberals who watch Fox News do worse on a general political knowledge scale than would be expected if they were watching no news at all. Such findings are surprising, to say the least, so the chapter explains exactly how watching some news, for some people, can leave them worse off than watching no news at all.

In Chapter 6, survey data is used to examine the effects of exposure to Fox News and other media sources on belief in various conspiracy theories. The results show that particular types of coverage – types commonly found in ideological media sources – lead viewers to be more likely to endorse anti-scientific and conspiracy beliefs, such as the belief that Barack Obama isn't a citizen of the United States, that vaccines cause autism, or that global warming is a fabrication created by scientists.

Chapter 7, the final substantive chapter, looks at how the content of coverage on Fox has impacted non-political behaviors and attitudes in society. For instance, FBI statistics reveal that statements about gun control on Fox – especially in the wake of the shootings at Sandy Hook elementary school – led to hundreds of thousands of additional gun sales. Fox coverage has also led to a now widespread belief in the United States about a "War on Christmas," and a number of false beliefs about the Common Core curriculum.

Finally, Chapter 8 concludes the book by taking a broad view of the findings outlined throughout it, and looks at how, and why, the findings here differ from the results of other studies of the effects of Fox News and ideological media. It ends with a discussion of why this matters – and why it's vital to understand how powerful media coverage can be.

2

THE MEDIA AND PRESIDENTIAL APPROVAL

Presidential approval is the most frequently cited metric for how well a President is doing, so it's a logical place to begin the search for the effects of media coverage on American politics. This chapter looks at how the media covers the President, and how that coverage tends to push Presidential approval ratings up or down. It also looks at the extent to which coverage on Fox has a greater impact on Presidential approval than coverage on the broadcast networks – despite the evening news's much larger audience – and how these effects change based on the political environment. While the general positivity or negativity of the coverage is the most important predictor, it seems that coverage of some topics – such as the President's personal life – can also move approval ratings. Finally, the analyses turn to the only other administration for which there is enough data to draw conclusions – that of President George W. Bush – to see if the outsize effects of Fox are limited to the Obama administration, or are a more general feature of modern American politics.

The Importance of Presidential Approval

Since the late 1930s, Gallup and other polling houses have been asking Americans the same question, with sometimes alarming frequency: "Do you approve or disapprove of the way [the President] is handling his job as President?" (Edwards and Gallup 1990). This question is important for two reasons. First, it's been part of political polls, and asked in the same way, for so long that there's reliable data on it going back to Franklin Roosevelt, allowing for direct comparisons between Presidents in a way that no other measure does. For instance, George H.W. Bush had higher approval ratings after the American victory in the first Gulf War than Truman did after the American victory in World War II; more

Americans disapproved of George W. Bush in October 2008 than did of Nixon just before his resignation. Second, it's used as the general gauge of the popularity of the President in a way that simply doesn't exist in other countries. Only in the US is there a real-time measure of the popularity of the executive that comes out several times a week, and it reveals a great deal about what power the President actually has at that time.

Presidential scholars generally divide the powers of the President into "hard" and "soft" powers. Hard powers are those things the President can carry out of his (the masculine pronoun is used solely because all Presidents up to this point have been male, and will, hopefully, have to be revised in future editions of this work) own accord: executive orders, military commands, vetoes, pardons and the like. These powers don't rely on the cooperation of Congress or the goodwill of the people. Most of the powers of the President, however, are soft powers, those which are contingent on the President's support in Congress and among the public – factors which are rather closely related. The President's ability to pass legislation, appoint officials for anything other than a temporary term, shape public opinion and set the priorities of the country and the polity are all dependent on his ability to convince Congress to go along with him.

This leads to the question of why members of Congress would go along with the President and pursue his priorities. Some of it might be down to goodwill, but if we make the reasonable assumption that members of Congress are rational actors primarily interested in winning re-election (they may well have policy preferences, but won't be able to pursue any of them if they lose re-election), the most reasonable conclusion is that members of Congress will do what the President wants only to the extent that doing so will help them get re-elected. So imagine a district or state in which the local member of Congress has higher approval ratings than the President (at least among the member's constituents): the member has little reason to go along with the President's preferred priorities or legislation unless they're something they would have wanted to do anyway. On the other hand, in a district in which the President is rather more popular than the member of Congress, the member is likely to do what the President would like. The President can offer substantial benefits to such a member – district appearances, public endorsements and the like – but the fact is that the member's constituents like the President's policies, and a member of Congress who ignores the wishes of his or her constituents frequently or obviously won't stay a member of Congress for long.

This is necessarily a simplified model – there are many ways a President can gain favor among members of Congress aside from relying on his popularity, and party leaders in Congress have some sway, but decreasing amounts of it – however, the effects of these actions are generally agreed to be marginal compared to the overwhelming effect of his popularity. A President with high approval ratings is much more likely to be able to push through desired legislation and get Congress to work on desired policy areas (Marshall and Prins 2007, Eshbaugh-Soha and Peake 2011).

A President with low approval ratings will have trouble getting members of Congress to pursue his policy agenda or pass his preferred legislation. It's no surprise, then, that the Presidents with the highest approval ratings have been the most productive legislators: President George W. Bush was able to leverage high approval ratings (peaking at 90 percent) after the 9/11 attacks to enact significant bills on tax law and Medicare expansion, not to mention reforms of the national security landscape. Once the continuing war in Iraq sapped his approval ratings (he reached a low of 25 percent approval and 71 percent disapproval in October 2008), his attempts to get Congress to address Social Security reform and immigration law fell completely flat. Similarly, it's not a coincidence that Harry Truman, who had the lowest mean approval ratings of any President (averaging 45 percent throughout his time in office, just below that of Jimmy Carter), was also able to run against a "do-nothing Congress." To some extent, Congress wasn't doing anything because Truman didn't have the popularity to get it to do anything.

All of this means that the Presidential approval rating is more than some score that's mostly of interest to Washington insiders. Rather, it tells political scientists about the ability of the President to exercise his most significant powers: the ability to set the policy agenda and push through legislation (Canes-Wrone and De Marchi 2002, Druckman and Holmes 2004, Eshbaugh-Soha and Peake 2005, Prins and Shull 2006, Barrett and Eshbaugh-Soha 2007). High approval ratings – such as those enjoyed by Franklin Roosevelt (mean approval of 63 percent), Lyndon Johnson (mean of 55 percent), Bill Clinton (also mean of 55 percent) and Ronald Reagan (mean of 53 percent) – correspond to periods in which legislation fundamentally reshaped the American government. This makes approval ratings a direct measure of the attitudes of the public, but an indirect measure of the capacity of the government. As such, understanding what factors influence Presidential approval ratings is enormously important for understanding how the government works, and the results here indicate that media coverage plays a large role in determining them.

In many ways, the dynamics of President Barack Obama's approval ratings (see Figure 2.1) are fairly typical for modern American Presidents (MacKuen 1983, Edwards and Gallup 1990, Brace and Hinckley 1991, Beck et al. 2012). When he took office, he had near 70 percent approval – a level he was able to maintain for the first few months of his term, what Presidency scholars call "the honeymoon period" (Beckman and Godfrey 2007). Once the honeymoon was over, Obama's approval fell quickly to about 50 percent, and fluctuated around there before peaking again after his re-election in 2012. Most recent Presidents, from Carter to George W. Bush, follow approximately the same pattern. Individual events like the Iran hostage crisis or the assassination attempt on Ronald Reagan or the end of a war can increase or decrease approval, but in the end approval ratings tend to revert back to where they would have been in their absence (Lebo and Cassino 2007).

So a lot of the movement in Presidential approval ratings is structural, or based on factors outside the control of the President – or the media, for that

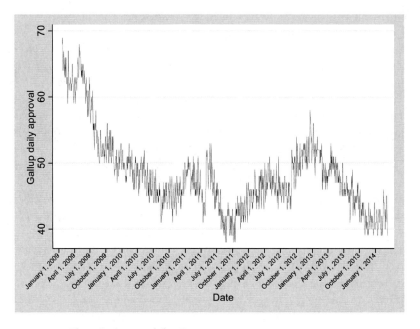

FIGURE 2.1 Obama's Approval, by Day

matter (Brace and Hinckley 1991, Canes-Wrone and De Marchi 2002, Gronke and Brehm 2002). However, there is also a great deal of day-to-day fluctuation in these numbers. Since 2009, Gallup has been measuring Presidential approval on a daily basis, though the figures released are actually a 3-day rolling average. Essentially, it's very difficult to get a good sample of the American public on a particular night: Democrats are less likely to answer their phones on week-ends, Republicans are less likely to answer their phones on weekdays, and so on. Averaging the results across 3 days not only gives a larger sample – and so a smaller margin of error – but also evens out the worst of these effects. Even with this averaging, though, there's a great deal of day-to-day fluctuation in the figures. On 44 percent of the days since Obama has taken office, his Gallup approval ratings have gone up or down by 1 point; on 20 percent of the days, 1 day has meant a gain or drop of 2 points. On a little more than 5 percent of the days since he's taken office, he's gained or lost 3 or more points. Five percent may sound like a rare occurrence, but it works out to a large 1-day shift in his approval rating about 1 day every 3 weeks.

Of course, some of these changes are simply random error: it probably doesn't make sense to ascribe too much importance to a 1 point increase or decrease. But fourteen times between 2009 and 2014 there was an increase or decrease of 4 or more points in a single day, and it's difficult to imagine that those sorts of fluctuations are meaningless. A President with a 48 percent approval rating is middling, one with a 53 percent approval rating is doing well, and if 1 day can make the difference between them, it's important to find out what was happening on that day. In essence, any change in Presidential approval must be the result of one of three things: random error, endogenous characteristics and exogenous factors. Some degree of random error is unavoidable, but because it's random, it doesn't bias the results one way or the other. In fact, if there are enough data points – and at the time these calculations were carried out, President Obama had been in office for nearly 2,000 days – the random error tends to average out to zero, so it can be pretty safely ignored.

The endogenous characteristics are a little more problematic. Endogenous characteristics are the degree to which the series is changing without being acted on by any outside forces. For instance, big swings in approval tend to fade over time: what goes up must come down, so what looks like a falling approval rating could be nothing more than a temporary spike that's fading away. Fortunately, there's enough data here to identify the type and extent of these endogenous factors, and then correct for them (details on this process are in methodology note 2.1). Endogenous factors also include things like regular weekly or monthly shifts, or even the fact that the figures for any particular day include the numbers for the previous 2 days (because Gallup is using a three-day rolling average for its numbers). It's vital to correct for these endogenous effects, for two reasons. First, in order to isolate real changes in approval, it's necessary to remove everything that isn't those real changes, and the movement caused by endogenous characteristics is a big part of that. Second, these endogenous characteristics can themselves reveal something about how Presidential approval works. For instance, in this case Obama's Presidential approval is shown to have strong memory characteristics, implying that it has a natural level that it tends to return to.

Once the corrections have been made that account for the endogenous characteristics, any changes that are left are due to a combination of random error and exogenous factors: events in the actual world that are moving Presidential approval up or down (Simon and Ostrom 1989, Brace and Hinckley 1991, Canes-Wrone and De Marchi 2002). These events might be things that the President does, or is perceived to have done, but this is also where media coverage of the President may play a role. The media coverage data used here was provided by Media Tenor, and looks at the net positivity of the coverage of the President on a daily basis (the calculation and justification for the net positivity measure are in methodology note 2.2), disaggregating the coverage to the number of negative and positive statements when appropriate.

Effects of Media Coverage of the President

Not surprisingly, Obama receives a great deal of coverage in television media. On the three network evening news broadcasts, there are an average of 13.7 statements about Obama a night; in the comparable hour of Fox News, there are an average of 23.3 statements. These statements are mostly neutral: factual statements that aren't directly positive or negative, and don't carry strong positive or negative connotations. For instance, all of the networks covered Obama's first physical exam after becoming President in March 2010, simply reporting his weight, cholesterol level and that the doctor told him to quit smoking. In addition to these neutral statements, the average hour of Fox contains 1.6 positive statements about Obama, and 6.1 negative statements. For instance, on the same night that the networks covered Obama's physical in 2010, Hannity asked his guests about a hypothetical connection between Obama and Nation of Islam leader Louis Farrakhan:

> In Chicago, we know that the President hung out with radicals – Pfleger and Wright and all these guys, and Bernadine Dohrn, Bill Ayers. No one ever asked if he hung out with Louis Farrakhan. No, really. Is that a fair question?

The combined network evening news broadcasts have 1.2 positive statements about Obama, on average, and 2.3 negative statements. The negative slant of the news about the President – a phenomenon that's not limited to Obama, but seems to be a feature of news coverage of the modern presidency in general – means that the positivity measure is generally below zero, indicating that there are more negative statements about the President in the news than positive ones.

In an average month of evening news broadcasts, the President can expect to see more negative than positive statements on 15 nights, an even balance on 12 nights, and more positive than negative statements on about 3 nights. In that same average month, the Fox broadcast would have more negative than positive statements on 20 nights, and an even balance on the remaining nights. There are expected to be more positive than negative statements on Fox only about 1 night every 3 months. The single worst night for Obama on Fox was September 20, 2011, after a day when he outlined a deficit reduction plan that included taxes on wealthy Americans, marked the end of the military's "don't ask, don't tell" policy and was accused of "appeasing" Palestinians by Texas Governor Rick Perry – an accusation that was almost entirely ignored in the network coverage in favor of discussion of ongoing negotiations at the UN. That confluence resulted in forty-eight negative and three positive statements about Obama in a single hour. In contrast, his best night of coverage on Fox was February 24, 2009, the night of his first joint address to Congress, when there were twenty more positive than negative statements about him. Obama's worst night on the networks came on February 3, 2009, when he had to rescind a troubled nomination, and his best night was that of his first inauguration. Put another way, if someone had told Obama on that first night that it would have been all downhill from there, they wouldn't have been wrong.

Like Obama's approval, the positivity of media coverage starts out high, and declines pretty quickly thereafter, as seen in Figure 2.2. This decline comes in both

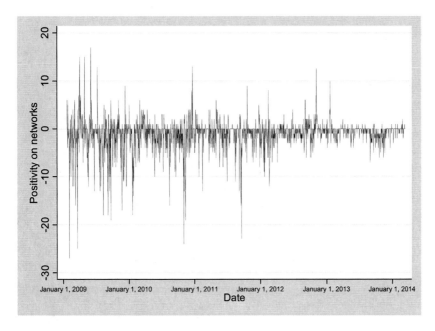

FIGURE 2.2   Positivity of Network Coverage of Obama (Excluding Day of
Inauguration)

the positivity and the total volume of coverage: in the President's second term in
office, the mean amount of coverage is less than half of what it was during the first
term. The positivity of Fox News coverage, seen in Figure 2.3, follows a similar
pattern, though it starts off lower, and goes much lower, much more quickly.

However, the fact that the two series share similar large-scale properties does
not mean that one is causing the other. Presidential approval and coverage of
the President could be moving at the same time, caused by some other factor,
or Presidential approval could be causing media sources to be more positive or
more negative in their coverage. Thankfully, it's possible to sort out the direction of causality – what's the cause, and what's the effect – through statistical
analysis (see methodology note 2.3). These analyses show that past values of
media coverage have an effect on present values of Presidential approval, but
past values of Presidential approval don't have any impact on present values of
media positivity. In statistical terms, this is called Granger causality (as mentioned
in Chapter 1; see Granger 1980, 1988a, 1988b), and means that media coverage
seems to be causing approval, and approval is not causing media coverage.

While some researchers have argued that the main effects of media coverage
on Presidential approval arise from priming and framing (Miller and Krosnick
2000), research on political psychology provides good reason to believe that
media coverage could have a significant direct effect on Presidential approval.
The most relevant research on this comes from lab work on online processing,

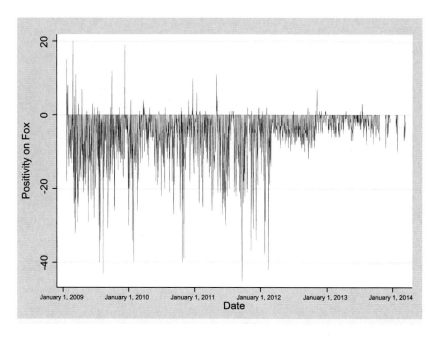

FIGURE 2.3   Positivity of Fox News Coverage of Obama

a model pioneered by Milton Lodge and his colleagues (Lodge et al. 1989, McGraw et al. 1990, Cassino et al. 2007). Online processing holds that individuals form an impression of a political figure by extracting the affective content of relevant information, incorporating that affect into their evaluation of the figure, and generally discarding the initial information. This model was initially promoted as a way to explain a puzzling discrepancy in political science: voters seem to know very little about candidates, but in general have the feelings towards those candidates that would be expected if they knew all of the relevant information. Put another way, people like the candidates they should like, despite the fact that they don't seem to have the information that would lead them to those feelings in the first place. In this view, the fact that voters can't actually tell researchers very much about the candidates they're casting ballots for doesn't really matter: voting, after all, is a multiple-choice question, not an essay question. The voters only look ill-informed because the researchers are asking the wrong questions: as long as the voters are going to cast a ballot for the candidate that aligns with their preferences, it doesn't matter why they say they're doing so.

In terms of Presidential approval and the media, online processing leads to the expectation that the tone of media coverage should have a direct effect on how the public evaluates the President. More positive coverage of the President should lead individual viewers to assess him more positively, which, in the aggregate, should lead to an increase in his approval rating. However, there seem to be some problems with this sort of approach. The most notable arises from motivated reasoning (Kunda 1990, Lodge and Taber 2000, Redlawsk 2002, Taber and Lodge 2006, Lebo and Cassino 2007). Rather than rationally updating affect towards political figures – impartially liking them more or less as new information comes in – individuals with very strong existing views seem to engage in a number of processes that serve to protect their existing affect. This makes sense: people who very much like, or very much dislike, the President tend to ignore information that's contrary to their existing affect, or find reasons to decide that it isn't relevant, or simply forget that they heard it in the first place (Taber and Lodge 2006). Because of this, it seems likely that the effects of the media on viewers will vary between groups, having a greater impact on groups that are less motivated to maintain their present views. Motivated reasoning doesn't mean that the information won't have an impact on evaluations of the President, just that the effects will be distributed unevenly. Such a viewpoint is supported by past research as well: Baum (2002), for instance, finds that tonality of media impacts evaluations of issues more among less-educated Americans than among those with more education.

Statements in the Media and Presidential Approval

The most basic way to test this relationship is by looking at the marginal effects of positive and negative statements on Fox and the networks on changes in President Obama's approval numbers. First, though, it's necessary to control for other factors that might also impact views of the President. For instance, Obama's approval ratings increased by 5 points, from 47 to 52, in the 2 days after the raid on Osama bin Laden's compound which resulted in bin Laden's death. Now some of this increase could be due to other factors (Obama's approval rating was already on an upswing at the time, having increased by 4 points in the prior 5 days), and some of the increase could have been due to increased positive media coverage of Obama after the raid (the day after the raid, the networks made seven positive statements about Obama, and only one negative one; Fox made eleven positive statements, and no negative statements; on the previous day, there were no positive statements about Obama on any of the broadcasts). However, it seems probable that some of the bump in approval is the effect of the killing of bin Laden, independent on how it was reported in the media. These sorts of independent effects were found for just four events over the course of Obama's term in office: the announcement that he had been awarded the Nobel Peace Prize, the end of the Congressional stand-off over extension of unemployment benefits, the raid on bin Laden's compound, and the Boston Marathon bombing. Each of these events, controlling for the general trends present at the time and the media coverage of the events, increased Obama's approval by 2.2–3.6 points.

Controlling for these major events, all of endogenous factors, and the general positive or negative trend of Obama's approval up to that day, the effect of media coverage on Obama's approval ratings can be isolated (the full regression results are in methodology note 2.4). The results indicate that, as expected, positive stories about Obama in the media increase his approval rating, and negative stories decrease his approval. However, the effects of the statements vary widely, depending on their tone and source. All else being equal, a positive statement on Fox is expected to increase Obama's approval by about 0.01 points per day for the following 5 days; a positive statement on the networks increases his approval by 0.007 points per day for the following 5 days. The effects of negative statements are so small as to be insignificant. These figures seem small, but it's important to remember that they often come in multiples, and the effects are compounded over several days. For instance, a pretty good day for Obama (in this case, March 3, 2009, a day when Obama gave a speech talking up the stock market) meant eleven positive statements about him on Fox – such as Bill O'Reilly's admission that "Obama may well be trying to fix the economy" (along with six negative ones, many centering on the headline that the Dow Jones Industrial Average had dropped 25 percent since Obama had taken office), and eight positive statements (along with six negative ones) on the networks. All told, this would be expected to increase his overall approval rating by 0.17 points per day for the following 5 days, for a total of about 0.9 points. If one not especially good day can increase his approval rating by nearly 1 point, very good days (and very bad days) can do much more. The day Obama won the Nobel Peace Prize, for instance, was expected to result in a 2.4 point increase in his approval rating over 5 days, not counting the 2.5 point gain that was independent of the media coverage. It's also important to remember that this is the effect of a small portion of the media environment on Obama's approval: there are plenty of information sources, from newspapers to websites, which simply aren't included here. The total direct effects of the media on Obama's approval ratings are certainly even greater than this.

Media Effects Change Based on the Political Environment

However, the effects of news coverage on Obama's approval ratings may actually be more complicated than it seems from this basic analysis. To understand why, it's necessary to remember that people aren't as rational as we might like. Ideally, individuals would see positive statements about the President, incorporate them into their overall view of his performance, and have more positive feelings about him as a result. The marginal impact of that one statement might not be enough to push a particular individual from being disapproving to neutral, or neutral to approving of the President, but, in the aggregate, it would be expected that positive statements would lead to higher approval ratings, and negative statements would lead to lower ones. Perhaps unfortunately, though, the best evidence is that people don't actually deal with new political information in this way. Rather, they engage in motivated reasoning, selectively incorporating or failing to incorporate new information in order to maintain their existing attitudes.

So people who dislike the President should be more likely to ignore positive statements about him and glom on to negative statements, as this allows them to maintain their current attitudes. People can also maintain attitudes by strategically seeking out or avoiding new information. So someone who likes the President might be less likely to watch the news when the President is having a bad week, and more likely to watch the news when the President is having a good week. Part of this – the differences between people who like and dislike the President – can't be tested with just the daily overall approval numbers (the breakdowns by group are released on a weekly basis, mostly because of all of the problems with getting good samples of all of the subgroups on a daily basis). However, the avoidance or seeking out of information can be tested, by looking at how the effects of news items change depending on whether the President is having a relatively good or relatively bad week. A relatively good week, for these purposes, is one in which his approval rating is increasing; a bad week is one in which it's decreasing. Moreover, it may take some time for the media coverage to be included in the approval ratings, so coverage for the previous 5 days is pooled when predicting changes in approval rating, as in the previous model (details in methodology note 2.5).

In the most general sense, the results show the same pattern as in the simpler analysis. Positive statements about Obama on Fox tend to increase his approval rating over the next several days, and negative statements about Obama on Fox tend to decrease it. In addition, coverage on the networks doesn't seem to have any significant effect, though the effect of positive network coverage on Obama comes closest. However, it also shows how conditional these effects are on the current trend of Obama's approval. When Obama's approval is down, both positive and negative statements about Obama on Fox have effects in the expected direction, and these effects are much larger than they are when Obama's approval is on the upswing. When Obama's approval has gone down over the prior week, each positive statement about him on Fox increases his approval by 0.02 points per day for 5 days. When his approval has been going up over the prior week, the effect is about one-third that size. Similarly, when Obama's approval has been declining, each negative statement about him on Fox decreases his approval by 0.07 points per day for the following 5 days. When his approval has been increasing, the effect is negligible. The effects of statements about Obama on the networks are smaller, and while they're not statistically significant, they also appear to be much less conditional on the direction of Obama's approval at the time.

All of this indicates that Fox News not only has the biggest effect on Obama's approval, but that this effect is strongly conditional on the recent dynamics of Obama's approval ratings. To the extent that Fox News's audience is more Republican than Democratic, its viewers may be more likely to tune in, or more likely to pay attention to the news, when the media environment is less threatening. As a result, statements on Fox when Obama's approval is going down have much greater force than they do when Obama's approval is increasing.

It's also interesting to note that while the network evening news broadcasts have a much larger combined audience than Fox News, they have no substantive effect on his approval ratings. This also highlights exactly how big an impact Fox News actually has on Obama's approval. After a week of falling approval ratings, 1 day's worth of positive coverage on Fox, consisting of twelve positive statements, and two negative statements, would be expected to increase Obama's net approval by more than a full point over 5 days. In an area where a few points mean the difference between success and failure, between being able to push through a policy agenda and not, Fox News coverage plays an outsize role.

Effects of Media Coverage by Political Group

These results all look at the effect of media coverage on changes in daily approval of the President, and for good reason. The degree of fractional integration found in the approval series indicates that changes caused by exogenous factors – like media coverage – tend to fade relatively quickly. As such, the best estimates of the effects of media coverage will be those that account for the effects before they have a chance to fade. However, there's also a problem with this: it doesn't allow for the estimation of differential effects of media coverage by groups within the population. As mentioned previously, this is a necessary flaw in the data: it's simply not possible to get valid estimates of subgroups on a daily basis. However, Presidential approval among such groups can be estimated on a weekly basis, and this may be frequent enough to pick up some of the effects of media coverage before they fade entirely.

Past research indicates that approval among the party opposite the President is most responsive to new information, and this seems to be the case here as well. Lebo and Cassino (2007) find that when Republicans hold the Presidency, approval among Democrats is driven by objective information about the economy. When Democrats are in office, economics only impacts approval among Republicans (see also McAvoy and Enns 2010). The reasoning behind this is simple: members of the President's party generally have very high approval of him, which doesn't drop too low except in the direst of circumstances. Approval among the opposition party generally isn't quite as low as approval among the President's party is high, giving it more room to fluctuate.

Using the weekly data, it's possible to divide up the public into ideological and partisan groups: conservative Republicans, moderate Republicans, moderate Democrats and liberal Democrats. Because the data for these groups is present only on a weekly basis, there's much less data available than there is for the daily model: a total of 144 weeks. This means that the models need to be simpler, but there are still interesting results (more information about these models can be found in methodology note 2.6). News coverage has absolutely no effect on Presidential approval among liberal Democrats or moderate Democrats, but it matters a great deal to Republicans. Moderate Republicans respond in the expected direction to coverage of Obama on Fox News (though not on the networks). Each positive statement about Obama on Fox News over the course of a week is expected to increase his approval rating among moderate Republicans by 0.04 points the following week, with each negative statement expected to reduce his approval among that group by the same. Since the net positivity of statements on Fox News is generally negative, this means that in an average week, coverage on Fox drives down approval of Obama among moderate Republicans by a bit more than half a point.

Surprisingly, conservative Republicans are also responsive to media coverage in their approval of Obama, though the effects are weaker than they are for moderate Republicans. Coverage on Fox, but not coverage on the networks, increases or decreases approval among conservative Republicans in the expected directions, by about 0.01 points for each positive or negative statement.

Media Effects Differ by Income Group

Of course, there are more ways to break up the results than by political group. The effect of media coverage on white Americans mirrors that of Republicans, and that of non-white Americans mirrors that of Democrats. More interesting, perhaps, is how the effects of the media differ between income groups. Past research has shown that stock market performance, among other economic indicators, impacts approval and electoral results (for example, Fauvelle-Aymara and Stegmaier 2013), and since groups perceive economic conditions differently (Hopkins 2012), approval patterns should differ by income group. Among poorer Americans – those in households earning less than $24,000 a year – coverage on Fox News and coverage on the networks are significant predictors of approval, and rather stronger than for any of the partisan groups. For Americans in the poorest quartile, each statement on the networks about Obama increases or decreases approval by 0.15 points, and each statement on Fox News increases or decreases it by 0.14 points. For individuals in the second income group (household annual income of $24,000–60,000), coverage on the networks has the expected effect (though a smaller one than for the poorest group), but coverage on Fox doesn't have a significant effect. Finally, for the third and fourth income groups ($60,000–90,000 annually, and $90,000 annually and up), coverage on Fox matters (with approval increasing by about 0.10 points per positive statement, but network coverage doesn't (full results for all of these analyses are in methodology note 2.7).

These results reveal a great deal about how media coverage from Fox and the networks differentially impacts Americans. As might be expected, coverage of Obama on Fox News has a much greater impact on Republicans than on Democrats, and a greater impact on self-identified conservative Republicans than on moderate Republicans: about twice as much. Among Democrats, none of the media coverage indicators has a significant impact on approval ratings, though the coefficients for both groups of Democrats hint that something interesting is going on. Statements about Obama on the networks have effects in the expected direction – increasing approval for positive statements, and decreasing for negative statements. However, for statements about Obama on Fox, the direction of the effects is reversed: positive coverage of Obama leads to decreases in approval, and negative coverage leads to increases. Since there is so little positive coverage of Obama on Fox News, this indicates some degree of partisan defensiveness among Democrats: the more critical coverage on Fox becomes, the more they rally in support of Obama.

Media coverage of Obama also has the greatest effect on people at the lowest rungs of the socio-economic ladder. Changes in the approval series of the economic groups are not very tightly correlated (see methodology note 2.7), indicating that these groups are responding to different kinds of information. Approval among the poorest group increases or decreases in response to positive and negative statements on both the networks and Fox News, and at a much greater rate than for any of the other income groups. Statements about Obama on Fox News have 50 percent more impact on approval ratings among the poorest group than they do among any of the other income groups, and statements about Obama on the networks have two to three times greater impact. Approval among the lowest income group also moves around more, as evidenced by the higher standard deviation of approval; together, these figures suggest that poorer Americans are less tied to existing views of the President than wealthier ones (in statistical terms, they would be said to have weaker priors). Among the two highest-earning groups, coverage on Fox News has a significant impact on approval, though coverage on the networks doesn't. This could be because these groups tend to be more Republican than the other income groups, or it could be because topics which lead Fox News to report positively or negatively about Obama are more important to these groups.

Topic Coverage and Obama Approval

To dig deeper into these questions, it's necessary to disaggregate the data in a different way, looking at the topics covered rather than the tone of the coverage. This presents some challenges, mostly because the number of statements about Obama in relation to any specific issue is very low for any particular day, and even lower when the statements are broken apart by their positive or negative tone (a problem that's of limited concern, given that the majority of statements on any particular issue have a neutral tone). As a result, analyses based on the topics of coverage are best carried out on a weekly basis, and show how approval among a subgroup, or the whole population, changes when discussion of the President is framed around certain topics in the news.

While the data includes several thousand topics, these are aggregated in twenty-six areas for the purpose of these analyses, with the frequency of each topic shown in Table 2.1. These broad areas include budget and tax issues, education, crime, women's and lesbian, gay, bisexual transgender and queer

(LGBTQ) issues, guns, education, scandals and so on (details of what these categories contain is in methodology note 2.8). Based on the analysis in Chapter 1, it should come as no surprise that the most frequent topic of statements about Obama is elections: mostly, what would normally be considered horserace coverage. However, more substantive matters – the state of the economy, and political matters (which includes the process of making laws) – come in second and third, and, combined, are actually more common than the horserace coverage. Discussion of healthcare also ranks highly, with an average of 4.4 statements about Obama dealing with healthcare per week, and as many as thirty-eight in weeks when it's a major topic of discussion. Note, of course, that these counts are only for statements that are actually about Obama, not discussion of healthcare or policy making or military matters in general. So a statement about healthcare would be more like "President Obama touted healthcare reform on Capitol Hill today" than "The healthcare.gov website remains broken," which would be coded as being about healthcare, but not about the President.

TABLE 2.1 Topics of Coverage of Obama, 2009–14

Topic of Obama coverage	Mean statements/week	Max. statements/week
Elections	6.00	73
Economy	5.19	36
Political matters	4.88	41
Healthcare	4.37	38
Military matters	3.60	75
Scandals	3.29	59
Personal matters	3.05	13
Other domestic issues	2.72	21
Terrorism	2.11	39
Public opinion	1.97	17
Environmental issues	1.65	18
Guns	1.16	39
Women's/LGBT issues	1.05	29
Immigration	0.80	11
Disasters	0.59	23
Crime	0.51	13
Education	0.40	6
Legal matters	0.33	12
Technology	0.28	4
Inequality	0.26	9
Media	0.15	8
Racial/ethnic issues	0.15	10
Sports	0.13	2
Regulation	0.12	2

To the extent that different groups within the population respond to different issues, it should be the case that the aggregate approval among these groups is responsive to different issue frames surrounding the President. For instance, if women are more concerned with healthcare or women's issues, approval among women should go up when these topics are mentioned in conjunction with the President, while approval among groups that don't care about these issues should remain unchanged.

In the overall approval series, controlling for the positivity of coverage on Fox News and the networks, two of these topics have significant impacts on the President's approval ratings: crime and personal matters. In general, when the news coverage links the President to discussions of crime rates or individual criminal acts, his approval rating increases by 0.16 points per statement in the following week. This is probably because Obama has presided over a period of historically low crime rates, and when he talks about individual crimes, he's most likely condemning the offenders. For instance, the biggest spike in coverage for this topic came in the Summer of 2010, when the President spoke about more seriously prosecuting white-collar criminals at financial firms. The other area that seems to help Obama's approval is statements that focus on his personal or family life: each one of these increases his overall approval by 0.1 points in the following week.

Typically, the statements coded as being about his personal life involve his relationship with his wife and children, or, in an instance that received a great deal of media attention, getting a new dog (the dog, Bo, was featured in the "Pinheads and Patriots" section of *The O'Reilly Factor*, in which he was warned that chewing up *Sports Illustrated* would make him a pinhead; Australian model Miranda Kerr was that night's "patriot"). These statements are fairly common in the media – there are about three statements like this per week, on average, in the coded broadcasts – and if they're intended to increase the President's approval by making him more personable, they're working (all of the regression analyses by topic are in methodology note 2.9).

However, it would be expected that these issues would have the greatest impact on specific groups, rather than on the public more generally. For instance, discussions of President Obama's healthcare plan might help his approval among Democrats, but hurt him among Republicans, meaning that it would have no net effect on the overall series, but significant impacts on approval among particular groups. Using the same ideological-partisan groups as in the previous set of analyses, it's possible to estimate the effects of linking the President to particular topics on approval ratings among distinct portions of the American public, and the results of these analyses are enlightening.

While statements concerning healthcare or healthcare reform don't have an impact on the President's overall approval rating, they do hurt Obama among certain groups – moderate Democrats and conservative Republicans – and don't seem to help his approval among any of the groups. The two most ideological groups, conservative Republicans and liberal Democrats, were also responsive to statements that linked President Obama with scandals, while moderates in both parties didn't seem to respond to such statements at all. Statements about Obama's personal life increased his approval among all of the groups except for liberal Democrats, and some of the issues only resonated with a particular group. Statements about Obama dealing with guns, for instance, had a significant impact on his approval only among moderate Democrats, and statements dealing with women's and LGBTQ issues only mattered to liberal Democrats.

Similar divisions can be found among the four income groups. Statements that posit Obama doing something about healthcare reduce his approval significantly among three of the four income groups (all but the second group – $24,000–60,000 annual income). Statements about the budget or taxes don't seem to have a significant impact on approval ratings among any of the income groups, but coverage of Obama's views on inequality does increase his approval among the poorest group by a fairly substantial degree. Unfortunately, coverage that discusses Obama's views on racial issues, which come up almost as much, tend to hurt him among this group more than discussion of inequality helps him. As seems to happen throughout, stories about his personal life help Obama among all of the groups.

Findings like this tend to illustrate the challenges politicians and candidates face when deciding what issues to focus on. A speech about inequality would tend to help Obama among poorer Americans, but mentioning the racial component of inequality in America would basically undo any gains he would get from the discussion of inequality. These results are also, in an odd way, very optimistic about how Americans consume media coverage. In cases such as these, Americans seem to be paying attention to the actual content of what's being said, and responding rationally to it. Poorer Americans would likely benefit financially from programs that would reduce inequality, so when politicians bring these issues up, they're rewarded.

Are These Just Framing Effects?

In sum, while the general tone of media sources has a differential impact on Obama's approval among various political and economic groups, the topics of the coverage matter as well. Media coverage that focuses on Obama's personal life will tend to increase his approval, and coverage that links Obama to scandals, or to his plans for healthcare reform, will tend to decrease it. There are two potential explanations for the link between approval and which topics are covered in the news. The first is the familiar argument of framing effects. In essence, this argument holds that no one is really changing their mind as a result of the coverage, and what looks like opinion change as a result of certain topics receiving more coverage is actually the result of those topics becoming more relevant when individuals are deciding whether or not they approve of Obama.

The media isn't changing any minds according to this view, simply making some attitudes more relevant. The second explanation is that information about certain topics is weighted more heavily by certain groups than others: simply put, they care about some topics more than others. If this is the case, then the media is having a direct effect on evaluations of the President by covering topics that weigh more heavily on the evaluations made by certain groups. In either case, coverage of the President is having an impact on the aggregate views of the American public: the question is how. Differentiating between these mechanisms is important because they tell very different stories about how the media is impacting approval: is it doing so by activating existent but latent attitudes, or is it doing so by changing the attitudes that individuals hold? Most likely, there's some of both, but to show the direct effects of media content on Presidential approval, it's necessary to show that the effects can't be explained entirely by framing.

It's impossible to differentiate between these explanations by looking at issues that are of importance to any particular group. If coverage of environmental issues leads some groups to be more likely, or less likely, to approve of Obama, it could be because they care about environmental issues, and give a lot of weight to statements about Obama's stance on them. Or it could be that they have strong existing opinions about Obama's stance on environmental issues, and these are activated by the coverage. To differentiate between them, it's necessary to look at the effects of coverage that doesn't have any content, and fortunately, there's a lot of it. While individuals might be more or less likely to approve of the President due to the country's economic performance, or his stance on social issues, horserace coverage of the President doesn't have any real-world implications. As operationalized here, horserace coverage includes all statements about campaign strategies, advertising buys (though not the content of the ads, which are coded along with other statements on that topic) and electoral results, but not statements about public opinion polls (they have their own category, and it's possible people could use overall public opinion as a cue to decide whether or not they should approve of the President). In a primary election, as discussed in Chapter 3, it may make sense to support a candidate based on how well that candidate has done in previous contests: in a competitive election, it makes sense to know who's likely to win. In the context of evaluating a President, however, it's not clear why any individual would be more or less likely to approve of the President because he or she likes or dislikes a particular campaign strategy or a particular ad buy. Essentially, horserace coverage is as close as media outlets come to making pure affective statements about the President, bereft of any content that would activate latent attitudes held by members of the public.

When the volume of horserace coverage in the previous week is used as a predictor in the approval models, it has a significant and positive impact on overall approval (increasing approval by 0.02 points for each mention), as well as on approval among both liberal Democrats and moderate Democrats (full results in methodology note 2.10). This indicates that, for members of the President's party at least, approval increases just because something about the President is being mentioned in the media. Since there's no content in the coverage to activate existing attitudes, framing alone can't fully account for them.

Fox News and Bush Approval

However, it's not enough to look only at how media coverage shapes approval of Obama: to examine the general effects of the media, it's necessary to look, to the extent that it's possible, at the effects of media coverage on other Presidents as well. While there is data on the approval rate for Presidents dating back to Franklin Roosevelt, there's simply more data about Obama's approval than there is for any of his predecessors, limiting the sorts of analyses that can be carried out. Even for President George W. Bush, daily data on approval simply doesn't exist, and even weekly data is limited: Gallup has data for much of Bush's Presidency, and only by combining results from a number of survey houses (see methodology note 2.11) is it possible to create a weekly job approval series for Bush (see Figure 2.4). Even then, there are some limitations on the series: subgroup data is only available by party (not ideological-partisan group, as for Obama), and even that isn't available for all of the data points in the series. In addition, while there is data on network coverage of Bush from the very start of his Presidency, Fox News was not even available in many areas until around 2003, so there's no data on its content until after that point.

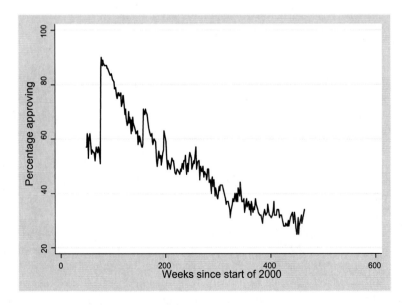

FIGURE 2.4 Bush Approval, by Week

Even this limited data, though, allows for the testing of some important hypotheses. The first has to do with the conditionality of the effect of Fox News. Earlier in this chapter, it was established that Fox News is far more influential in changing Obama's approval numbers than the networks are. What's not clear is exactly why this is the case. It could be something intrinsic about Fox News, or it could be that Fox News is more influential during the Obama administration because it serves as the voice of the opposition during a Democratic administration.

Like Obama's approval, the results of the analysis indicate a degree of fractional integration, meaning that the effects of exogenous factors tend to fade, dropping by about 20 percent each week. Controlling for major events in Bush's presidency – most notably the terrorist attacks of 9/11 (which increase his overall approval by 31.1 points), and the invasion of Iraq in 2003 (which has an estimated effect of increasing his approval by 9.1 points) – positive statements about Bush in the media increase his approval slightly (by 0.01 points per statement), but significantly (full results for all of these analyses are in methodology note 2.12), and negative statements have a similar small but significant effect. So, overall, there's evidence for the effect of media coverage on Bush's approval: less than for Obama, but part of that difference is certainly due to the differences in the data available. Remember that the fractionally integrated nature of the daily Obama data means the effects of the media tend to fade fairly quickly, so it may not be surprising that there is relatively little of the direct effect left when the analysis is carried out on a weekly basis. However, if the analysis is restricted to the period for which data on Fox News is available, the story is a bit different.

While there are fewer data points in which there's data on Fox coverage, the positivity of coverage on Fox has a significant impact on Bush's approval in the following week, with positive statements increasing his approval by 0.014 points per statement, and negative statements decreasing it by the same amount. Positivity of coverage on the networks has no significant effect: the estimated effect is only about a quarter the size of the effect of Fox News, and is in the wrong direction to boot. When the positivity of the statements is separated out into its components, there seems to be some degree of asymmetry between the effects of positive and negative statements about Bush on Fox, with positive statements having a much greater effect in increasing his approval than negative statements have on reducing it.

Put together, these results present a bit of a puzzle: statements about Bush on Fox News have a much larger impact on changes in his approval than statements about him on the networks, but there also seem to be significant effects of statements on Bush's approval for the whole period of his presidency, which includes several years before data on Fox coverage is available. There are two possible explanations for this: the first is that the overall results on the effect of coverage on Bush's approval are being driven largely by the effect of Fox, with the strong effects of Fox coverage outweighing the weak or non-existent effects from early in his term. The second is that network coverage has a variable effect, one that's stronger prior to Fox's ascension, and weaker afterwards. To figure out which, it's necessary to bifurcate the data into the periods before and after 2004, and see how the results differ in the two periods. Prior to 2004, network coverage has a significant effect on how Bush's approval ratings move in the following week, increasing or decreasing them by 0.03 points per positive or negative statement, with some indication that positive statements have a stronger effect on increasing them than negative ones do on decreasing them. In 2004 and after, the positivity of coverage on Fox has a significant effect in the expected direction (though one that's weaker than the effects of the networks prior to 2004), but the effects of the networks are tiny, insignificant, and in the wrong direction. Moreover, the lack of network effects isn't simply because of the inclusion of Fox coverage as a predictor: when Fox coverage is removed from the model, network coverage still fails to have a significant effect on Bush's approval.

The story here seems to be that while media coverage had a significant direct effect on Bush's approval, much as it has for Obama's approval, the nature of that effect changed over the course of the Bush administration. Early in his administration, his approval was impacted by the positivity of coverage on the networks, but some time around 2003 or 2004, networks became less influential. It's possible that statements on Fox had an impact on his approval prior to that period (though the data does not exist here to test for it), but what's certain is that after 2003, coverage on Fox is a significant predictor of changes in Bush's approval ratings, while coverage on the networks no longer is.

Such results lead to two important conclusions about media effects on Presidential approval. The first is that the effects of the media on approval aren't something that began with the Obama administration. Approval ratings for President Bush, and likely for Presidents before him, also fluctuated based on the coverage he received on television. However, during the Bush administration, network coverage became less important to overall approval, and statements on ideological media, such as Fox News, became relatively more influential. The second conclusion has to do with why Fox News is so influential in shaping approval of Obama. The results indicate that Fox News coverage of the President has been more influential than coverage on the network evening news broadcasts since at least 2004, meaning that Fox's effects on Obama's approval cannot simply be due to the fact that it's giving voice to the opposition party: even when Republicans held the White House, Fox coverage was still more important to approval ratings than network coverage, despite the much larger audience reached by the networks.

Media Coverage and Presidential Approval

The analyses in this chapter lead to six important conclusions about how media coverage impacts Presidential approval. First, coverage of Obama is more negative than positive on both Fox and the broadcast networks – but it's much more negative on Fox.

Second, actual events don't do much to change Obama's approval: the only events that have a significant impact are the raid on bin Laden's compound, the winning of the Nobel Peace Prize, the Boston Marathon bombing, and the end of the stand-off with Congress over unemployment benefits in December 2011.

Third, positive statements about Obama in the news increase his approval, and negative stories decrease his approval, with statements on Fox having a larger effect than statements made on the network broadcasts. However, these effects change along with the political environment. Positive statements matter more when he's down, and negative statements matter more when he's up.

Fourth, Republicans respond to coverage of Obama on Fox, but not on the networks, and Fox coverage even influences approval among conservative Republicans (though not by much). Poorer Americans change their views of Obama based on network and Fox coverage, but wealthier Americans only seem to respond to what's on Fox, and ignore the networks.

Fifth, some topics, especially crime and Obama's personal life, lead to increases in his approval rating. Coverage of healthcare hurt him among some groups, as did coverage of political scandals. But it's not just the content of the reports: horserace coverage has an effect as well.

Finally, the importance of Fox News in shaping Presidential approval pre-dates the Obama administration. As early as 2003, Fox coverage was a strong predictor of changes in President Bush's approval rating.

Presidential approval ratings are enormously important for the success of a President, and, taken together, these results indicate that media coverage of has an enormous impact on them. The thirty-seven statements the coded media make about Obama on an average night have a direct and measurable impact on the approval rating, with positive statements about the President tending to push his approval rating up, and negative statements tending to push it down. The main effects of these statements are relatively small, but are magnified by the days when there are a large number of positive or negative statements, and the fact that effects are incorporated into the President's approval ratings over the course of 3–5 days. Coverage on the best and worst days of Obama's presidency resulted in swings of up to 2–3 points over the course of a few days, not counting the effect of the events that led to the positive or negative cover-age in the first place. Winning the Nobel Peace Prize, for instance, increased Obama's approval by an estimated 2.5 points – but the positive coverage the prize engendered in the media doubled that effect. These sorts of dramatic shifts are pretty infrequent – two or three times a year, on average – but days of media coverage that push the President's approval rating up or down by a point or so are more frequent, happening two or three times a month.

It's also clear that Fox News has an effect on approval disproportionate to the size of its audience. While more Americans, by far, watch the network evening news broadcasts, coverage on Fox News has a much greater effect on Presidential approval than network coverage. This difference is exacerbated when the general trend of approval is taken into consideration. Past research has shown that individuals tend to avoid news when they expect that they won't like the content (Shepherd and Kay 2012, Garrett et al. 2013, Nam et al. 2013, Garrett and Stroud 2014): in this context, it means that Fox tends to have a greater impact on Presidential approval when the President has, in general, been having a bad week. When Obama's approval is down over the past week, both positive and negative statements about him on Fox have a greater impact than they do when his approval is up. This disproportionality is even more pronounced among subgroups of Americans: coverage on Fox or the networks is about equally influential among the lowest income group (in which media use is generally more influential), but Fox is far more influential among Americans in the higher income groups. There is also some evidence of ceiling and basement effects: among groups, like conservative Republicans, who already have very low levels of approval for Obama, media coverage has less of an impact than it does on groups like moderate Republicans. These same groups also respond negatively to statements about Obama's healthcare reform plans.

Using historical data, it's possible to estimate the effects of media coverage on George W. Bush's approval ratings. The results show that the general effects of the media, and the disproportionate influence of Fox News, pre-date Obama, and go back at least as far as data on Fox News content is available. The outsize importance of Fox News, it seems, is not conditional on which party controls the White House, but is a standing feature of the modern American political system.

In addition, it seems that these are direct effects of the media in changing the attitudes of Americans towards the President, rather than just a restatement of the framing effects that have been so well studied by scholars of political communication (Nelson et al. 1997, Bennett and Iyengar 2008, Iyengar and Kinder 2010, Iyengar 2014). These framing effects argue that media coverage is important because it changes the issues upon which a political figure is evaluated: so coverage of the economy makes those considerations more relevant to overall evaluations, which may change an individual's stated opinion without changing any underlying attitudes. It isn't that talking about the economy makes someone like the President more or less, just that it makes considerations about the economy – which may be more positive or more negative than the overall evaluation – temporarily more relevant to the overall evaluation. While these framing effects certainly exist, they cannot fully explain the effects of the media on Presidential approval demonstrated here. For one thing, a framing effects model would hold that the issues being covered would be more influential than the tone of the coverage. If framing is responsible for what appear to be changes in evaluations, it shouldn't matter whether the coverage is positive or negative, whereas these results show that it matters a great deal. Indeed, it doesn't seem to matter what the coverage is talking about so much as whether it's positive or negative. Second, even coverage that doesn't seem likely to activate any particular considerations – statements about President Obama's campaign strategy, or the results of elections – impacts Presidential approval in the expected direction.

The fact that the big driver of approval is the positivity of the coverage provides support for an alternative model of media effects, one based on the online processing model (Lodge et al. 1989, McGraw et al. 1990). This model holds that when individuals receive information about a political figure, they extract the positive or negative content of that information, use it to update their existing evaluation of the political figure, then, often, forget all about the information that started the process in the first place. As discussed in detail in Chapter 5, Americans don't know much about government or the people who run it, but online processing essentially allows people to have it both ways: to have rational attitudes about political figures without being able to access the information that led them to those attitudes in the first place.

Often, the online processing model is thought to be in opposition to a motivated reasoning approach (Kunda 1990, Lodge and Taber 2000), which holds that individuals who hold strong attitudes tend to reject information that would lead them to change or moderate their views. However, these results show that these models can easily co-exist, and there's evidence for both of them here. While the best estimates of the effects of the media are in the daily model of approval, the weekly model, which allows for the separate estimation of effects on political-ideological groups, indicates that the effects of statements in the media differ by group. Both this and past work (Lebo and Cassino 2007, McAvoy and Enns 2010) have shown that members of the President's party are less responsive to new information than members of the out-party, and this seems to be the case here as well. So individuals may be rationally updating their attitudes towards the President, as predicted by online processing, unless they're sufficiently motivated to avoid doing so, as predicted by motivated reasoning. Both models hold, just on different segments of the population.

Of course, any effects of media coverage on attitudes are going to be limited by the fact that many Americans simply aren't paying attention to politics all of the time. As such, it makes sense that there would be greater effects of the media on attitudes, and even behaviors, when there's an election going on, and the next two chapters look at exactly that.

3

FOX NEWS AND THE 2012 REPUBLICAN PRIMARY

The 2012 Republican Presidential primary election received an enormous amount of coverage in the media, more than any other single topic in the news during the beginning of 2012. Most of this was horserace coverage – discussion of who was winning and losing ground in the election, or in key states, without much actual content about the candidate.

Perhaps because it's a trusted source of news for Republicans, coverage on Fox pushed the standings of the candidates in national polls up or down, while coverage in the more broadly seen network evening news broadcasts had no measurable effect whatsoever. Fox coverage also led to huge shifts in the financial contributions to the candidates, but there are differences based on how well the candidate is doing in the polls, and whether the contributions are coming from large or small donors. Fox coverage matters more for candidates who are struggling in the polls, with any mention on Fox News being good news for the candidates at the bottom of the national standings. Fox also seems to drive the behavior of small contributors much more than large contributors, which may be one of the reasons why small contributors have less influence on the process than big donors do.

Coverage of the candidates on Fox didn't have nearly as much of an influence on Romney's campaign as it did on the others. It seems that negative coverage on Fox led his supporters to rally around him, though this didn't come up too often, as coverage of Romney on Fox was strongly positive throughout much of the campaign.

Primary Elections

So far, it's been established that the television media – and Fox News in particular – has a significant effect on Presidential approval, but these effects are limited by the characteristics of the audience for political news during the normal course of events (Arceneaux and Johnson 2013, Bolsen and Leeper 2013, Scacco and Peacock 2013, Birdsong et al. 2014, Garrett and Stroud 2014). Namely, the people paying the greatest attention to the news are strong partisans, who are the least likely to be persuaded by it. Very few strong Republicans are going to start approving of Obama, regardless of what the media says, and only a few more Democrats are going to start disapproving of him. With some short-lived exceptions – mostly driven by rally-round-the-flag effects, like George W. Bush's approval after the 9/11 attacks, or his father's spike after the first Gulf War (Baum 2002) – the views people have of politicians are constrained by their base partisanship. Political independents – real independents, that is, not just partisans saying that they're "independent" in order to look better in an interview (Keith et al. 1992) – might be more moved by the media, but they're also not paying attention to political news. This may lead to a difference between the effects of media on Presidential approval and on election results: during an election, these independents actually start paying attention, so the media may have more of an impact.

But what happens when partisanship no longer provides a guide for opinions? In Presidential politics, the only time this happens is during a competitive party primary. In these primaries, the various candidates are all members of the same party, being evaluated by members of their party, so voters need to know more than just their party identification to decide how they're supposed to vote. These elections also attract relatively high levels of public attention, making it more likely that voters will be paying attention to media coverage of the candidates, and increasing the probability that the media will have an impact.

To put it in terms of motivated reasoning, individuals voting in a primary election don't have as strong a motivation to support one candidate over another as they do in the general election. In the general election, party affiliation leads the most politically interested individuals away from actually changing their minds in the face of media content, diluting the effects of the media (Lodge and Taber 2000, Redlawsk 2002, Taber and Lodge 2006). In a primary election, party cues don't help, as all of the candidates are of the same party. There may still be motivated reasoning involved – individuals who are tied to one candidate or the other – but it's not likely to be as pervasive or as controlling as it is in a general election.

The 2012 Republican Primary

For all of these reasons, competitive Presidential primary elections make for a best-case scenario for media influence, and the 2012 Republican Presidential primary is no exception. The election featured eight major candidates (eventual nominee Mitt Romney, Rick Santorum, Newt Gingrich, Ron Paul, Jon Huntsman, Rick Perry, Michele Bachmann and Herman Cain), five of whom (Romney, Perry, Cain, Gingrich and Santorum) led at some point during the race (see Figure 3.1). While the debates between the candidates began in May 2011, Romney didn't take a final lead until 9 months later, in March 2012. Had there been just one or two candidates, voters might have been able to base their decision on their like or dislike of one candidate, or the perceived conservatism of the candidates, but with five viable candidates, there was no simple decision to be made. It should be noted that Bachmann is excluded from most of the analyses found later in this chapter: her poll numbers were near or at zero for the entire run of the series, as national coverage following her win in the Iowa straw polls quickly degraded her standing in Iowa and nationally (Christenson and Smidt 2012) – a finding shared by other analyses of this race (McGowen and Palazzolo 2014).

The decision for voters wasn't even as simple as Romney or whichever other candidates happened to be doing well at the time: even outside the top two candidates at any point during the primary, the other candidates totaled an average of 25 percent support. So, even during the period in August 2011 when Perry was leading the field, he and Romney together were polling less than 50 percent, more than 25 percent of voters were supporting one of the other candidates, and more than 30 percent of Republican voters were undecided. Even if voters were simply looking to support the candidate who seemed to have the best chance of beating Romney for the nomination, they would need to be paying close attention to the polls to figure out who that was at a given moment.

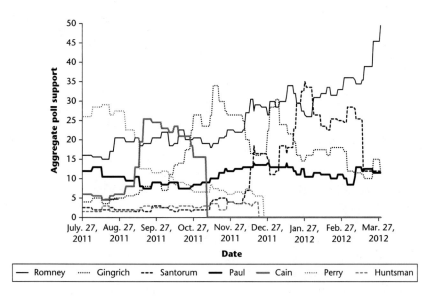

FIGURE 3.1 Republican Primary Poll Support, July 2011–April 2012

Perhaps because there was no compelling race in the Democratic primary, in which Obama was without a serious challenger, the Republican race attracted intense media attention. For the period between the start of 2012 and the end of the competitive period at the end of March, coverage of the Republican primary was 26 percent of all of the news covered on the network news, and 28 percent of the coverage on Fox. By way of comparison, coverage of Obama and the White House was only about 10 percent of the coverage on network news, and 16 percent of the coverage on Fox. So an individual who was watching one of the 22-minute network evening news broadcasts could expect to see about 5½ minutes a day about the Republican primary process; someone who was watching a 44-minute Fox would see, on average, 12½ minutes of coverage.

Predictably, this coverage peaks on the days immediately before and immediately after an actual nominating contest (mostly primary elections, but there are still plenty of other "contests," like caucuses around the country). Coverage for the candidates other than Romney peaked on January 3, 2012, the day of the Iowa Caucuses, in which Romney was initially declared the winner, only to have the contest later declared a tie between him and Santorum. On that day, Santorum, Romney, and Paul all had more than twenty statements about them on the evening news broadcasts, with Perry and Gingrich receiving a bit less. Total coverage peaked on the day of the New Hampshire primary, when the evening news broadcasts recorded a total of ninety-five statements about the candidates: 72 percent of all of the coverage on that night (Bashar al-Assad and a Supreme Court decision took up most of the remainder). While Romney receives more coverage than any of the other individual candidates, it isn't until he secures the nomination at the end of March that Romney begins to entirely dominate the coverage, as shown in Figure 3.2.

All of this coverage has a potentially enormous impact on the political choices made by Americans, in terms of which candidate they choose to vote for, as well as the decision to contribute money. The contentious nature of the primary also meant that it was one of the major stories in the news in early 2012, with Republican primary coverage representing more than a quarter of the statements in the media over that period. While there was more coverage on Fox than on the broadcast networks, the sheer volume of coverage outweighed all other topics on all of the networks, including coverage of the White House and President Obama, as shown in Figure 3.3.

In such a crowded field, with such complex dynamics, media coverage is essential to the candidates as they seek to differentiate themselves from the competition. But how much of an impact does the coverage really make? Does it matter if the coverage is on Fox or one of the network broadcasts? Could a difference in coverage actually have changed the outcome of the election? Data on campaign contributions also allows for the monetization of media coverage: how much is a positive statement on Fox, or another channel, really worth to a candidate?

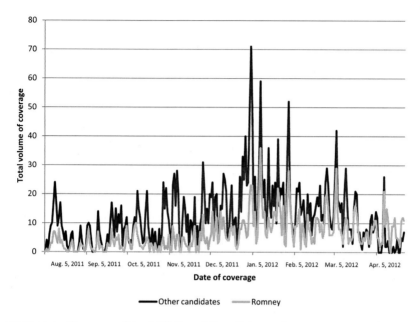

FIGURE 3.2 Coverage of the 2012 Republican Primary: Romney versus Other Candidates, August 2011–April 2012

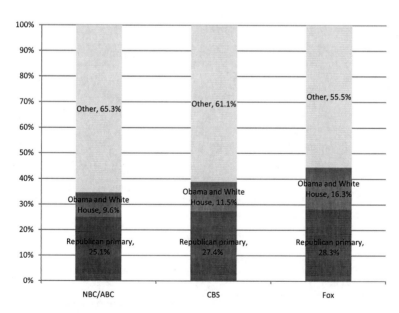

FIGURE 3.3 Coverage of the 2012 Republican Primary by Broadcast, January–March 2012

Note: See methodology note 3.1 for details.

What's in the Coverage?

No one who's followed media criticism over the last 20 years will be surprised with the general content of the coverage: it's mostly about the horserace (Patterson 1980, Robinson and Sheehan 1983, Buell 1987), a description of who is winning right now, and how this is likely to change (or not) – what Patterson (1993) has termed "the strategic game." This sort of coverage has been considered problematic by media scholars because it doesn't do anything to actually inform voters about what the candidates stand for, or give them any basis on which to make a decision about which candidate to support (Farnsworth and Lichter 2011). ABC and NBC were the worst offenders: 82 percent of their coverage of the candidates dealt with horserace issues, significantly higher than the 77 percent of the coverage on Fox, and 78 percent on CBS (as shown in Table 3.1). This sort of coverage is rarely scintillating after the fact, featuring lines like: "Republicans in the poll overwhelmingly say Mitt Romney is the candidate with the best chance of beating Barack Obama, but still, only 24 percent want him to be the Republican nominee" (ABC, November 7, 2011). There's no reason given in the coverage as to why someone would choose to support Romney, or anyone else.

At first glance, this seems to be good news about coverage on Fox: less horserace coverage means more time for coverage of substantive issues. However, it doesn't quite work out that way. While ABC and NBC spend substantially less time on the horserace than Fox, Fox spends the difference talking about the personal characteristics of the candidates: whether they make good leaders, their families and so forth. Again, this isn't information that's terribly helpful to voters in deciding how to cast a ballot, and this is 11 percent of the coverage on Fox, compared with 6 percent on NBC and 9 percent on CBS. On the other matters – foreign policy, domestic policy, healthcare policy – there isn't much difference between the media outlets. When the topics are broken down further, there are a few more differences: nearly all of the coverage of women's issues and abortion in discussions of the primary came from NBC (1.2 percent, compared with 0.2 percent on the other outlets). Fox leads

TABLE 3.1 Topics in Coverage of 2012 Republican Primary Candidates, January–March 2012: 2,195 Statements

	% All	*% NBC*	*% CBS*	*% Fox*
Horserace	79.5	82.4	77.9	77.3
Personal qualities	9.2	5.8	9.1	10.5
Domestic policy	9.0	7.6	10.7	8.5
Foreign policy	2.0	1.2	1.8	2.3
Healthcare	1.4	1.2	0.9	1.7

Note: See methodology note 3.2 for details.

the way on coverage of energy and tax policy issues, both of which are ignored entirely by NBC. Of course, much of this is negative coverage – criticisms of subsidies for solar energy production are frequent, as are mentions of Obama's "attacks" on coal producers – but such coverage is, at least, about *something*.

When the coverage is divided up by the candidate being discussed, as in Table 3.2, a clear pattern emerges. The better the candidate has done in the election, the more time the media spends actually discussing his or her policy views. Michele Bachmann, who bowed out in January 2012 after a disappointing sixth-place finish in the Iowa caucuses, was covered only in terms of the horserace. After all, since it was clear that she wasn't going to be the nominee, there was no reason to pay any attention to her actual personality characteristics or policy views (of course, there's also less coverage of her in the data than for any of the other candidates: just twenty-four statements in the January–March period). Similarly, Paul and Huntsman didn't have much of a chance once the voting started, so their coverage was about 85 percent about the horserace. The one exception to this is coverage of Texas Governor Rick Perry. While Perry also didn't have much of a chance in the polls, this was largely because of a serious of gaffes, starting in November 2011, with a failed attempt during a debate to remember the cabinet departments he would eliminate. He finally dropped out in January 2012, after another gaffe in which he publicly called Turkey's leaders "Islamic terrorists" and said that they should be kicked out of NATO (Perry later stood by his statement). Not surprisingly, nearly a quarter of the coverage of Perry focused on his personal qualities, especially his leadership capabilities.

Among the candidates who did relatively well during the period analyzed – Gingrich, Romney and Santorum – there was less horserace coverage, and more coverage of their personal characteristics and domestic policy views. As much as media critics might dismiss the general content of the coverage as being overly focused on the horserace aspects of the campaign, there is something to be said for the way the candidates are presented here. In a race with a large number of candidates, voters might rightly be more concerned about throwing away their votes by casting a ballot for a non-viable candidate than choosing the candidate who is closest to themselves on the issues. As such, it makes sense that the least viable candidates get the least amount of coverage, and that this coverage is

TABLE 3.2 Coverage Topic by Candidate, 2012 Republican Primary

	% Bachmann	% Gingrich	% Huntsman	% Paul	% Perry	% Romney	% Santorum
Horserace	100.0	79.5	83.6	84.9	71.8	73.3	79.5
Personal qualities	0.0	9.9	13.1	4.7	23.9	15.2	9.1
Domestic policy	0.0	8.6	3.3	7.3	0.0	9.0	7.7
Foreign policy	0.0	3.2	0.0	3.0	0.0	1.1	1.4
Healthcare	0.0	0.8	0.0	0.0	4.2	1.6	2.4

most focused on election results and their standing in the polls. If a voter were thinking about voting for Michele Bachmann, the most important thing for that voter to know would be that Bachmann didn't stand a chance, and that the vote should probably be directed to someone else. The greater focus on the issue positions and personal characteristics of the candidates doing well could easily help voters choose from among them. The practice of focusing on the horserace is far less defensible in the general election, in which there are only two viable candidates, but it's not necessarily as bad as media critics generally contend.

The Impact of Coverage on the Primary Election

Sorting out the effect of all of this media coverage on the outcomes of polls and elections is far from straightforward. The first problem is that media coverage and movement in the polls are very closely linked. Both of them tend to move in response to actual events, whether it's one of Rick Perry's numerous gaffes on the campaign trail or Michele Bachmann's disappointing finish in the Iowa caucuses. In the current media environment, coverage of such events begins immediately, and can continue for days until another topic displaces it (Farnsworth and Lichter 2011). The measurable reaction of public opinion to these events moves comparatively slowly: the most-watched media coverage of an event goes on in the early evening, at about the same time poll interviewers are making their calls. As a result, the measured impact of these events and the media coverage don't show up until the following day, but there's no guarantee that respondents will even have seen it then. Traditional models of media influence hold that the greatest impact of the media occurs as it filters through opinion leaders (Lazarsfeld et al. 1948, Katz and Lazarsfeld 1955), who talk about it with their friends or co-workers, or today, post about it on Facebook or Twitter. Alternatively, survey respondents may just fail to notice the news for a few days: while political news and discussion is central for a small portion of the population, it's a sideshow for most people.

The second problem is that the effects are expected to be relatively small. While the media is certainly responsible for some of the change in evaluations of candidates during a primary, there are lots of other factors that may be just as, or more, important. Campaigns, at least, believe that political advertising is influential, even if there isn't a lot of proof of that (Ridout and Franz 2011). Personal contact is thought to be the most influential factor: knowing that a friend or relative is supporting a certain candidate (or even seeing signs on neighbors' lawns) seems to strongly drive preferences (Gorecki and Marsh 2012, Sokhey and McClurg 2012, Lupton et al. 2014). So the proportion of change in vote preferences that's driven directly by the media is likely to be fairly small. That doesn't mean it's not important – elections are often decided by small margins, and American politics is replete with speculation about how a change of a few votes here or there could have altered history.

Related to this is a data issue. Because the direct effects of the media on candidate preferences are expected to be relatively small, a lot of data, and a lot of variance, is needed to distinguish between media effects and candidate preferences that are moving around just because of random error, weird survey samples and all sorts of other factors that don't really reveal anything meaningful. The more data is available, the easier it is to distinguish between media effects and random error, and in this case, more data means a longer primary season. Because the 2012 Republican primary started so early, and continued so long, there's enough data to sort out the difference. The second part, variance, is just as important. It's possible to sort out even small direct effects of the media in the 2012 Republican primary because the numbers for the candidates change so much. If the numbers for the candidates didn't move very much, there would be few changes in support to explain, and therefore less of a chance to see the effects of the media on these changes.

The analysis here is based on the Media Tenor data from ABC, NBC, CBS and Fox, from August 5, 2011 until April 25, 2012 (a total of 265 days), when the Republican National Committee declared Romney the presumptive nominee. It might have been nice to start earlier, but the ability to do so is limited by the availability of frequent polling data. While there are a number of sources for survey data on the candidates, the analyses here use just two: Gallup and YouGov. These two polled the question the most consistently, and included the greatest number of candidates – something that's a problem with many of the other polls, and therefore a problem with poll aggregations. While it's generally better to use poll aggregations like Pollster or RealClearPolitics, they don't work as well when they're dominated by just one or two sources, or when the different polls being aggregated ask the questions in materially different ways (in this case, the big problem is the inclusion of candidates, or pollsters using an "other" category to lump together a number of minor candidates). Both conditions exist here, so using just two polls that both gathered a lot of data, proved reliable and asked the question in the same way works in this case.

The most important predictors here are the number of positive and negative stories on Fox and on the various non-Fox evening news broadcasts, the latter aggregated into one non-Fox measure. Given how similar the content on these various broadcasts is, it's easier to pool them all together than to try to determine the effects of the individual channels on how well a candidate is doing in the polls. The coverage for each candidate is then pooled over the previous 3 days, so, for instance, the analysis looks at what effect the coverage on Monday, Tuesday and Wednesday had on the change in a candidate's standing in the polls on Thursday. Because a lot of candidates are included in the analysis – including some, like Huntsman, who was the subject of a total of 148 statements over the entire campaign, and others, like Perry, who dropped out relatively early – the number of statements used here is skewed towards zero (full details for this analysis are in methodology note 3.3).

Fox Coverage Drives Candidate Support

The results show a huge impact of Fox coverage on the fortunes of candidates. On average, a single positive statement on Fox about a candidate in the 2012 Republican primary increased that candidate's standing in the polls by 0.07 points; each negative statement decreased it by 0.05 points. Now, those numbers seem pretty small: but candidates aren't getting just one statement at a time (with the exception of Huntsman). At the peak of his campaign, towards the end of September 2011, Herman Cain was seeing nine positive statements and no negative statements over 3 days, with many of them noting his strong performance in polls and speculating that he could take the nomination, as in this exchange between Kimberly Guilfoyle and Dana Perino on Fox's *The Five* on September 29, 2011:

> Guilfoyle: In a new Rasmussen poll, Cain comes within five points of beating President Obama among likely voters. So, Dana, do you think he can keep this going, or is this just a flash?
>
> Perino: I think he can and he will. He *Cain*. He's got the best name, because it rhymes with so many things.

He received similar amounts of coverage on MSNBC, much of it mocking. All told, it wasn't huge coverage, but it's enough that it increased his standing in the polls by more than half a point per day – a situation that lasted most of a week. Later, when the coverage turned strongly negative over allegations of sexual harassment, he was on the receiving end of eight negative statements, and no positive statements over a 3-day period. In addition to the actual allegations, and his responses to them, which certainly hurt his popularity, the coverage on Fox cost him about half a point per day. All told, positive coverage during his peak gave Cain about an extra 2.5 points in the polls; negative coverage around his fall cost him an extra 2 points.

These effects of Fox's coverage on the standing of the candidates are even more remarkable when they're compared to the lack of effects for all of the other news outlets, which have a far larger audience than any program on Fox. Positive stories about a candidate on ABC, NBC or CBS do correspond to increases in a candidate's standing down the line, and negative stories correspond to decreases, but the effects are so small that they can't be distinguished from no effect at all. Positive stories about a candidate on any of the evening news broadcasts have about one-fifth of the effect of a positive story on Fox, and while negative stories have an effect almost as large as those on Fox (only about 20 percent smaller), the effect still isn't statistically significant. In sum, any effect the evening news broadcasts have on the candidate's poll numbers in the primary election is so small that it might well be zero.

Interestingly, Fox seems to have a much more muted effect on Romney's poll numbers. Positive stories about Romney on Fox don't have any significant effect

TABLE 3.3 Tone of Romney Coverage during Primary, by Source, Type of Coverage

	Horserace		Non-horserace		Horserace % of coverage
	% Negative	% Positive	% Negative	% Positive	
ABC/NBC	30	47	48	18	69
CBS	22	59	29	17	73
Fox	18	53	41	17	74

Note: See methodology note 3.4 for details.

at all, while negative stories have a strong impact in what seems to be the wrong direction. A negative story on Fox about Romney corresponds to a later increase of about 0.09 points in Romney's poll numbers, in what looks to be the result of a rally effect among his supporters (Cohen et al. 2008). Moreover, since Romney was higher in the polls for longer than any of the other candidates, who came and went fairly quickly, he received a great deal more coverage on Fox and the other media outlets than his opponents. As a result, the positive effects of negative coverage on Fox have the potential to drive up his numbers significantly.

As it turns out, that didn't happen, mostly because the coverage of Romney on Fox was strongly positive, with about twice as many positive as negative statements about him. Most of that is driven by horserace coverage: a candidate who wins an election is going to receive positive coverage about it, and Romney won more elections than any of the other candidates, as shown in Table 3.3. This advantage doesn't extend to non-horserace coverage: on Fox, as well as the evening news broadcasts, coverage of Romney that wasn't centered on election and poll dynamics was generally negative. For coverage on Fox, though, this was largely drowned out by the positive horserace statements: the horserace was 74 percent of the coverage of Romney, and more than half of that was positive.

During Romney's worst days – around the end of January of 2012, when it became clear that he wasn't going to be able to run away with the nomination – he was recording nine or ten negative statements a day on Fox, balanced out by only a handful of positive statements. Such days would be expected to *increase* his poll numbers by nearly 1 point per day as long as the tide of negative coverage continued – a period which lasted a little more than a week. That tide of negative coverage on Fox seems to have increased Romney's margins by 5.7 points (and, in reality, he reversed a downward trend and began to gain again shortly after the negative coverage began).

Why Romney Is Different

All of this raises the question of why Romney is so different from the other candidates in the race. It seems likely that the difference is due to Romney's privileged position in the election – a position that researchers studying the primary process have found to be increasingly important. William Mayer has been the leading proponent of a model of the primary process in which the frontrunners at the start of the process wind up winning the nomination (Mayer 1996, 2000, Mayer and Busch 2004), with voters choosing from what Steger (2000) has called a "stacked deck." This system is thought to have been accelerated by a series of reforms in the nomination process after 1972, which seemed to lead to a less chaotic, more managed series of nominating contests (Aldrich 1980, Barilleaux and Adkins 1992, Mayer 1996). It might seem that the decline of controls on campaign spending post-*Citizens United* upset this balance, with the 2012 Republican Presidential nominating contest showing wild swings in support between a number of candidates in the pre-primary and through the start of the nominating contests, but in the end, the pre-primary leader – Romney – wound up being the winner of the nomination (Norrander 2013). This process seems to be even more influential on the Republican side: as Berggren (2007) points out, the only elections between 1972 and 2004 in which the early frontrunner did not win (and the only one since, Obama in 2008) were all on the Democratic side. This seems to be evidence of the hybrid approach proposed by Steger (Steger et al. 2004, Steger 2013), in which the invisible primary dominates the nomination process if party elites are able to unify behind a candidate during the pre-primary period. If they are unable to do so, early nominating contests, such as those in Iowa and New Hampshire, take on additional importance. In this case, because party elites were able to unify behind Romney early on, signs that he was slipping – such as the negative coverage on Fox – led to increases in support. Other candidates were pushing to be the more conservative alternative to Romney, the establishment favorite who was in one of the top two positions for the entire race (McGowen and Palazzolo 2014). The dynamic in the polls is pretty clear: a challenger overtakes Romney, the support for the challenger falls off, and Romney emerges with more support than he had going into the challenge, before facing the next challenger. This pattern was repeated several times over the course of the race, and suggests that these challengers actually pushed support towards Romney, perhaps at the expense of the non-ascendant challengers. So, for instance, when then frontrunner Rick Perry's support collapsed, Herman Cain quickly took over in the polls, but this didn't have much of an impact on Romney's numbers, which steadily built as support for the candidates other than Cain and Romney (especially Ron Paul) fell away. This is consistent with Romney being the second-favorite candidate of a large number of voters: there might have been someone they liked better, but they preferred Romney to whoever was taking the lead at that time. As a result, negative horserace coverage was a signal that another less-preferred candidate could win, pushing these voters to strategically support Romney over Cain, Gingrich or whoever.

Importantly, the data doesn't support the various claims made during the campaign that Fox was unduly supportive of Romney at the expense of other candidates. The tone of the coverage of Romney on Fox is broadly in line with what was on the evening news broadcasts, and while the coverage of Romney was generally more positive than the coverage of the other candidates, that was driven by the horserace coverage. Romney received more positive horserace coverage in all of the broadcasts – but that's because he led in the polls more and won more elections than his competitors.

In sum, Republican primary voters in 2012 were strongly influenced by the content of the coverage on Fox, but didn't seem to respond to coverage on the other broadcasts at all. Since most of this coverage was about the dynamics of the election itself, it had the effect of magnifying the already large swings in the polls. A candidate who did well in a poll, or in a primary contest, received a great deal of positive coverage for that win, and that coverage further increased standing in the polls until unignorable gaffes or a resurgent Romney turned the coverage negative, exaggerating a collapse in the polls. The relatively small amount of coverage the non-Romney candidates received for most of the primary means that these effects are generally fairly small – but they become large when the dynamics of the race shift. Generally, coverage on Fox didn't help or hurt Herman Cain or Rick Perry or Rick Santorum very much, but when that coverage did come, it was at a critical juncture for their candidacies, and accelerated their rise and fall.

The magnitude of these effects is more impressive because they don't include the effects of whatever actually caused the news coverage in the first place. Because the analysis controls for the content of the mainstream evening news broadcasts – which are covering the same major election events as Fox is – the estimated effect of Fox on the poll numbers of the candidates is on top of everything that was covered in the other broadcasts. So the effects seen here aren't the effects of, say, winning a primary contest: that would be covered in all of the media sources. At most, it's the indirect effects of how that victory is spun on Fox, or what's said about the candidate on Fox about the victory that isn't said on the other media outlets. Despite the fact that Fox has a much smaller viewership than the evening news broadcasts (as discussed in Chapter 1), its status as a trusted source of information for conservative Republicans, the group most likely to vote in the Republican primary, gives it outsize influence on the course of the election.

Campaign Contributions

In addition to effects on the polls, it's also possible to look at how media coverage of the candidates impacts the amount of money they're able to raise from the public, and how that money's divided between large and small donations. Thanks to campaign finance disclosure rules administered by the Federal Election Commission (FEC), candidates are required to give the names, addresses and occupations of all donors who give more than $200 to their campaigns (the disclosure includes individuals who gave less than $200 if they gave money via websites or text message – a group which includes most of the contributors in the 2012 Presidential election). The resulting dataset is enormous – about 22 million entries for the 2012 primary and general elections – and is freely accessible to anyone with the necessary hard drive space who wants to download it. While there's a perception that campaign contributions are the province of the wealthy, Pew data from the 2012 election shows that 13 percent of Americans gave money to one of the Presidential candidates, making the overall pool of donors much more like voters in general than in past elections (Lipsitz and Panagopoulos 2011). Since media coverage, especially on Fox, drives support to candidates, it makes sense that it would also drive some proportion of voters to donate money to those candidates.

From a data perspective, this is fantastic. First, this is not a sample of voters, but rather a list of everyone who gave directly to the candidates. When looking at the effect of the media on poll numbers, there's always the chance that a group that was heavily influenced by a particular piece of information was underrepresented in the polls. For instance, researchers have shown repeatedly that evangelical Christians are less likely than the average American to take part in political telephone polls (Bader et al. 2007), perhaps because they don't trust them, or fear that their beliefs will be ridiculed. So, if media coverage of Rick Santorum drove these evangelical Christians towards him, the spike of support for Santorum would be underreported in the aggregate poll numbers. While pollsters commonly use techniques like weighting and stratifying to account for these sorts of differences, they can't account for all of them, introducing extra error into any model of what drives the polls. Since the contribution data doesn't rely on samples, there isn't any concern about systematic underrepresentation or overrepresentation: it's all there.

Second, time elements aren't nearly as much of a problem when looking at campaign contribution data. Political polls are generally taken over the course of 3–7 nights, with pollsters working during elections trying to bring that time down as much as possible in order to keep the data timely. This is important for our purposes because it means that any impact of the media on a candidate's support isn't going to be evident until the poll is finished calling people, and the effects may be diluted by the fact that some of the people in the sample may have been exposed to that news, while others were called before it happened. When looking at campaign contributions, this isn't as much of a problem. According to Pew data, 60 percent of donors to the candidates in the 2012 Presidential election made their contributions via email or text message (both campaigns had systems set up to accept donations via text in 2012, the first election in which the FEC allowed it). These techniques are as instant as it can get: while there's no way to be sure, it seems likely that many of these donations were in direct response to something seen on television, potentially happening while the information was being presented.

Of course, there are some serious limitations to this sort of analysis. For one thing, while candidates are required to report all donations over $200 to the FEC, the 2012 election saw enormous amounts of money contributed to outside groups – such as so-called Super PACS (political action committees) – that didn't have to disclose their donors. These groups are able to spend money on behalf of the candidates as long as they don't actively coordinate with the candidate's campaign. There's no central clearinghouse for these sorts of donations, even when they are disclosed, and even if there were, it's not entirely clear how they should be credited to the candidates. Some of the PACs are no more than alternative ways of donating to campaigns, while some may have legitimate aims of their own. Similarly, some of the donations are motivated by a desire to give to a candidate, while some may be driven by allegiance to the people running the PAC, or its stated goals. The difference is important, and since there is no clear way of establishing it, it's better to use only contributions that are sure to have been intended for the candidate.

In addition, not all of the donations are instantaneous. According to the Pew data, 60 percent of donors made contributions online or via text, and most of the remaining donations were made in person at campaign rallies or smaller local meetings. The final group – contributions made via mail – constitute a relatively small and shrinking portion of contributions (campaigns don't like them as much as online contributions because of additional processing costs), so while they're registered by the campaigns on the date they were received, which may well be a few days after they were sent, they're not a big problem. The larger issue comes from the checks given in person. In many cases, these checks are given to a bundler, who pools donations from a large number of contributors. When these checks go to the campaign, they're registered as a large number of smaller donations, despite the fact that they're more likely to represent the preferences of the bundler, who may be strategically deciding which candidate to raise money for, and when (Stromer-Galley 2014). Unfortunately, there's no mechanism for telling the difference between checks given to the campaign via a bundler and those given directly to the campaign, so the process may well introduce some error into our calculations of how media impacts the contributions decisions people make (see methodology note 3.5 for more on why this isn't too much of a problem here).

The final problem with the FEC contribution data is that some contributions aren't included at all. While small donations given via electronic means are included in the data, small contributions that come in via checks from donors who give less than $200 over the course of the campaign to the candidate and meet various other requirements aren't always included. To understand what drives small contributions versus large contributions – which are always recorded – this is a potential problem, but not a big one. While small checks aren't always recorded in the FEC data, there are fewer of these than there were in the past: small donors are increasingly likely to give money online or via text. From a data perspective, this means that the FEC data on small donations includes more of those people who gave money online, but since the goal here is to see the immediate effects of media coverage, that's not necessarily a bad thing.

The decision to make a campaign contribution is more complicated than the decision to tell a pollster that you're supporting a particular candidate. There's reason to believe that voters' campaign contributions may be more strategic, with some contributors wanting to give their money to those candidates who have a chance of actually winning the nomination (Mutz 1995a describes two different kinds of donors, with large donors expected to be more strategic). These strategic elements make the analysis rather more complex (details on the contribution analyses in general can be found in methodology note 3.6). There are two different basic measures that can be taken from the FEC data: the amount raised by a candidate on a given day, and the number of contributions given on that day. As with the analysis of the effects of media on poll results in Chapter 4, the analyses control for the time element by only using media coverage data from the 3 days prior to the actual contribution. While contributors may be giving money in the moment when they see media reports about a candidate, there are plenty of examples of good fundraising days leading to positive coverage. A campaign that raises a lot of money on a given day might well publicize that amount on the news that night; so including same-day news coverage could potentially credit the amount raised to the coverage of the amount raised – something that would undercut the causal story.

Media Coverage and Contributions in the 2012 Primary

The simplest way to model the data is to look at how the number of contributions a candidate receives on a given day is driven by media coverage over the few days prior, and the results here are straightforward. On average, candidates other than Romney receive seventeen contributions for each positive statement about them on Fox news in the past 3 days, and lose six donations for each negative statement on the non-Fox broadcasts. Positive statements on the evening news broadcasts and negative statements on Fox don't seem to make a difference. This is all in addition to the effects of how well a candidate is doing in the polls: the better the poll numbers, the more contributions a candidate can expect to receive (for full results, see methodology note 3.7). For Romney, news coverage doesn't make any difference in the number of contributions received: the better he's doing in the polls, the more contributions he receives, but that's about it. The results are about the same in an analysis of the amount of money that a candidate receives, rather than the number of donations: for the candidates other than Romney, a positive mention on Fox nets about $4,700 a day for the next 3 days, while a negative mention on another channel costs the candidate about $6,900 a day for the next 3 days (full results in methodology note 3.8).

While a model like this has the virtue of simplicity, it's actually a bit too simple. First, it treats all donations as the same, when there could easily be differences between what leads people to make small donations and what leads them to make large donations. Second, it ignores the likelihood that donors behave differently when a candidate is doing well in the polls than when that candidate isn't. To begin with, the analyses divide the contributions into four categories, depending on their size: small contributions of $250 or less (a bit more than half of all of the registered contributions, totaling 20 percent of the money the candidates raised), moderate contributions of $251–1,750 (38 percent of the contributions, and 39 percent of the money), large contributions of $1,751–2,499 (9 percent of all contributions and 4 percent of the money) and very large contributions of $2,500 or more (the top 1 percent of contributions, but about 37 percent of the money).

When the analyses allow for the effect of news stories varying by how well the candidate is doing, and divide up the contributions by size, the results are much more interesting. A few patterns emerge across all of the contribution categories. First, statements about the candidates on Fox have a significant impact throughout, but statements on the non-Fox channels only have a significant impact on larger contributions. Looking at small donations – those of $250 or less – positive statements on Fox about the candidate bring in more contributions than would be expected based just on the candidates' standing in the polls, and negative statements lead to less money in donations, as shown in Figure 3.4. Statements on any of the other channels have an effect that's so small – a few hundred dollars a day, at most – that they're indistinguishable from no effect at all. Looking at the big contributions – $2,500 or more – all of the statements start to matter (see methodology note 3.9 for more information on these analyses), as shown in Figure 3.5.

This is the first sign that part of what's happening here is down to differences in how large and small donors are making the decision to give money. The small donors are highly responsive to Fox, but don't pay any attention to the other media outlets: they're looking for ideological cues, signs that the candidate is favored by their party, but paying less attention to whether that candidate's acceptable to the wider polity. This is line with past research, such as Mutz (1995a), who argues that big donors are generally more strategic, and looking for indications that a candidate will win before making a contribution. Larger donors aren't making a statement – they're making an investment. As such, they're paying attention not just to the ideological cues that might be provided by Fox, but also to the networks, and what they might be saying about electability.

Second, positive statements on Fox help candidates who aren't doing very well, but don't do much to help candidates who already are. For a candidate languishing at 5 percent in the polls, a single positive mention on Fox News leads to a $4,500 bump in small donations per day for 3 days, as well as an extra $2,700 per day in large donations. A candidate currently polling at 10 percent can only

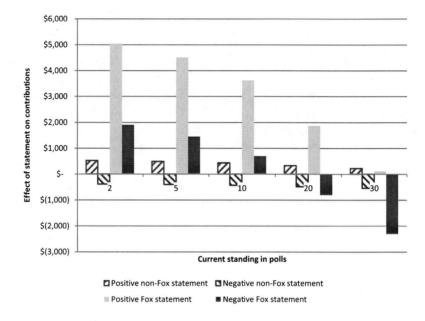

FIGURE 3.4 Effects of Media Statements on Money Raised in Donations of $250 or Less for Non-Romney Candidates, per Day

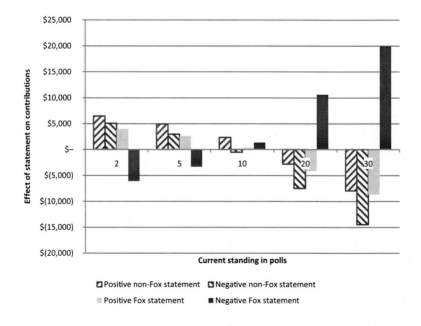

FIGURE 3.5 Effects of Media Statements on Money Raised in Donations of $2,500 or More for Non-Romney Candidates, per Day

expect a bump of $3,600 per day from small donors, and no real increase among large donors – only about an extra $350 per day. If the candidate's doing very well, at 30 percent in the polls, the increase in small donations is negligible – about $100 per day, and there's actually a negative impact on large donors.

Third, for candidates who aren't doing well, any news is good news. If a candidate's at 10 percent or less in the polls, any statement on Fox News, positive or negative, leads to an increase in donations. Positive statements bring in more money than negative statements, but it seems that merely reminding potential supporters that a candidate's in the race is worth something to candidates at the back of the pack. If a candidate's at 2 percent in the polls, a positive statement on Fox is worth a bit more than $5,000 extra in small donations, and even a negative statement is worth about $1,900 dollars in small donations. The same holds true for large donations in response to non-Fox coverage. Large donations increase for candidates polling at 2 percent if they're mentioned at all in non-Fox broadcasts, to the tune of about $6,500 in large donations for a positive mention, and $5,100 for a negative one. At the same time, Fox coverage has the expected impact on large donations to these candidates, increasing with positive mentions (by about $4,000 per day), and declining by about $6,000 for a negative mention. It seems likely that large donors see mainstream media coverage – positive or negative – as a sign that an investment in a long-shot candidate might pay off, while seeing the tone of coverage on Fox as an indicator of whether a candidate will be accepted by the party.

Media Coverage and Leading Candidates

The world is very different for candidates doing well in the polls. The analyses discussed so far only cover the non-Romney candidates – as with the effects of media coverage on poll numbers, Romney's campaign follows very different rules – and for all but a few days of the campaign, one of these candidates was at 25 percent or better. It makes sense that the media would impact the main challenger to Romney differently, but it's surprising how differently donors act. While small donors give money in response to struggling candidates in response to any mention on Fox broadcasts, the leading candidate of the moment loses donations in response to negative coverage. For a candidate polling at 20 percent, a negative statement on Fox reduces expected small donations by about $800 a day for 3 days; for a candidate at 30 percent, that negative statement costs about $2,300 per day. On the flipside, positive coverage on Fox doesn't help these candidates nearly as much: a positive statement on Fox is worth half as much to a candidate at 20 percent as it is to a candidate at 10 percent, and is worth almost nothing if the candidate's at 30 percent.

When a candidate's leading in the polls, large donors are especially sensitive to coverage on Fox, but not in the way you might expect. If a candidate's at 20 percent in the polls, negative statements on the mainstream evening news broadcasts reduce large donations by about $7,500 per day; but positive statements reduce contributions as well, just by a smaller amount. The only sort of coverage that increases large donations is negative coverage on Fox. The candidate challenging Romney for the lead could expect to get an extra $10,600 a day in contributions after a negative statement on Fox. What's going on here?

While coverage – even some positive coverage – is expected to reduce contributions to candidates doing well in the polls, there's no reason to feel bad for them, as their baseline level of contributions is much, much higher than for candidates doing poorly. All told, a candidate polling at 2 percent who hasn't received any media coverage in the previous few days can expect to bring in just about $25,000 a day in contributions. A candidate polling at 20 percent can expect about $240,000 extra a day; at 30 percent, that goes up to more than $350,000 a day while those poll numbers last (which wasn't too long for any of the candidates in the 2012 Republican primary). So, while most types of coverage tend to reduce contributions for candidates who are riding high in the polls, it reduces them from a much higher level. These candidates also get a lot more coverage in the media – and a lot more criticism from their opponents – than the candidates who aren't doing as well, which may well explain the oddly reversed effects of Fox coverage on their contributions from donors writing big checks. Donors giving $2,500 or more may well regard attacks on Fox as a reaffirmation that their candidate is seen as the leader, or perhaps that the candidate needs reinforcement to stay in the lead. Either way, attacks on Fox lead candidates who are flying high in the polls to get more money from big donors, and less money from small ones.

All of this analysis is for candidates other than Romney, and for good reason: media coverage just doesn't have that much of an impact on Romney's fundraising. Rather, the biggest influence on how much money the Romney campaign brought in was how well he was doing in the polls, and what direction the polls had been moving during the previous week (a factor which had absolutely no impact on the fundraising totals of the other candidates) – a pattern observed for frontrunners in previous elections as well (Mutz 1995b). Basically, the better Romney was doing in the polls, the more money he brought in, especially from large donors, and declines in those poll numbers led large donors to give even more: a 3 point drop over the course of a week led big contributors to chip in an extra $16,000 a day in contributions, while not impacting small donor behavior at all.

Conclusions about the Media and Fundraising

All of the evidence on the effects of media on contributions to candidates in the 2012 Republican primary points to three overarching conclusions. First, coverage of the candidate, especially on Fox News, has an enormous impact on how much money the lower-tier candidates are able to raise. One positive statement about a candidate from Fox about a candidate at 5 percent in the polls nets that candidate more than $13,000 in small contributions, and a total of nearly $38,000 over the course of 3 days. That's not a lot of money in terms of a national political campaign: the Romney campaign wouldn't have sneezed at it, but probably wouldn't have worried too much about it either. For these smaller campaigns, though, it's a lot. Not counting money that went to Super PACs or money the candidate lent to his own campaign, the Huntsman campaign raised about $2.3 million in total over the period studied. The increased contributions related to that one positive statement amount to more than 1.5 percent of all of the money raised from individual donors during the period studied. All told, Fox made twenty-one positive and fifteen negative statements about Huntsman over the course of the campaign – not a lot of coverage, but enough to represent a sizeable portion of the total amount he was able to bring in, especially when it's remembered that even negative statements on Fox help out candidates who are as low in the polls as he was for much of the campaign. Huntsman also got some coverage on the non-Fox broadcasts – but given his standing in the polls, this doesn't seem to have made much of a difference in the amount of money he was able to bring in. Simply put, the lower-tier candidates lived and died by coverage on Fox News.

Second, in a primary campaign like this one, the non-Fox broadcasts just don't seem to matter that much. It's only among the biggest donors – those giving $2,500 or more in a shot – that ABC, CBS and NBC consistently matter at all, and even among them, the effects of negative and positive statements are much smaller than the effects of statements on Fox. For small donors, at least, Fox is literally the only news that matters.

Finally, large and small donors behave very differently. Large donors not only respond to news that isn't on Fox, they also pay a great deal more attention to how well the candidate's doing in the polls. For all levels of contributions, the impact of a statement depends strongly on how well the candidate's polling: a positive statement on Fox nets a candidate polling at 2 percent more than $15,000 extra in small contributions over 3 days, but only nets a candidate polling at 30 percent about an extra $350. However, this interaction between a candidate's poll numbers and the effect of statements in the media gets stronger as the contributions get bigger. Small contributors are making a statement; big contributors are making an investment.

Necessarily, these investments are only going to pay off if the candidate being invested in actually wins. So it makes sense that people writing a check for $2,500 or more (and sometimes a lot more: the two biggest days for contributions in the dataset are for nearly $2 million each, both of them for Perry, who has a disproportionate number of the biggest contribution days; Romney's best day among the large donors was a little more than $500,000, and the biggest day among them for any other candidate was $225,000 to Gingrich) are going to pay attention to the polls, and favor the candidate who seems likely to win at the time. Small donors, however, must have some idea that their contributions aren't going to make much of a difference to candidates who are on top of the polls, and probably not much of a difference to candidates who aren't doing so well. They're likely contributing for what Kayden (1985) calls "moral reasons." These small donors seem to be using their money to make a statement that they're ideologically aligned with the candidate to whom they're contributing. If you know your donation isn't going to be making much of a difference, and you're giving money just to express your support for a candidate who has said or done something you like, there's no reason to worry too much about how well the candidate's doing in the polls.

Conclusions

Looking at the effects of the media on both polls and fundraising in the 2012 Republican primary, it becomes clear that when it comes to Republican politics, at least, Fox News has not only far greater impact than the broadcast networks, but a real impact on the dynamics of the race. There's no evidence that the outcome of the primary would have been any different had Fox covered the race in a different way; after all, Fox coverage simply didn't have that much of an effect on Romney, so he likely still would have won. But the story of the 2012 Republican Presidential primary isn't primarily the story of Romney winning: what characterizes the race is the series of candidates who went from also-ran to frontrunner status and back again in record time, and Fox's coverage does play a big role in that.

The results can't say that Cain or Perry or Gingrich or Santorum wouldn't have made a run at the lead in the absence of Fox coverage, but they can say that Fox coverage makes a huge difference in the ability of minor candidates to raise money, and money certainly helps candidates move up in the polls. More directly, Fox's coverage led candidates to gain and lose ground in the polls faster than they would have otherwise – a process which loops back to cause shifts in the amount of money that candidates were able to raise. Candidates in races like this are always fighting for momentum, for the perception among opinion leaders, the media and the public that they're on the way up. This momentum may start with an electoral win in a small state – as it did for Barack Obama in the 2008 Democratic primary – but it can also start with a jump in the polls (Mutz 1997, Steger 2008, McGowen and Palazzolo 2014). Such gains turn into increased media attention and increased fundraising, and all of that lets a candidate buy more advertising, more people on the ground, and a bigger campaign operation, fueling a further rise in the polls. It doesn't seem that coverage on Fox News was enough to sustain that upward spiral of success, but it seems likely that positive coverage – or, at low levels of polling, any coverage – was enough to jumpstart the process. The gains in the polls and the bump in fundraising have to start somewhere, and coverage on Fox seems a likely place.

So, while media coverage does have a real impact on the dynamics of the campaign, these effects are limited, and the surest sign of this is the relative lack of media effects on the Romney campaign. For Romney, positive coverage on Fox didn't do anything, and negative coverage just served to mobilize supporters. Similarly, positive coverage on Fox seems to actually reduce large contributions to Romney's campaign, while having no impact at all on small contributors. Positive coverage on Fox mattered to the other candidates because they didn't already have a large campaign in place, because they needed a jumpstart to have a chance in the polls. Since Romney already had money, name recognition and organization in place, there wasn't much that the media could do to help or hurt him, aside from mentioning how well he was doing in the polls. As his poll numbers rose, so did his contributions among the large donors who were looking to make an investment, and when his poll numbers fell, contributions among this group increased even more, either to protect their investment or to ward off a less palatable challenger. Could Fox, or one of the other broadcasters, have taken Romney down? Almost certainly not. As powerful as the media is in influencing voters, that influence is on the margins: those margins can make or break a candidate who's already living on the edge, but can't do much to a presumptive leader like Romney. Instead, being the presumptive leader – or perhaps just the favored candidate of powerful parts of the establishment – seems to be a self-sustaining role. A dip in the poll numbers leads donors to give more; negative coverage pushes wayward supporters back to him. Romney's contributors and supporters are still responding to the content of the media, but not in nearly the same way as they do for the other candidates.

Fox's role in the 2012 Republican primary seems to be the arbiter of taste for rank-and-file members of the party. Its coverage doesn't impact the big donors terribly much, but it does seem to have created flavor-of-the-week candidates through a combination of attention and positive coverage. For a minor candidate, merely being mentioned on Fox was enough to set off a surge of small contributions, likely because of the way that coverage framed the race in the eyes of viewers. If a viewer perceived Romney as too moderate, or unelectable, Fox was presenting alternatives, candidates who might come closer to the viewer's preferred viewpoint. When one of these candidates jumped in the polls, Fox coverage increased the size of that jump, and pushed more small donors towards him. When that candidate began to flounder, as they all did, Fox accelerated the decline, and quickly substituted a new alternative to be built up and taken down. Fox didn't get Romney elected, or singlehandedly create the volatility that characterized the 2012 primary, but the extreme volatility and fundraising shifts were at least partially due to its coverage.

4

THE 2012 GENERAL ELECTION

Compared to the Republican primary, the 2012 general Presidential election was pretty dull. While the degree to which he led fluctuated over the course of the campaign, Obama held a lead in the poll aggregates for the entirety of the general election, and wound up winning by about the margin predicted by the aggregators (Panagopoulos and Cohen 2014). However, there's enough variation in the size of that lead to enable us to answer several important questions about the impact of the media on how voters make decisions about the candidates: How much does media coverage impact the polls? Is the election purely about the incumbent? How much do campaign events matter?

The results here indicate that while coverage of the general election doesn't matter as much as it did in the primary election, media coverage on the networks and on Fox does still play a role. Some of this role is direct – coverage on Fox matters a great deal during the first part of the general election, when fewer voters are paying attention, while coverage on the networks matters more as the election draws nearer – and much of it is indirect. The actual events of the campaign normally thought to drive voters towards one candidate or the other don't seem to actually make much of an impact, but they do seem to shift the tone of coverage, and *that* impacts the standing of the candidates in the polls.

Data on the General Election

As in the analyses of the Republican primary election, there are three main data sources that can be used to understand the interplay of the media and the pre-election polls. The first is the polls themselves: in this case, the Pollster poll aggregation, which included as many as five national polls per day over the course of the election, and averaged a little more than three national polls per day over the course of the general election (starting from when Romney became the presumptive nominee at the end of April 2012 until the actual election on November 6, a total of 195 days). While there are several poll aggregators that covered the 2012 Presidential election, with many using the same data, they each use slightly different algorithms to combine the various poll results into a single result at a given point in time. The Pollster average is used here because it came the closest to the actual results of the election of the major aggregators, predicting a 1.5 point margin for Obama (who actually won by 3.8 points; this may not seem terribly accurate, but 2012 was, in general, a poor year for polling accuracy in the Presidential race). While differences in question wording across the polls being aggregated makes the use of aggregators problematic in the analysis of the Republican primary election, this sort of variation isn't a problem in the general election, as all of the major survey groups used approximately the same wording. The second data source is, as before, Media Tenor data on the content of evening news broadcasts on the three major networks, as well as Fox News, for the same period, including all coverage of the two candidates. Finally, FEC data allows for the tracking of all registered campaign contributions, with the same caveats discussed in Chapter 3.

Obama's lead over the course of the election ranged from a high of 4.2 points over Romney (48.3 to 44.1) at the end of September to a low of 0.2 points at the end of October. Obama held a solid, though not huge, lead of 1–2 points from April until around the end of August, when his lead began to grow substantially – growth that coincided with the end of the Republican National Convention that officially nominated Romney, and was most notable for the speech given by actor and director Clint Eastwood to an empty chair – a speech which was reported very differently on the three main cable networks. CNN's John King noted that "if you don't like Barack Obama, you probably thought it was funny and scathing." Chris Matthews on MSNBC referred to the speech as "bizarre ramblings." Eric Bolling, one of the hosts of Fox News's *The Five*, called it "irreverent and sometimes outright funny . . . landing some hard-hitting blows." Shortly after this came the seemingly more successful Democratic National Convention, which included a positively reviewed speech by former President Bill Clinton. Immediately after the conventions, Obama's lead grew to more than 4 points, before declining again, beginning at the end of September, and accelerating at about the time of the first Presidential debate, which Obama was largely perceived to have lost to Romney. The timing of the rise and fall of Obama's poll numbers relative to Romney led many at the time to attribute these shifts to campaign events – a hypothesis that will be tested later in this chapter.

The most obvious characteristic of the general election polling is the extent to which Obama's numbers and Romney's numbers are mirror images. Because not everyone in a general election poll actually picks a candidate, with some saying that they're not sure, or refusing to answer the question, it's possible for one candidate to gain ground without the other candidate losing any. There's actually plenty of room for this: early in the election, about 10 percent of likely voters say that they don't know who they'll vote for – a figure which drops to about 5 percent just before the election. However, this doesn't seem to be happening: rather, gains for one candidate are almost perfectly reflected in losses for the other (changes in the two series are correlated at p = −0.64), as seen in Figure 4.1. This is important because it means that there's nothing to be gained from looking at changes in Obama's support and Romney's support separately: they're basically the same thing. Instead, the two can be combined into one measure, which looks at the difference between the two candidates in the poll aggregate.

Before addressing the first major question of the chapter – How much does media coverage impact these poll numbers? – it's necessary to sort out what is, and what is not, an actual change in the polls. While some of the fluctuations are probably meaningful, others probably aren't. For instance, suppose that an event in the campaign, or an especially successful advertisement, pushes some voters who previously had been on the fence to support one of the candidates. That candidate would see a bump in poll numbers: one that's meaningful, with a source that could be identified. However, after a time, some proportion of those voters who were swayed by that event or ad are likely to return to being on the fence, or favoring the other candidate. Maybe the memories of the event faded; maybe

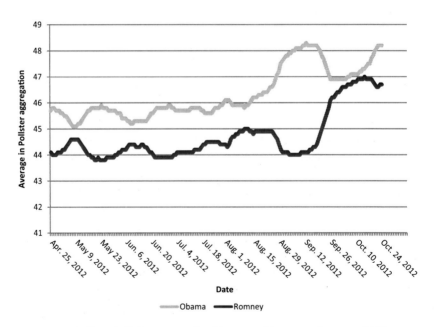

FIGURE 4.1 Pollster Poll Aggregates for Obama and Romney Support, 2012 General Election

it stopped being the most relevant issue when they were answering a poll interviewer's question about which candidate they were going to support. Regardless of what the reason is, a gain in the polls is likely to be followed by a drop in the polls, and while the gain might be driven by something that can be measured, it isn't clear that the following drop is (the same logic applies to gains following a consequential drop). When measured over time, poll numbers have their own internal logic – what researchers call endogenous characteristics – and it's possible to correct for the changes in the polls that are due to this internal logic, leaving only those changes that are consequential (see methodology note 4.1).

Media Coverage of the 2012 General Election

Given the amount of media coverage received by the Republican primary election, it makes sense that general election coverage would be overwhelming, and it was. Even if the definition of election coverage is limited to coverage centering on the Presidential or Vice-Presidential candidates (in order to differentiate it from coverage of the other elections going on at the same time), statements about Obama, Biden, Romney and Ryan constitute 27 percent of all the statements on ABC, NBC, CBS and Fox News over the period of the general election (April 25–November 6). This coverage was heavily weighted towards the Presidential nominees, rather than their running mates, but even they received substantial coverage, as shown in Table 4.1.

For reasons that will become clear, coverage on Fox has been separated out from coverage on the evening news broadcasts. Even on the network broadcasts, which are less focused on politics than Fox, coverage of the two candidates and their running mates constitutes more than a quarter of all statements on the evening news. This coverage is also pretty balanced: a bit more than 25 percent negative and a bit less than 20 percent positive for each candidate. This general balance between Republicans and Democrats extends beyond the candidates: the Republican and Democratic Parties receive almost identical coverage as well. As shown in Chapter 1, coverage of Democrats and Republicans on the evening news broadcasts isn't normally this balanced, indicating that the networks are taking special care to be evenhanded during the Presidential election.

This evenhandedness doesn't extend to Fox, however, as shown in Table 4.2. While the total amount of coverage focused on Obama and Romney is about the same on Fox as it is on the evening news broadcasts, the tone of the coverage is very different. Coverage of Romney is about the same as on the broadcast networks (29 percent negative and 22 percent positive on Fox, versus 26 percent negative and 20 percent positive on the other broadcasts), but coverage of Obama is much more negative. Fully 41 percent of all of the statements about Obama on Fox are negative (along with more than half of the statements about the Obama administration in general). Oddly, though, this doesn't seem to represent any sort of general anti-Democratic bias: Congressional Republicans

TABLE 4.1 The Top Twenty-Five Figures and Institutions Covered on ABC, NBC and CBS, April 25–November 6, 2012

Figure	% Negative	% Neutral	% Positive	% of all coverage
Obama, Barack	27	56	17	12.8
Romney, Mitt	26	54	20	10.3
Republican Party (USA)	20	71	9	2.3
Ryan, Paul	18	69	12	2.1
White House/Obama Administration	34	63	3	1.9
Assad, Bashar al	79	19	2	1.7
Democratic Party (USA)	20	65	15	1.7
Clinton, Hillary	6	89	4	1.3
Biden Jr., Joseph	21	70	9	1.2
NASA	4	64	32	1.2
George Zimmerman	75	25	0	0.9
Congressional Republicans	41	51	8	0.8
Taliban	74	23	3	0.8
Al Qaeda	75	23	0	0.8
bin Laden, Osama	89	11	0	0.8
Clinton, Bill	0	75	25	0.7
Stevens, Christopher	85	6	9	0.7
Holmes, James	69	31	0	0.7
US Secret Service	94	5	0	0.7
Federal Bureau of Investigation	3	78	19	0.7
Trayvon Martin	95	5	0	0.6
Sandusky, Jerry	87	13	0	0.6
McCain, John S.	19	74	6	0.5
Obama, Michelle	0	81	19	0.5

and Congressional Democrats (not individual members, just the parties within Congress) are treated about equally, each at about 30 percent negative and just under 10 percent positive. Coverage of the Republican and Democratic Parties is similarly even.

Coverage of the candidates during the general election is less focused on the horserace than coverage during the Republican primary, perhaps because there's simply less variation in the polls. About 43 percent of all of the statements about Romney focus on polls, elections and advertising, with the remaining coverage split between a variety of topics, including substantive issues, like taxes, the economy, and oddly, foreign affairs, which was the most discussed substantive policy issue for Romney, as shown in Table 4.3.

Foreign affairs was also the most covered substantive policy issue for Obama, constituting about 11 percent of all of the statements about him. As shown in Table 4.4, coverage of Obama is, in general, much less focused on horserace

TABLE 4.2 Coverage on Fox, April 25–November 6, 2012

Figure	% Negative	% Neutral	% Positive	% of all coverage
Obama, Barack	41	47	11	14.3
Romney, Mitt	29	49	22	10.4
White House/Obama Administration	51	46	3	3.9
Republican Party	23	67	10	3.1
Democratic Party	29	61	10	2.7
Ryan, Paul	17	67	17	2.2
Congressional Republicans	32	61	7	1.6
Biden Jr., Joseph	30	63	8	1.5
Clinton, Hillary	11	84	5	1.3
Assad, Bashar al	80	18	2	1.1
Congressional Democrats	28	64	8	1.1
Clinton, Bill	5	69	26	0.9
Al Qaeda	83	13	3	0.9
Bush, George W.	30	53	18	0.7
McCain, John S.	16	79	6	0.7
Carney, Jay	8	92	0	0.7
Stevens, Christopher	91	3	6	0.7
Holder, Eric	52	46	2	0.6
Boehner, John	8	90	2	0.6
NASA	7	63	30	0.6
bin Laden, Osama	92	8	0	0.6
George Zimmerman	78	21	0	0.5
US Secret Service	94	5	0	0.5
Romney, Ann	6	64	30	0.5

TABLE 4.3 Coverage of Romney, April 25–November 6, 2012

Topic	% Negative	% Neutral	% Positive	% of all coverage
Elections	18	56	25	30.5
Political parties	30	38	32	11.2
Personal qualities, awards and prizes	42	39	19	10.1
Public opinion and polling	30	34	36	7.5
Foreign affairs	45	46	9	5.6
PR, image, advertising	44	47	9	5.1
Economic policy	35	34	30	4.0
Healthcare system and policy	28	59	13	3.6
Tax policy	39	42	19	3.0
Budget, fiscal policy, including deficits	35	53	12	1.7

TABLE 4.4 Coverage of Obama, April 25–November 6, 2012

Topic	% Negative	% Neutral	% Positive	% of all coverage
Elections	35	50	15	19.3
Foreign affairs	40	54	5	10.9
Political parties	35	41	24	9.4
Public opinion and polling	35	33	32	6.1
Healthcare system and policy	46	46	8	5.8
Economic policy	64	27	9	4.7
PR, image, advertising	39	57	4	4.7
Personal qualities, awards and prizes	31	55	14	3.6
Business and economic climate	53	42	5	3.5
Tax policy	49	48	3	2.7

issues, which make up only about 30 percent of the statements about him. This makes sense: while Romney's only job during the campaign was running for office, Obama was also serving as President, necessitating some degree of substantive coverage. The reduced horserace coverage for Obama could also be due to the fact that he was in the lead for the entirety of the election: just as her poor showing in the polls meant that it didn't make sense to cover Michele Bachmann's substantive issue positions, Obama's lead makes his substantive positions more relevant, and horserace coverage less so.

As with the 2012 Republican primary, to determine the effect of the coverage on public opinion, it's necessary to take several factors into account. The most obvious is the amount of positive and negative coverage on Fox and the networks in the day prior to the change in public opinion (correcting for the internal characteristics of the poll numbers), and the trend in that public opinion data over the past 2 weeks. There are some differences between the analysis of the primary and the general election: the most obvious is that the analyses of the general election coverage consider just the previous day, rather than the aggregated coverage from the previous 3 days. The reason for this is twofold. First, because the analyses already control for the internal characteristics of the poll numbers, there's no reason to worry about the fact that the polls are taken over the course of several days. Second, the number of polls means that movement occurs much more frequently, so there's simply more variance for each day's worth of coverage to explain.

Direct Effects of the Media in the 2012 General Election

The analysis shows that coverage of Obama and Romney has a significant impact on the size of Obama's advantage in the polls throughout the course of the campaign (full regression results are in methodology note 4.2), with the results shown in Figure 4.2. When Obama has been losing ground in the polls over the past 2 weeks, positive coverage on the network news broadcasts has the biggest impact on the race: each positive statement on ABC, NBC or CBS increases the size of Obama's advantage by 0.09 the following day if Obama is down 2 points over the past 2 weeks, and by 0.05 if Obama is down 1 point over the previous 2 weeks. On a good news day for Obama, there are about three positive statements about him on the network evening news broadcasts. If he's been losing ground in the polls, that's enough to net him 0.15–0.3 points in the polls the following day, depending on how much ground he's lost. A day of very good coverage (in the top decile) – seven positive statements about him on the networks – would be expected to net him 0.35–0.63 points in the polls on the following day. This might not seem like much, but over the course of the campaign, Obama's poll numbers simply don't move very much on a day-to-day basis: even a movement of 0.1 points in either direction only happens on less than half of the days.

The story here seems fairly straightforward. When Obama has been losing ground in the polls, positive coverage on the network news broadcasts helps him gain that ground back. Coverage on Fox, meanwhile, has no effect, nor does

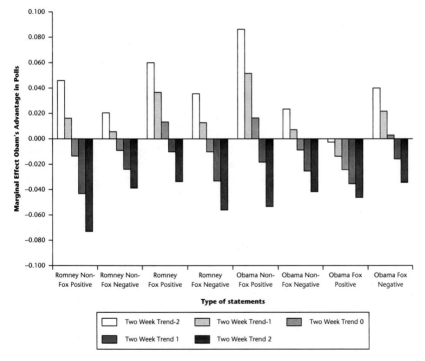

FIGURE 4.2 Marginal Effect of Media Statements on Obama's Advantage in Polls over Whole Campaign

negative coverage on the network broadcasts. Simply put, when Obama's poll numbers are down substantially, people who are inclined to turn against him already have, so more negative coverage isn't going to do much. However, positive coverage on the broadcast networks, which might serve to convert some of those lost supporters back, does make a difference, and a substantial one at that.

This isn't to say that coverage of Romney doesn't matter when Obama's lead has been declining; the only significant impact comes from positive coverage of Romney on Fox. When he's been gaining ground in the polls, Romney's progress is derailed, to some extent, by positive coverage on Fox, which costs him about 0.06 points for each statement if Romney has gained 2 points over the previous 2 weeks, and a bit less, 0.04 points, if Romney has gained 1 point on Obama in the past 2 weeks. Again, the story here isn't too complicated: when Obama's lead is well down in the polls, Romney gains many of the persuadable voters. Actions which endear him to Fox News, leading to positive coverage, seem to turn off some of the voters gained over the previous couple of weeks.

Similarly, when Obama is up in the polls over the past 2 weeks, he loses ground when Romney receives positive coverage on the network news broadcasts, which costs him about 0.07 points per positive statement about Romney on ABC, NBC or CBS. Most of the time, of course, Obama's lead now and his lead 2 weeks ago are about the same. When this is the case, positive statements about Obama on the network broadcasts help him a bit – an increase of about 0.02 points per positive statement on the following day.

However, there's a reason why this analysis of the effects of the media began with the line charts of the poll numbers. As is clear from them, there simply isn't much movement in the polls for the first part of the general election, with nearly all of the movement in the polls happening in its last 2 months. This makes sense: not only does the general public tend to pay more attention to the election in the weeks just before voting, but the amount of coverage also increases significantly during this period, as shown in Figure 4.3. The first big spike in coverage is at the start of September, and while there are fluctuations, the mean level of coverage after that point is nearly twice as high as the mean level of coverage beforehand (an average of thirteen statements a day for the last 2 months of the campaign, versus eight statements a day for the period before that). As such, it seems likely that media coverage has a greater impact on the public during those last 2 months than previously.

In those last 2 months of the campaign, media coverage has a much greater impact on the polls than has been calculated for the overall campaign. The size of the difference is enormous: for the entire period of the election, the combination of media coverage and the two-week trend explain 16 percent of the changes in Obama's advantage in a given day; in the last 2 months of the campaign, the combination of media coverage and the two-week trend explain 56 percent of all of those changes. Simply put, media coverage matters throughout the course of the campaign, but it matters a great deal more during the last 2 months.

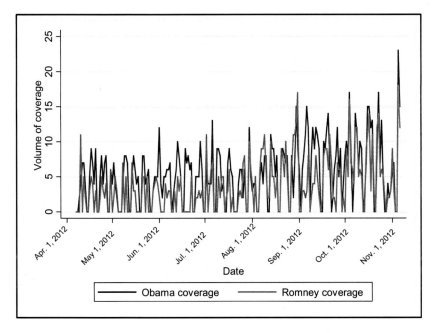

FIGURE 4.3 Number of Statements per Day about Obama and Romney

For the most part, the direction of the effects of the media on the polls are about the same during the last few months of the campaign as during the campaign overall, but the magnitude of the effects is much greater, as shown in Figure 4.4. When the size of Obama's lead has been declining over the past 2 weeks, positive statements about him on the network broadcasts have a huge impact on his poll numbers: as much as 0.11 points in the polls on the following day for each positive statement on the network news (depending on how much his lead has been declining). When the size of Obama's lead in the polls has been stable over the past 2 weeks, the gain from positive network coverage is smaller, but is still significant: about 0.03 points per positive statement. However, it simply doesn't seem to matter what sorts of coverage Obama receives on Fox – neither positive nor negative coverage of the incumbent has a significant impact on his lead in the polls.

The same cannot be said for coverage of Romney. While positive coverage of Romney on Fox doesn't make a significant difference, negative coverage on Fox does. When Romney has been gaining in the polls, negative coverage on Fox doesn't change the status of the race much. When he's been falling behind, though, a single negative statement about him on Fox is expected to lead to a gain of as much as 0.11 points in the polls the following day.

Oddly, the effects of negative coverage of Romney on Fox are almost identical to those of positive coverage of him on the network broadcasts. The story here seems to be that positive coverage of Romney on the networks

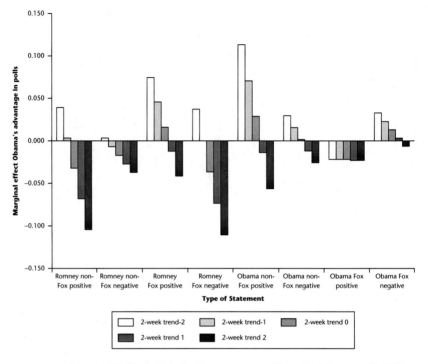

FIGURE 4.4 Marginal Effect of Media Statements on Obama's Advantage in Polls, Last 2 Months of Campaign

pushes persuadable voters back towards him, as would be expected. The perverse effects of negative coverage on Fox aren't as easily understood, but it seems likely that the criticism of Romney on an ideologically tinged outlet is seen as a sign that he's more centrist, less conservative, and thus more palatable to voters.

All told, the direct effects of the media play a substantial role in shaping the course of the general election, with the impact being greatest in the last 2 months of the campaign. The overall effects of the media on the dynamics of the race seem rather larger during the general election campaign than during the Republican primary, with individual statements about the candidates having the potential to push the race towards one candidate by 0.1 points or more, depending on how the race has been going up to that point. Still, the biggest impact of media coverage seems to be bringing the race back to equilibrium. In general, when Obama's lead has been growing, statements in the media about either candidate tend to help Romney, to the extent that they have a significant impact at all. When Obama's lead has been shrinking, statements in the media tend to reduce support for Romney. While there are differences in the size of the effects of positive and negative statements, the pattern remains about the same throughout. The most likely explanation for this relies on the preferences of the persuadable voters, those who are on the fence during the campaign. When the race has shifted strongly towards one candidate or the other – a trend that has Obama's numbers or Romney's numbers up by 2 points over the past week – it means that many of these persuadable voters have been pushed into one camp or the other. But just because they've been pushed into that camp doesn't mean that they're going to stay there: additional coverage of the campaign, seemingly regardless of the tone of that coverage, tends to push them back towards the other candidate, or into the undecided camp. The stronger the recent trend is, the more voters are susceptible to being pushed around by media coverage in this way.

Because of the ways the recent dynamics of the race interact with the effects of the coverage, it might be reasonable to look at how the media impacts the race when it's been stable over the past couple of weeks, as in Figure 4.5. By this standard, the largest effects are due to positive coverage of the candidates on the network evening news broadcasts: each positive statement about Obama is expected to increase his margin by a bit less than 0.03 points, and each positive statement about Romney is expected to decrease Obama's margin by about the same. The effects of negative statements about the candidates on the network broadcasts are in the same direction, but aren't large enough to be considered statistically significant. Some coverage on Fox is significant when there hasn't been any movement in the polls over the past 2 weeks, but not in the direction that might be expected. Negative statements about Romney on Fox significantly decrease Obama's margins in the polls, helping Romney to the tune of about 0.04 points per negative statement. Still, these effect sizes tend to underestimate the actual effects of media coverage on the race. The direct effects are there, but they're most sizeable when the race has been shifting over the previous few weeks, and this makes sense. A large shift in the polls means that one of the candidates has won over a lot of the persuadable voters, which makes that candidate's support more susceptible to shifts in media coverage.

What Media Matters?

In the general election, the differences between the effects of the networks aren't nearly as stark as they are during the Republican primary. Looking at the whole course of the election, coverage on Fox seems to be more influential than coverage on the network news broadcasts: positive and negative statements about Romney on Fox have a significant impact on the difference between the two candidates in the polls, as do positive statements about Obama. In contrast, the only statements on the networks that seem to matter are positive statements about the incumbent.

However, when the analysis is narrowed to the last 2 months of the campaign, the network news broadcasts become more influential. Generally, it seems that

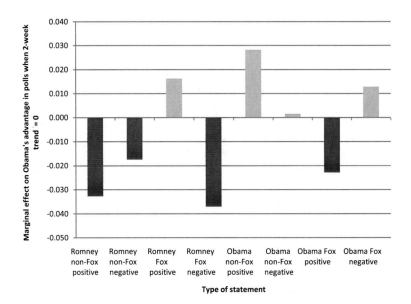

FIGURE 4.5 Marginal Effect of Media Statements on Obama's Advantage in Polls When 2-Week Trend Is 0, Last 2 Months of Campaign

coverage of Obama on the network broadcasts is more important than coverage of Romney on the network news, and coverage of Romney on Fox is more important than coverage of Romney on the networks.

The story the data's telling is twofold. First, people who are watching Fox are purposely seeking out political news, at a time before much of the country is really interested (as in DellaVigna and Kaplan 2007, Feldman et al. 2012). As a result, in the early stages of the election, coverage on Fox is much more influential than coverage on the networks, which don't cover political news as much, and have an audience that's probably less interested in a general election 5–6 months before ballots are cast.

However, once the voting nears and the general public becomes more interested, statements about the candidates on the networks become more influential. Remember that the networks have a much larger viewership than Fox News does, and since their viewers may be less interested in politics overall, they're more likely to be persuadable. As such, the question of which media source matters most becomes a question of what stage the election is in: early on, it's Fox, later, the networks. This lines up nicely with the results from the analysis of the Republican primary: in a primary, participation is much lower, and the politically engaged are the ones most likely to take part. Since much of the country isn't paying attention yet, Fox winds up being much more influential.

Second, the question of which media sources are most important depends on which candidate is being considered. Romney's coverage on Fox seems to matter more than his coverage on the network broadcasts, and Obama's coverage on the networks matters more than how he's covered on Fox. Again, this likely has to do with the different audiences of the broadcasts. While Fox's audience isn't monolithically conservative, it's much more weighted towards conservatives than the relative ideological balance of the network evening news broadcasts. As such, to the extent that Fox's audience is persuadable, it's more likely to be vacillating between supporting Romney and being undecided than between supporting Obama and being undecided. It makes sense, therefore, that coverage of Romney would be more influential than coverage of a candidate about whom many of the voters have already made up their minds.

A final point to bear in mind is exactly how much direct impact of the media depends on the dynamics of the race at that point. All of the broadcasts – and Fox, to a greater extent than the networks – have a much greater impact on the race when it's been shifting strongly one way or the other than when it's been stable. It seems that in the general election, broadcast media's biggest effect is pushing back against the current trend and towards the previous equilibrium. In the 2012 Presidential election, the media's biggest direct effect comes from slowing down the gains made by the candidates, making sure that a few weeks of gains don't turn into a landslide.

Incumbent Bias

These results also allow an answer to the question of whether voters are paying more attention to the incumbent or to the challenger. Traditionally, elections in which an incumbent is running are seen as a referendum on the incumbent: if voters think the President has been doing a good job, they'll re-elect him. If they think he's done a bad job, they won't. As such, it would make sense for coverage of the incumbent to have a greater impact on the race than coverage of the challenger. On the other hand, if it's assumed that voters are using the media to gather enough information about the candidates to make an informed decision, it would make sense for coverage of the challenger to have a bigger impact. After all, in a Presidential election, voters have had four years to get to know the incumbent, and probably have all of the information they need to decide whether or not they like him. The challenger, however, is a relatively unknown quantity, so media coverage of him has a greater potential to move the opinions of voters.

While either is plausible, during the 2012 election, coverage of the challenger had a larger impact on the race than coverage of the incumbent. Whether the analyses look at the direct effects of the media throughout the course of the campaign or concentrate on the last 2 months, media coverage of Romney has a larger direct effect than coverage of Obama, and those effects are less contingent on the existing dynamics of the race. This isn't to say that this is the case in every Presidential election, or even every Presidential election in which there's an incumbent running: it's entirely possible that Obama's campaign strategy was successful in turning the election into a referendum on Romney, or that voters had such polarized opinions about Obama that further information about him didn't make much of a difference.

This is the general problem with studying Presidential elections: there simply aren't enough cases to be able to draw major conclusions about what does and does not matter, and even if those conclusions could be drawn, there's no guarantee that they would remain valid in the next election. Importantly, the fact that media coverage of the challenger has a larger impact on the race than coverage of the incumbent doesn't mean that statements about Obama on the news don't matter at all: they still matter, it's just that statements about Romney tend to matter more. This result isn't driven by coverage on Fox either: statements about Romney on the network broadcasts are more influential than statements about Obama.

Campaign Events

All of this analysis of the effects of the media on the polls seemingly overlooks one thing: when media sources cover a candidate, they're talking *about* something. When the analyses look at coverage of the candidates in the abstract, it's as if the statements in the media are something like "Obama did something bad," when it's more likely that the statement is along the lines of "Obama did very poorly in the first debate." If that's the case, it seems possible that the direct effects we've been attributing to the media are, in fact, the direct effects of the campaign events the media's reporting on. There's no question that after the first Presidential debate, Obama's margin in the polls, which had already been shrinking, fell precipitously, eventually making the race the closest it would ever be, before Obama's lead widened again a few weeks before election day. There are three things that are potentially going on here, and in any circumstance in which an event during the campaign might be pushing the race one way or the other. The first is the direct effect of the event. Across the networks covering it, nearly 60 million people watched the first Presidential debate. It's likely that some of those viewers changed their minds about which candidate they were going to support as a direct result of what they saw during the debate. The second is the effect of media coverage of the event. Immediately after the debate, and for days afterwards, coverage of the debate dominated discussion of the campaign. This coverage – which was strongly negative towards Obama (CNN's body language expert said that Obama was "moving quickly like a hummingbird," indicating that he was "feeling powerless and frantic") – could easily have moved the polls, independent of the debate itself. That is, people could be responding not to the debate, but to the response to the debate in the media. Finally, it's already been established that Obama's margin in the polls has some endogenous characteristics, most notably that it tends to revert back to an equilibrium state whenever the margin gets too big or too small.

All three of these things are happening at once, but using statistical controls, it's possible to isolate the direct effects of the campaign events. Controlling for the endogenous characteristics is the easiest, as that's done in the same way as in the analysis of media effects earlier this chapter. In addition, the direct effects of media coverage – including coverage of campaign events – have already been modeled, so it's no problem to determine how much of the change in the poll numbers following a campaign event is due to coverage of the event. What we're left with is the question of whether the campaign event itself corresponds with a change in the polls beyond that which can be attributed to the other factors. Each campaign event can be treated separately, but it's first necessary to determine which events during the campaign are most likely to have made a real difference. The easiest cases can be made for the debates and the conventions: they're widely viewed by the public, and generally thought to be opportunities for the candidates to make their cases for the general election. To these, we can add the announcement of Romney's Vice-Presidential nominee, and the East Coast landfall of Superstorm Sandy.

The general perception in the public and the media is that these events made a huge difference in the campaign, and it's easy to see why that is. If we take a naïve model, one in which we don't correct for the endogenous characteristics of Obama's margin in the polls and don't look at the impact of media coverage or the trends in the race, it seems like these events have a big effect. In such a model, the Democratic Convention increases Obama's margin by nearly 0.4 points per day for 4 days: increasing his lead over Romney by about 1.5 percent in total. The first Presidential debate, which was perceived to have been a disaster for Obama, corresponds to a drop of 0.4 points in Obama's margin. Sandy has a smaller effect, not statistically significant, but even it corresponds to an increase of 0.21 points in Obama's lead (regression models for this analysis in methodology note 4.3).

So, for observers watching the election as it happens, and without the benefit of media coverage data, it certainly seems like these events are making a difference. Something happens, and Obama's margin in the polls drops or increases accordingly. The cause-and-effect story seems to make sense; but it ignores the other factors that play a part in the dynamics of the race. Sure, Obama did badly in the first debate, and his poll numbers dropped afterwards – but how much would they have been expected to drop anyway? If they were expected to go down by 0.3 points anyway, the drop of 0.4 points attributable to the first Presidential debate no longer seems like a big deal.

Once the other factors are controlled for, these campaign events seem to have very little impact on the race. Of the eight campaign events included, only one of them – the Democratic National Convention – has any significant impact (full models and explanation in methodology note 4.4). During the convention, Obama's margin over Romney increased by about 0.2 points per day for 4 days, for a net increase of a bit less than 1 point.

All of this seems to be very much at odds with the way the media reports on the Presidential campaign, and the general public perception of it. If none of these things really matter to the poll numbers, why does the media spend so much time reporting on them? The first answer is that these campaign events *do* matter – but they do so almost entirely by impacting media coverage. As shown in Table 4.5, on the 3 days before the first Presidential debate, there were two negative statements about Obama on the network news broadcasts, and four negative statements about him on Fox. In the 3 days after the debate, there were eleven negative statements about him on the network news broadcasts, and twenty-one on Fox. Coverage of Romney became similarly positive, going from no positive statements in 3 days before the debate to seven positive statements on the networks, and twelve on Fox. Of course, not all of this coverage was about the debate – some of the negative coverage on Fox dealt with accusations that Obama had manipulated the release of unemployment numbers – but the shift in coverage is enormous.

Generally, this sort of negative coverage for Obama would be expected to decrease his margin in the polls by a fairly large amount; but at that point, Obama's advantage had already been dropping significantly – 2.8 points in the previous 2 weeks. The conditional effects of the media – the effects that interact with the trend in the polls – tend to work against the current trend in the polls, increasing Obama's margin when he's been down, and increasing it when he's been up. This means that the high volume of coverage actually would be expected to *increase* Obama's margin in the polls. Essentially, he'd been falling in the polls enough, and lost so many of his supporters, that negative coverage seems to have pushed some Obama voters back towards him, rather than away from him (as it would have if he had been gaining in the polls). Even if the debate itself didn't have any effect on Obama's margin in the polls, the media coverage resulting from it might have, if not for the trends that were already pushing his poll numbers down substantially.

None of this means that the rest of these events didn't have an impact on the polls; it just means that they didn't have a *direct* impact. These events led changes in the tone of media coverage of the candidates, which does have a large impact on the race. For instance, the Republican National Convention resulted in an increase in positive coverage for Romney, especially on Fox, at a time when

TABLE 4.5 Shift in Coverage, 3 Days prior and 3 Days after First Presidential Debate

	Non-Fox positive	Non-Fox negative	Fox positive	Fox negative
Romney, before first debate	0	2	0	0
Romney, after first debate	7	4	12	5
Obama, before first debate	4	2	2	4
Obama, after first debate	2	11	0	21

Obama's margin had been increasing in the polls. This spike in coverage is esti-mated to have cut Obama's margin in the polls (or at least slowed down the rate of increase) by about 0.4 points.

The key, though, is that people aren't being persuaded by the actual events, but rather by the media coverage of those events: the response to the campaign event is shaped by the way the media covers it. It seems like the campaigns know this: there's a reason why every campaign spends the time after the debate sending surrogates onto news shows to explain why their candidate won. They know that it's not the debate itself, but rather the media coverage of the debate, that determines how the public will respond.

Conclusions

The enormous amount of coverage of the general election campaign doesn't have as great an impact as the coverage of the primary election did, but has a significant effect nonetheless. Interestingly, the biggest effect of news coverage is when it runs in the opposite direction to the overall trend in the polls. So, when Obama's lead over Romney is down, positive coverage of Obama matters more. When Obama's lead over Romney is increasing, negative coverage mat-ters more. Fox also matters a great deal more early on in the general election, when fewer people are paying attention, with coverage on the networks mat-tering more as the election draws nearer.

While it turns out that very few events during the campaign actually have a significant effect on the standing of the candidates in the polls, coverage of those events does seem to matter a great deal. For instance, the first Presidential cam-paign didn't have an impact on Obama's standing in the polls, but after the first debate, coverage of Obama turned strongly negative, and this shift in coverage did have an effect on the polls.

In a campaign like the one in 2012, media coverage simply doesn't impact the vast majority of voters: like pretty much everything in a political campaign, the direct effects of media are all about persuading a small segment of the popu-lation that's not tied too closely to either candidate (McKee and Shaw 2003, Hillygus and Shields 2014). However, this doesn't mean that media coverage is not, in itself, important in the dynamics of the election: these persuadable vot-ers are the battleground over which campaigns are fought, and media coverage is turning them one way or another. Moreover, Fox News coverage does still matter in these elections. Remember that while the actual campaign events don't significantly impact the race in most cases, the way in which those events are spun in the media matters a great deal, and the evidence in this chapter is that Fox News had a much stronger anti-Obama spin than the broadcast net-works. In 2012, as in recent Presidential elections, there have been far fewer Republican crossover voters than Democratic crossover voters, and this Fox coverage seems to be one reason why that's the case. The effect of Fox on the general election is limited by the fact that its viewers, many of whom are searching for political information, seem to have made their minds up relatively early. As such, while Fox coverage has a large impact on the polls early in the general election, it's overtaken by the networks later in the process. As with the primary election, it doesn't seem as though the coverage of the race turned the electorate one way or the other: but 2012 was also not a particularly close race. In a tight race, the documented effects of the media coverage could be enough to push it one way or the other.

5

FOX NEWS AND POLITICAL KNOWLEDGE

If Fox News were only having an effect on Presidential elections and Presidential approval, it would be enough to establish it as a major force in American politics. However, the effects of Fox news coverage on its viewers go well beyond electoral behavior. The next few chapters deal with the effect Fox News has on its viewers and how it changes their attitudes and behaviors outside of elections, and this begins with how it impacts their political knowledge.

This is a contentious topic because it's easy to confuse Fox News having a negative impact on the political knowledge of viewers with Fox News viewers having low levels of political knowledge. As the results in this chapter show, people who report watching Fox News do worse on a political knowledge scale than people who are otherwise similar to them, but report consuming other media sources, or even no media sources at all. However, this doesn't mean that Fox viewers know less about politics than the general population, just that they would know more if they were watching some other news program.

These results are easy to oversimplify, but they're actually fairly subtle. As might be expected, the effect of Fox News viewership on political knowledge depends, to some extent, on the viewer: Fox News doesn't hurt political knowledge among conservative viewers, but does among the sizeable contingent of moderates and liberals who tune in. Moreover, it isn't even that Fox News viewers wind up knowing less about everything in politics. Rather, the best explanation for these effects is that Fox viewers concentrate so much on topics that aren't discussed in other media outlets that they simply don't pay attention to the sorts of general, neutral questions asked in political knowledge scales.

This is a controversial enough finding – later in the chapter, the views of other scholars and Fox News's own response to the findings are discussed – that much of this chapter will be spent looking for other potential explanations for the effect of Fox on political knowledge. However, the same results are found in the analyses of multiple national surveys carried out by different groups, in different ways, and at different times, leading to the conclusion that it's Fox News viewership, rather than some other characteristic of the viewers, that's leading to the effects on political knowledge.

Political Knowledge in America

Political knowledge is not something that social scientists study very much, for two major reasons: first, we've spent the last 20 years showing that people can generally get by without actually knowing too much about politics, and second, because when it is measured, the results are depressing.

How depressing is that state of political knowledge in America? It's bad, and it's been that way for a long time. In data from the American National Election Study – the multi-million-dollar 2-yearly survey that's considered the gold standard in American political science – in 1985, less than a quarter of Americans knew who the Secretary of Defense was, or who Thurgood Marshall (then a long-serving Supreme Court Justice, and the first African-American to hold that post) was. Not many more knew where the headquarters of the UN is, or what NATO is, and less than half knew whether Poland was part of the Soviet Bloc. The researchers who are most associated with the study of political knowledge, Scott Keeter and Michael Delli Carpini (Delli Carpini and Keeter 1991, 1993, Delli Carpini et al. 1994), note that in the early 1990s, the most commonly known attribute of President George H.W. Bush was that he hated broccoli. Similarly, more people were able to name the host of *The People's Court* than an actual justice of the Supreme Court.

Even from this low start, things haven't gotten much better. In the middle of a Presidential election in 2012, surveys carried out by the PublicMind poll showed that only about 40 percent of Americans knew who won the Iowa caucuses, and only about half knew who had won the New Hampshire primaries, despite these contests being the major stories on all news broadcasts for weeks (in Chapter 3, it was noted that election coverage like this constituted about a quarter of all news being reported at that time). Asked about specific policy measures, like the extension of a payroll tax cut that had been in the news, less than 10 percent knew what was going on. Even if people weren't paying much attention to the news, only a little more than half of Americans know who the Vice-President is in various surveys over several administrations, most recently in 2010 (details in methodology note 5.1).

This is important because representative democracy seems to require a certain level of knowledge on the part of voters (Galston 2001). Ideally, when people are deciding which candidate to vote for, they're supposed to figure out where the candidates stand on the issues of importance, compare them, and use that information to decide how to cast their ballot (Carmines and Stimson 1980,

Alesina 1988). And if people are bad at even knowing who the candidates are, they're really bad at knowing where the candidates stand on the issues. A 1996 study found, for instance, that about 33 percent of Bill Clinton's supporters were voting for him because of his strong (non-existent) anti-abortion views (Abramowitz 1995). According to the 2010 ANES data, 33 percent of Americans thought that the Democratic Party was on the liberal side of the ideological divide; 39 percent thought that it was conservative (though they did better at understanding that Democrats were more liberal than conservatives). These sorts of errors really call into question the ability of the American public to make the sorts of political calculations that voting requires. How is someone supposed to decide which party to support – never mind which candidate to support – if they don't even know whether that party is conservative or liberal?

In the face of findings like these, political scientists have put a great deal of effort into finding ways in which democracy can co-exist with a very low level of knowledge in the public, and they've been more or less successful in a few approaches. Milton Lodge, a political psychologist at Stony Brook University, found that people tend to forget the actual facts they hear about politicians, but remember whether or not they like them (Lodge et al. 1989, McGraw et al. 1990, Cassino et al. 2007), as discussed in Chapter 2. David Redlawsk, now at Rutgers, and his colleagues have shown that people who just vote on the basis of party generally pick the candidate they would have selected if they had done all of the research rational choice theories would desire (Lau and Redlawsk 2001, 2006, Lau et al. 2008).

Still, even if Americans can get by without too much information about candidates and issues, there's very little argument that democracy would work better if people had more information, and that's where the news comes in. After all, it isn't necessary to design a system to try and teach people about what's going on in politics, and what candidates are doing: it already exists. As of 2015, there were at least six 24-hour news channels on cable in the US, and at least three of those available on nearly every tier of cable, with CNN, MSNBC and Fox News available in more than 82 percent of homes (TV by the Numbers 2013). Moreover, Americans watch a lot of news these days. While primetime viewership of these channels is generally only a few million a night (as discussed in greater detail in Chapter 1), a majority of Americans (53 percent in a December 2013 PublicMind poll) say that they've watched Fox News in the past week, with another 46 percent saying that they've watched CNN (details on the measurement of such questions are in methodology note 5.2); the full results are shown in Figure 5.1.

Such findings have been criticized for overstating the number of Fox viewers, the idea being that some respondents will state that they are watching Fox as a way of asserting a Republican or conservative political identity. To mitigate this problem, PublicMind polls have made use of a modified list format (described later in this chapter) that only brings up Fox to those respondents

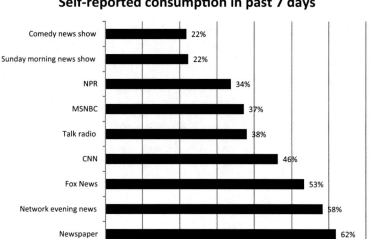

FIGURE 5.1 Percentage of Americans Saying That They've Gotten News from Each Source, December 2013

who already say that they get information from cable news in general. While Americans may be reading newspapers and watching evening news broadcasts a lot less than they used to (although the use of online resources means that newspapers are actually being read by more people, even if fewer are paying for them), there's little doubt that there's more news out there than in the past, and that lots of Americans – if not most Americans – are taking advantage of it. The problem is that all of this extra news content doesn't seem to have done anything to actually teach Americans more about politics and current events. While it's difficult to directly compare knowledge questions over time, there are some constants. When researchers ask Americans to name the Secretary of State or the Prime Minister of the UK or the Vice-President, the percentage who can respond accurately has stayed remarkably stable over time, and this is the puzzle. On some measures, like whether Americans know which party has a majority in the House of Representatives (shown in Figure 5.2), Americans are doing worse now than in the past. If we're getting more news from more sources than ever before, why aren't Americans learning more?

In Chapter 1, it was established that there's bias in the content of some of these cable news channels, especially Fox, but that doesn't necessarily mean that they're not informational. A story about what the Secretary of State is doing should still inform viewers as to who the Secretary of State is and what's going on in foreign policy regardless of whether that story is positive or negative. But it just doesn't seem to work that way. The results indicate that exposure to ideological media sources – like Fox News, MSNBC and talk radio – does very little

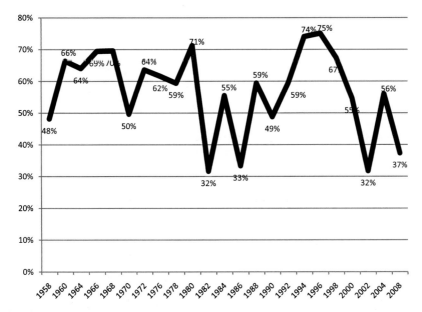

FIGURE 5.2 Percentage of Americans Who Know Which Party Controls the House of Representatives, ANES Data

to give people more information about the world around them. In some cases, more exposure to ideological news actually makes people less knowledgeable.

Media Sources and Political Knowledge

Of course, figuring out the informational effects of various media sources is more involved than just looking at how much knowledge the consumers of those sources have. In the data from the 2012 PublicMind political knowledge survey, Americans were asked eight political knowledge questions – four about domestic issues, and four about international issues. The domestic political questions asked which party held the most seats in the House of Representatives at the time, the terms of the payroll tax cut extension that had just been passed (which required action on the Keystone XL pipeline), the eventually named winner of the Republican Iowa Caucuses, the winner of the New Hampshire primary, and the approximate unemployment rate at the time. The international questions asked respondents whether protests in Egypt had removed Hosni Mubarak from power, whether Syrian protests had removed Bashar al-Assad, which country was most responsible for bailing out failing European states, and why the US was considering increased sanctions on Iran. The easiest of these questions was about the leadership in the House: 65 percent answered correctly. The hardest concerned the payroll tax cut: only 9 percent were able to mention anything about oil or a pipeline.

The most informed respondents were those who said that they got their news from NPR: on average, they were able to answer 4.9 of the questions correctly, compared with *Daily Show* viewers, who answered 4.4 correct; FOX News and MSNBC viewers were at the bottom of the pack, averaging only 3.4 questions correct, beating out only viewers of local news broadcasts, which typically don't talk about national or international issues. Results for all media sources are in Figure 5.3.

From this alone, it might be tempting to conclude that NPR and *The Daily Show* are the most informative news sources – after all, they have the most informed audiences – but that's not really fair. Political knowledge results from a lot more than just watching, reading or listening to the news: education matters, as do age, political views, race and any number of other factors. If nothing else, most Americans claim to watch more than one of these sources, so uncovering the informational value of each individually means using statistical controls to isolate the effect of each of these sources on political knowledge (details in methodology note 5.3).

When the analysis is carried out in this way – estimating the effects of exposure to each news source on the number of political knowledge questions answered correctly – the results are striking. Not only do some news sources have a stronger effect than others, but the differences are enormous. All else equal, a politically moderate respondent who doesn't watch any of the listed news sources is expected to answer about 2.5 questions correctly – not great, given that it's an eight-question scale – but not too troubling,

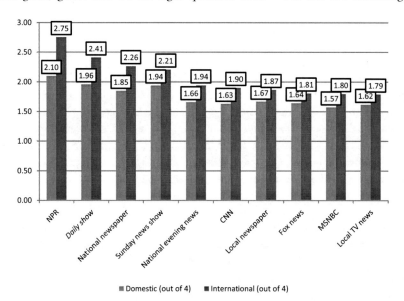

FIGURE 5.3 Mean Number of Correct Answers, by Area of Question and Media Source

given that almost everyone in the sample watches something. If that respondent only listened to talk radio, and didn't consume any other news, he or she would be expected to get about 2.9 correct – a small but significant difference. If that respondent watched only *The Daily Show*, he or she would do about as well. On average, *Daily Show* respondents did much better on the knowledge scale than people who listen to talk radio – but these results indicate that difference isn't because they're watching that particular show, but because of other shows they're watching, or other characteristics that lead them to be better able to answer the questions. Still, the biggest positive effect comes from listening to NPR: politically moderate respondents would be expected to answer an extra 0.8 questions correct if they listened to Terry Gross instead of staying up late to watch *The Daily Show*, as seen in Figure 5.4.

Nor are these effects some artifact of this particular poll. Reproducing these results using the more limited knowledge scale from the 2010 ANES gives very similar results, as shown in Figure 5.5. For political moderates, exposure to Fox News has a significant negative effect, NPR, *The Rush Limbaugh Show* and *The Daily Show* have significant positive effects. The biggest difference is in the effect of Sunday morning political news shows, which have no significant effect in the ANES data. The story being told by both datasets, though, is very similar (details for the ANES analysis are in methodology note 5.4).

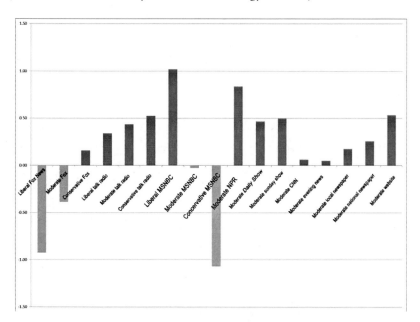

FIGURE 5.4 Marginal Effect of Consuming Various News Sources on Questions Answered Correctly, with Ideology When Significant, from PublicMind Data

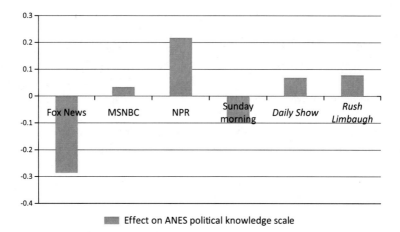

FIGURE 5.5   Marginal Effect of Consuming Various News Sources on Questions
Answered Correctly from ANES Data

The most surprising thing in these results is the marginal effect (the change from the baseline) that comes from watching Fox News. A political moderate who watches only Fox News is expected to answer only 2.1 questions correctly – fewer than the baseline of 2.5. If political moderates watch just Fox, it seems that they're less able to answer questions than they would be if they were watching nothing at all. Now, this doesn't mean that watching Fox News leaves everyone worse off. Conservatives who watch Fox News end up a little better able to answer the political knowledge questions, getting about an extra 0.2 correct. Liberals who watch Fox News, though, wind up much worse than they would be otherwise, answering 0.9 fewer questions correctly than they would otherwise.

By the same measure, MSNBC doesn't do well either. The effect of MSNBC on moderates is so small that it's no different than zero. Liberals who watch MSNBC get a little more than one extra question correct, but conservatives answer 1.1 fewer questions correctly than they would otherwise. Talk radio, too, seems to have these ideologically moderated effects, in which people from one political persuasion get more information out of it than people from another. In the case of talk radio, though, at least all of the marginal effects are positive.

It's also important to remember that these effects do pertain to a large number of people. While more politically informed liberals are less likely to watch Fox, and more informed conservatives less likely to watch MSNBC, there are still plenty of people who do. About a quarter of liberals say that they watch some Fox, and about a quarter of conservatives say that they've watched some MSNBC: in both cases, they seem to be at a real disadvantage (a discussion of the causality concerns of this analysis can be found later in this chapter). In the 2012 PublicMind data, 32 percent of self-identified liberals say that they've gotten news from Fox in the last week. Now, that's lower than the figures among moderates (54 percent) or conservatives (76 percent), but still sizeable. Similarly, 34 percent of self-identified conservatives say that they've watched MSNBC in the last week, compared with 48 percent of moderates and 53 percent of liberals. So, while there's sorting of viewers based on ideology, there's still a large counter-ideological audience for both of these sources. Therefore, if an effect pertains to liberals who say that they watch Fox News, for instance, it isn't a hypothetical group: it's about 12 percent of US registered voters.

Other News Sources

In contrast to the effects of ideological media, political moderates learn the most by turning to NPR, *The Daily Show* and Sunday morning news programs (leaving aside the category of "websites," which is too nebulous to analyze very deeply). What all of these sources have in common is an eschewing of the debate format: they're much more likely to feature longer interviews with individuals holding a particular point of view. Because there's no opposition to that individual presented on the program, it falls on the host to ask questions, to poke and prod, and the individual being interviewed has the opportunity to make complex arguments without being interrupted. This, it seems, gives viewers a great deal more information than the programs on ideological media.

This may explain why NPR and *The Daily Show* are more informative than other media sources – but why are Fox News and MSNBC so bad for viewers' level of information? One possible explanation comes from the amount of news people are watching. There are only so many hours in a day, and one spent watching MSNBC can't also be spent listening to NPR. So, if a conservative were not watching MSNBC and getting no informational value out of it, he or she might be watching or listening to something else. As a result, MSNBC viewers wind up with less knowledge than those not spending part of their news watching budget on that channel. However, the data just doesn't seem to bear this out. Using the 2010 ANES data, it's possible to examine the relationship between how much time someone spends watching Fox News or MSNBC, and how many nights per week spent watching a non-ideological news source: network evening news broadcasts, as in Figure 5.6. If the negative effects of Fox and MSNBC are driven by less overall news consumption among their viewers, then people who watch more shows on those channels should be less likely to watch the evening news broadcasts – but it's actually the opposite.

Actually, the more Fox News and MSNBC people watch, the more nights they're likely to watch the national evening news broadcasts. There's also a significant interaction with ideology – at least for MSNBC viewers – such that ideologues who watch more news that matches their ideology wind up watching more non-ideological news in general. This holds true no matter what measure is

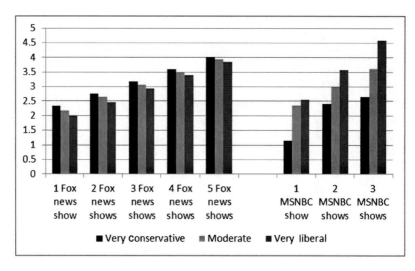

FIGURE 5.6 Mean Number of Nights Respondents Reported Watching Evening News Broadcasts, by Ideology and Number of Fox and MSNBC Programs Watched

used for the total amount of political information consumed: people who consume more ideological media also consume more non-ideological media. It also holds when the analysis divides up ideological and non-ideological sources on ideological channels. For instance, Fox News viewers who watch *The O'Reilly Factor* rather than *Fox Report* (a less ideological program), but watch the same number of Fox Shows overall, seek out more non-ideological news. As such, it can't be that they're spending less time on more informative news sources: rather, the negative informational effects of the ideological media sources (especially on viewers with clashing ideologies) must be a function of the content of the media.

Responses to These Findings

Not surprisingly, these results have proven controversial. Fox News put out a press release stating that myself and the other researchers should focus on improving the academic quality of our university (incorrectly citing a study which actually placed it rather favorably), and didn't address the findings. More seriously, Arceneaux and Johnson (2013: 46–9) argue that such findings are simply not reliable outside the laboratory. Some of their problems with the results are accounted for in the analysis: for instance, they worry that conservatives who do and do not watch Fox may be different in ways other than their use of ideological media. In the analysis, political ideology is interacted with viewership, allowing there to be differences in the impact of the ideological news sources by ideological group. More generally, though, they argue that the control variables present in the analyses can't possibly control for factors that would make individuals choose to watch ideological media sources. The general claim is that there must be some other, unmeasured, factor that leads individuals to choose ideological media, and that it is this factor, rather than exposure to the ideological media (or perhaps in conjunction with exposure to ideological media), that leads to the observed lower levels of knowledge. Addressing this issue, and pinpointing the mechanism that makes exposure to ideological media lead to lower levels of political knowledge, first requires an examination of the other factors that lead individuals to have more or less political knowledge.

Other Predictors of Political Knowledge

One of the most common objections to these findings is that the causal arrow is going the wrong way. It isn't that exposure to Fox News or MSNBC leads individuals to be less knowledgeable, but that people who watch these channels are less knowledgeable to begin with (especially those watching counter-ideological channels – liberals watching Fox, conservatives watching MSNBC). It's impossible to use observational data to fully disprove this argument. Using a long-term experiment – rather than the short-term studies carried out by Arceneaux and Johnson (2013) and others, which are likely unable to capture such effects – would mean randomly assigning participants to watch a news channel they otherwise might avoid; given the evidence presented here that this tends to reduce the amount of political knowledge people have, even with exposure to other news sources, this would probably be unethical. Also, it wouldn't actually reveal much about the way these news channels impact viewers in the real world. A crucial part of the effect of ideological media is the fact that viewers have to opt in to watching it: it's not at all clear that viewers forced to watch it would be impacted in the same way. The fact that the audience isn't randomly selected is also why there's the specter of the reversed causal arrow.

To sort this out, it helps to take media exposure out of the equation entirely, and see what characteristics lead individuals to have higher or lower levels of political knowledge in general. The first factor that seems to matter a great deal is age (Delli Carpini and Keeter 1993): older individuals are typically much better able to answer political knowledge questions than their younger counterparts. This makes sense: older Americans are more likely to vote, more likely to have a strong attachment to one party or another, and have simply had more time to build up reservoirs of political information (Neundorf and Niemi 2014). In the 2012 PublicMind poll measuring political knowledge, for instance, 29 percent of respondents under the age of 30 couldn't answer *any* of the eight political questions posed to them, compared to just 10 percent of voters over the age of 60. Similarly, only 11 percent of the youngest voters answered six or more questions correctly – a figure that rises to 17 percent of 30–44-year-olds, 29 percent of voters aged 45–59 and 27 percent of the oldest voters, as shown in Figure 5.7.

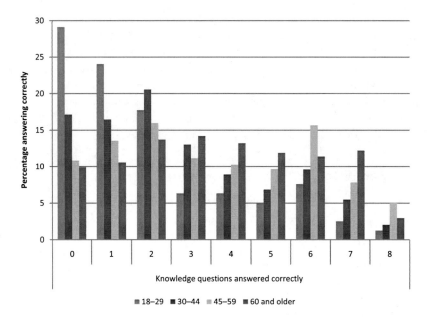

FIGURE 5.7 Percentage Answering Each Number of Questions Correctly, by Age, PublicMind Data

Not surprisingly, education leads respondents to be more able to answer questions correctly: respondents with at least some post-graduate education have a mean score of nearly five out of eight questions correct. Respondents with only a high school education or less only answer about 2.3 correctly.

Gender, race and other demographic considerations also play a part in the ability to answer these questions correctly. The median man in the sample is able to answer four of the eight questions correctly; the median woman is only able to answer two. Whites, on average, can answer 3.5 questions correctly, compared to 2.5 for African-Americans. Married people are also more aware of what's going on in the news than unmarried people: currently married respondents were able to answer 0.9 additional questions, on average, compared to unmarried respondents. Finally, men do quite a bit better than women: the average woman in the sample answered 2.7 questions correctly, the average man 4.1.

Partisanship and Political Knowledge

Perhaps most surprisingly, party identification doesn't play much of a role in how much Americans know about politics either, as seen in Figure 5.8. Independents do worse than people who identify with either party, but Republicans and Democrats both do about the same, with no significant differences between partisans. Leaners – respondents who initially say that they aren't members of either party, but admit to "leaning" towards one party or another when pressed – do better than partisans or independents, but that's to be expected. Past research on leaners has shown that they are motivated to present themselves as being independents because they're aware of negative stereotypes about partisans. This alone is probably enough to sort more knowledgeable people into these "leaner" categories.

However, while party identification doesn't play much of a role in how much people know about the news, political ideology does. On average, liberals are able to answer 3.8 questions out of the eight asked; moderates score 3.5, and conservatives 3.4.

Putting all of these effects together, it's possible to predict the expected knowledge levels of Fox News and MSNBC viewers based solely on the demographics of the viewership. Viewers of both networks are a bit older than the mean, and Fox viewers are a little more Republican and more conservative, while MSNBC viewers skew in the opposite direction. Fox viewers are also more likely to have a college degree than most Americans and MSNBC viewers, and more likely to be male, married and white, all of which tend to increase levels of political knowledge. Based solely on these factors, the mean Fox News viewer would be expected to answer 2.8 questions correctly: a lot more than the mean respondent's score of 2.1. MSNBC viewers would be expected to answer 2.3 correctly. In the actual data, though, Fox News viewers and MSNBC viewers get almost the exact same number of correct answers as the mean respondent. The difference is chalked up to what's been left out of the demographic model: media exposure, and its interaction with ideology. The fact that all three groups – Fox viewers, MSNBC viewers and respondents overall – wind up at about the

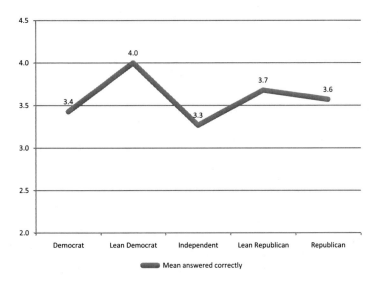

FIGURE 5.8 Mean Number of Knowledge Questions Answered Correctly, by Partisanship, from PublicMind Data

same place while their demographic compositions are so different demonstrates the strong effects of media exposure: controlling for all demographic factors, individuals who report watching Fox News score lower on the knowledge scales than people who don't, especially if they're liberal or moderate. While the average Fox News or MSNBC viewer knows just as much as anyone else, demographically, Fox News viewers should know rather more, and MSNBC viewers should know rather less.

The Attentional Explanation

So, if it isn't demographic factors, and it doesn't seem to be purely driven by selection effects, what could possibly be leading individuals who consume ideological media to wind up being *less* informed than if they weren't watching anything? One explanation is offered by research carried out by economists Elizabeth Schroeder and Daniel Stone (2014), using the huge three-wave Annenberg studies (each wave consists of more than 50,000 interviews) that measure, among other things, political knowledge. They break down respondents to these surveys by year and geographical area (something that's only possible because of the huge sample sizes in the Annenberg studies), and see how these change as Fox News becomes available in that area. Essentially, they're treating the introduction of Fox News to an area as if it's a field experiment: individuals don't really control when they get a new channel on their cable systems, and it's hard to imagine people moving in order to get Fox News, so differences between people who get Fox early and later are likely due to its availability. They found that the introduction of Fox News into an area had no *overall* effect on the ability to answer knowledge questions, but it reduced the ability of respondents in the area to answer questions that would be disconcerting to Republicans (for instance, knowing that President Bush in 2004 favored extending the federal assault weapon ban, or that John McCain in 2008 favored a cap-and-trade program to reduce carbon emissions). They compared the content of these questions to Fox transcripts, and found that it isn't that the availability of Fox made respondents less able to answer questions about politics and current events; it's that it made them less able to answer questions about topics that weren't covered on Fox.

As discussed previously, ideological news sources tend to focus their attention on certain issues that may not be of relevance to other news organizations. In 2013, for example, the top ten stories mentioned on Fox News included the attack on the US Embassy in Benghazi and the scandal over the "Fast and Furious" program in which the ATF unwittingly turned over weapons to Mexican drug cartels. Anyone watching Fox with any frequency would be forgiven for thinking these were the most important news stories of the day – but neither of them were in the top ten subjects for any of the other news sources in the Media Tenor database.

As such, it seems likely that frequent consumers of ideological media sources would assume that these stories are important, and pay more attention to them, at the expense of other topics in the news. Given that the questions used to measure political knowledge reflect stories that may be more prevalent in non-ideological media, it isn't that consumers of ideological media know less about politics than others – just that they know less about the stories others are interested in. For instance, if the questions had asked about the "Fast and Furious" scandal, Fox News viewers might have done very well. It isn't that they aren't exposed to information about other issues that would help them answer the questions posed to them, but rather that they're not worried about those other topics, and don't absorb the information.

Motivated Reasoning

This reshapes the question about ideology: rather than ask, for instance, why conservatives watching MSNBC do worse on knowledge questions, it makes sense to ask why liberals watching MSNBC do better. In addition to the attentional explanation, motivated reasoning and counter-argument may play a role as well. The best research on this comes from political psychologists Charles Taber and Milton Lodge at Stony Brook University (Lodge and Taber 2000, Taber and Lodge 2006, Cassino et al. 2007). In one study (Taber and Lodge 2006), they had people examine statements about a controversial issue: gun control or affirmative action. The statements they saw had been pre-tested to ensure that they were balanced – the arguments in favor of gun control were just as convincing as the arguments against, the two sides were equally understandable, and the statements were even about the same length. Some of the arguments were strong, and some weak. When evaluating the statements, participants were even told to be even-handed and fair, and that they would have to explain the controversy to other students (in reality, they wouldn't have to – but the potential for social embarrassment if they did a bad job of understanding and explaining worked as a potent tool to get the students concerned about their accuracy). When they were asked to rate the strength of the arguments – and remember, they were trying to be as fair as possible – participants with high levels of political knowledge rated statements that were against their position as much weaker than arguments that were in agreement with their position.

The kicker, though, is the amount of time they took to decide whether the statements were weak or strong. When participants with high levels of political knowledge read a strong argument that they agreed with, it took them about 18 seconds to decide that it was strong. When they read a strong argument they didn't agree with, it took them an extra 6 seconds to decide that it wasn't strong at all. So what were they doing with those extra 6 seconds? Counter-arguing: figuring out reasons why they shouldn't believe the (objectively) strong argument they had just seen, an argument that might cause them to change their minds on an issue they felt strongly about. They didn't need the time when they were dealing with a weak argument – they could just discount that immediately – and they didn't need it when dealing with an argument they agreed with. It's also important to note that exposure to these strong arguments didn't make the participants any less confident in their views. People with strong views still had them, no matter how many strong arguments against those views they heard.

While Taber and Lodge are much more worried about cognitive processes – how people deal with incoming political information – than they are with the media, their counter-argument results say a great deal about what people with strong views are doing when watching ideological media. Rather than passively accepting information that's presented to them, they're counter-arguing the information as it comes in – a cognitively taxing process that makes it less likely that they'll retain the information. As a result, they're not only learning about a biased subset of the political information they could be exposed to, and primed to think that those stories are more important, but they're not even learning much about the stories they're hearing. As such, conservatives watching MSNBC and liberals watching Fox News wind up with less knowledge than they'd be expected to have if they weren't watching any news programming at all.

Criticisms of These Findings

When this research was initially reported by the press, it was treated as evidence that Fox News viewers know less about politics than other Americans. In addition to being a massive oversimplification, that's also wrong. While the median Fox News viewer does worse at answering political knowledge questions than he or she would be expected to in the absence of Fox News, Fox News viewers, on the whole, aren't any worse at answering political knowledge questions. Remember, while exposure to Fox and MSNBC reduces levels of political knowledge among viewers whose beliefs run contrary to the network's ideologies, Fox increases levels of knowledge among conservatives, and MSNBC does the same among liberals. Since Fox and MSNBC viewers are disproportionately drawn from the ranks of conservatives and liberals, respectively, the loss in knowledge among some viewers is made up for by the gains among others.

It's certainly possible that these effects aren't driven by exposure to these media sources, but rather by some other factor these models haven't accounted for (as in Arceneaux and Johnson's criticisms), but the weight of the evidence makes it seem very unlikely. In this view, there's something that correlates with political knowledge and viewership of ideological media that isn't partisanship or ideology or race or age or gender or marital status or education. It could be that this other trait leads people to do worse at answering knowledge questions, and people with that trait are simply over-represented in the population of Fox News viewers. But there are a couple of problems with this explanation. The first is that it's not at all clear what that factor could be: it can't be anything demographic, or related to the amount of news being consumed. Other factors used in social psychology that might predict political knowledge levels, like openness or authoritarianism, are correlated fairly strongly with the characteristics that have been measured, like education, ideology and partisanship, so it seems unlikely to be one of those. There may well be some difference between viewers of ideological media and non-viewers, but until it's determined what that is, and how to measure it, the simplest explanation is that viewers of ideological media are different from non-viewers because they're exposed to the ideological media. Second, it's important to remember that the effects of ideological media on reducing political knowledge are present for both Fox News and MSNBC viewers. As such, the hypothetical factor, whatever it is, would have to lead viewers to be more likely to watch Fox News and MSNBC, or would have to be two factors, both unaccounted for by the control variables, that separately lead Americans to choose to watch Fox News and MSNBC. Given the unlikeliness of such a factor existing, the explanation offered here, and in Schroeder and Stone's (2014) analysis – increased attention to information that would otherwise be considered irrelevant, leading to increased knowledge in those areas – seems rather more likely.

Non-Ideological News Sources

While the focus of this analysis has been on ideological media sources, there are plenty of other ways Americans get news about politics – what impact do these sources have on political knowledge? While the PublicMind surveys, using a detailed political knowledge index, only include the most popular media sources, the 2010 American National Election Study asked participants about more than forty news sources, including some that aren't exactly hard news, like *The Ellen DeGeneres Show*. These sources, excluding websites, were ranked according to the mean number of knowledge questions their audiences answered correctly (on a 0–1 scale).

There are a few patterns that are immediately evident from the rankings presented in Table 5.1. The first is that media sources with the widest audiences – in terms of the percentage of ANES respondents who indicated that they had consumed them recently – have lower mean levels of knowledge. The programs with the most knowledgeable audiences also tend to have the smallest audiences – the *New York Times*, *The Mark Levin Show* (a right-leaning talk radio show originating in New York City), the *Wall Street Journal* – all have audiences of one-eighth the size or less of network news programs. This could be due to a selection effect – small groups of more informed people choosing different media sources – or simply because programs with large audiences will almost certainly have audiences with characteristics closer to the mean.

The second obvious feature is that ideological news programs don't fare very well. MSNBC programs like *Hardball* and *The Rachel Maddow Show* make the

TABLE 5.1 Mean Knowledge Levels of Audience, by News Source and Percentage
Consuming It, from 2010 ANES Data

Knowledge rank	Source	Mean knowledge
1	New York Times	0.85
2	Mark Levin (radio)	0.84
3	Morning Edition (NPR)	0.81
4	Wall Street Journal	0.81
5	Fresh Air (NPR)	0.80
6	PBS News Hour	0.79
7	All Things Considered	0.78
8	Hardball with Chris Matthews	0.77
9	The Daily Show	0.76
10	Rachel Maddow	0.76
11	Sean Hannity (radio)	0.75
12	This Week	0.74
13	Colbert Report	0.74
14	Hannity	0.74
15	O'Reilly Factor	0.73
16	Late Edition with Wolf Blitzer	0.73
17	Rush Limbaugh	0.73
18	Frontline	0.72
19	Meet the Press	0.72
20	The Situation Room	0.72
21	Laura Ingraham (radio)	0.72
22	Fox & Friends	0.71
23	Neal Boortz (radio)	0.71
24	Face the Nation	0.70
25	USA Today	0.70
26	Glenn Beck (radio)	0.70
27	MSNBC Live	0.69
28	Piers Morgan	0.69
29	Anderson Cooper 360°	0.68
30	CNN Newsroom	0.67
31	Michael Savage/Savage Nation (radio)	0.67
32	Tonight Show	0.64
33	Late Show with David Letterman	0.64
34	NBC Nightly News	0.63
35	60 Minutes	0.63
36	Today Show	0.62
37	Fox News	0.61
38	ABC World News	0.61
39	20/20	0.60
40	CBS Evening News	0.59
41	Dateline	0.59
42	Good Morning America	0.57
43	Ellen DeGeneres	0.55
44	Early Show	0.55

top ten, but with the exception of *The Mark Levin Show* on radio, the most informed audiences are for relatively ideologically neutral sources like the *New York Times*, the *Wall Street Journal* and NPR radio programs.

Of course, as with the ideological media sources already discussed, much of this may be due to the composition of the audience, rather than the content of the program. When all of these media sources are used jointly to predict levels of political knowledge, along with demographic indicators for race, gender, age, partisanship, political ideology, income and education, only a few have independent effects. Exposure to the *New York Times* and the *Wall Street Journal* tends to increase levels of political information, as does exposure to *The Daily Show* and PBS's *News Hour*. Viewers of *CBS Evening News* tend to have lower levels of political information, controlling for all other media exposure, than their demographic characteristics would otherwise predict. Finally, two of the ideological media sources – *The Mark Levin Show* and *The O'Reilly Factor* – have positive effects on levels of political knowledge. Further analysis, though, shows that these effects are identical to those identified earlier. While these media sources have positive effects for most people who watch them, that's because the audiences for these programs are so ideologically skewed towards conservatives. O'Reilly's audience consists of nearly 70 percent self-identified conservatives, and Levin's audience includes more than 95 percent self-identified conservatives (and exactly zero self-identified liberals in the ANES data). So, while liberals and moderates do worse on political knowledge scales if they watch these programs, the audience is sufficiently conservative that the overall effect is positive. Listening to *The Mark Levin Show* might well have negative effects on the political knowledge of moderates and liberals, but since there are almost no moderates and liberals listening, there's really no way to tell.

The most ideologically polarized media audiences are for conservative talk radio programs: all of the top five, and seven of the ten most ideologically polarized programs, are conservative talk radio shows. The remaining three are shows on Fox News. While there are plenty of shows whose audiences skew liberal, the skew isn't nearly as strong. The program with the most liberal audience in the ANES data is MSNBC's *Rachel Maddow Show*, with an audience that's 66 percent liberal and 14 percent conservative. If these figures were flipped, it would be the eleventh most conservative audience. Interestingly, while the effects of the liberal programs on knowledge are still dependent on ideology, these effects don't seem to pertain to the programs with the most liberally skewed audiences. *Rachel Maddow* has no independent effect on political knowledge, and the NPR shows listed have only small ideologically based effects. Listening to *All Things Considered*, for instance, leads liberals and moderates to have rather higher scores on the ANES knowledge scale, and has essentially no impact on the political knowledge of conservative listeners. The program with the second most liberal audience, Comedy Central's *The Daily Show*, has positive effects on knowledge that aren't at all contingent on ideology.

In fact, *The Daily Show* is one of only four media sources in the dataset that have strong positive effects on political knowledge that aren't at all conditional on ideology: the other three are PBS's *News Hour*, the *New York Times* and the *Wall Street Journal*. The fact that a comedy news show informs its audience about as well as two of the most respected newspapers in the country and the only hour-long network newscast says something very good about *The Daily Show*, something bad about other news sources, or both.

In general, then, other media sources follow the same patterns in their effects on political knowledge as the cable news channels. When they have any impact at all, conservative sources tend to have strongly ideological effects, increasing political knowledge among conservatives, and reducing it among moderates and liberals. Liberal sources have weaker ideological effects, increasing knowledge among liberals and moderates, and having very little effect on political knowledge among conservatives. If the effects of these other sources are about the same as the impact of cable news channels, why focus on Fox News and MSNBC? The answer lies in the reported consumption of these sources. Some radio shows have large effects on political knowledge, but their audiences are very small compared to those of cable news programs. The most popular talk radio show in the data is *The Rush Limbaugh Show*: 10 percent of the ANES sample report listening to him at least once a month. In contrast, 34 percent of the sample says that they watch Fox News at least once a month. While these programs may have a deleterious effect on the political knowledge of Americans, their impact is limited by the size of their audience. For cable news, however, the size of the audiences makes the impacts on political knowledge much more important.

Conclusions

While most of the chapters in this book have dealt with a number of areas in which Fox News could be having an impact on American politics, this chapter dealt with just one major finding: that exposure to Fox News leads some viewers to do worse at answering political knowledge questions than they would otherwise. The evidence for this claim is strong: the finding crops up in both the PublicMind and ANES surveys, and studies based on the Annenberg data seem to confirm what's being seen in the surveys. Fox News viewers seem to know less about general topics of political interest than they otherwise would, partly because they're not paying attention to the sorts of topics included in the political knowledge scales, partly because they're motivated to ignore some topics that might be disconcerting to them.

The main alternative explanation is that Fox News viewers are different from non-viewers in some way that's not controlled for by the regression models. However, it's not at all clear what this could be: partisanship doesn't make much of a difference, and age, gender and the other characteristics associated with Fox viewership can't explain the difference either. It's always possible that there's some other difference that no one is measuring, but it's not clear what that could be.

So is Fox News actually leading viewers to know less about politics? It depends on who you are. It seems very clear that liberals and moderates who watch Fox and conservatives who watch MSNBC wind up with less political knowledge than they would be expected to have otherwise. Mostly because of the popularity of Fox News, that's not an insignificant proportion of the population: in the 2010 ANES data, it's 23 percent of Americans. In that same dataset, they're more likely to say that they're going to vote (their mean reported likelihood of voting is 85 percent, compared to 83 percent) more likely to talk about politics with friends and co-workers (2.4 days a week at the mean, compared to 2.3 days), and more likely to personally engage in politics, as measured through an index of civic participation (mean score of 1.5 versus a mean score of 1.4). All told, these people seem like they're interested and engaged in politics – but their ability to engage in the political world is being limited by the fact that their viewing habits leave them with less information about politics than they would have if they cut Fox out of their media diet.

6

CONSPIRACY THEORIES AND OTHER FALSE BELIEFS

In addition to changing attitudes towards politicians, behaviors like campaign contributions, and even levels of political knowledge, individuals who report watching Fox News also wind up holding very different beliefs about the state of American politics than non-viewers. Nowhere is this more evident than in the effects of Fox News on the willingness of viewers to endorse conspiracy theories and other false beliefs. Controlling for other factors that are expected to make a difference – like levels of political knowledge – individuals who report watching Fox News are more likely to say that global warming is a hoax cooked up by scientists, that weapons of mass destruction were found in Iraq, and that Barack Obama is not actually an American citizen.

What's especially interesting about these beliefs is that for Republicans who watch Fox, many of these beliefs become more prevalent with increases in political knowledge, while most social science models of conspiracy beliefs say that knowledge should decrease them. Fox News is not the only media source that leads people to endorse conspiracy theories – in the case of the discredited vaccine–autism link, CNN seems like the worst offender – but for political conspiracies, it plays an enormous role.

Conspiracy Theories in American Politics

America has a long history of political conspiracy theories. When George Washington was still President, newspapers on one side were claiming that John Adams wanted to make himself king, while those on the other side claimed that Thomas Jefferson was keeping a family he had fathered with his dead wife's slave half-sister (no one ever said that all of the conspiracy theories were false). One of the earliest third parties in American history was formed around the theory that the Masons were running the country and covering up murders in upstate New York (Kruschke 1991, George and Wilcox 1996) – it might seem crazy to us now, but at one point the governors of both Vermont and Pennsylvania were members of the Anti-Masonic Party. Even Abraham Lincoln wasn't above injecting a little bit of conspiracy theory into his speeches. At some point in school, most Americans have heard about Lincoln's famous 1858 speech in which he declared: "A house divided against itself cannot stand. I believe this government cannot endure permanently, half slave and half free."

Most of the time, Americans talk about this speech in the context of Lincoln's devotion to the Union: the United States has to be one as a country, it can't be divided, and so on. However, that's not really what he was talking about. In modern political parlance, this would be called a "dog whistle," a line that's designed to signal a controversial stance to one group while not revealing that stance to others. For instance, when Richard Nixon campaigned for "law and order" in 1968, it's generally agreed that he was talking about suppressing black riots in urban areas (Perlstein 2000, Flamm 2005). People who cared about that issue knew exactly what "law and order" meant, while it seemed like a general statement of principle to everyone else. In Lincoln's case, the "house divided" line was a reference to the slave power hypothesis, a popular conspiracy theory of the 1850s, in which it was thought that slave states weren't content to simply retain slavery, or even advance it into new territories being added to the country, but wanted to make all of the states slave states. There was no real evidence for such a position – just like there isn't any real evidence for 9/11 truthers or Newtown shooting theorists today – but that didn't stop a large swath of what was then the left wing of the Republican Party from believing passionately in it. Some of Lincoln's rivals for the Republican nomination had explicitly endorsed the slave power hypothesis, and thus made themselves seem too extreme for the country as a whole. Lincoln, however, used lines like the "house divided" speech to signal the extremes of his party that he was on their side without doing so too overtly and killing his chances of being elected.

The normal social psychology explanation for belief in conspiracies is that people feel that important events must have important causes (Hofstadter 2008/1966). The killing of John F. Kennedy is a watershed event, so it feels like there should be more to it than a lone gunman. When people look deeply into any situation, they can find patterns that don't seem to fit the accepted version of the truth – these patterns and inconsistencies form the basis of conspiracy theories that become impossible to dispel. Indeed, in the most recent survey results on that question, only 19 percent of Americans said that one man was responsible for the assassination. After all, any evidence against the theory could just have been produced by the conspirators, and the more people argue against the theory, the more evidence there is that some people are trying to quash the truth. Social psychologists have also argued that conspiracy theories help people make sense of an otherwise nonsensical world: it may be easier to believe that an evil cabal is behind an event than it is to admit that it's random. Trying to understand the conspiracy is a way for people to try and regain control and understanding of the world (van Prooijen 2012, Oliver and Wood 2014).

What these models have in common is a built-in solution to conspiracy theories: information. The more people know about the world, and what's really going on in it, the less likely they should be to buy into these theories. Understanding gives people a sense of control, and facts lead to the truth, which typically isn't a conspiracy. A belief that the 1969 moon landing was a hoax doesn't stand up to much scrutiny, and normal social psychology explanations would argue that other conspiracy theories should go the same way. And while this might work for most conspiracies, there are a couple of reasons why it doesn't work for political conspiracies in the modern era.

The first is that most political conspiracies aren't driven by the normal social psychology explanations, but by something mentioned earlier: motivated reasoning. Everything researchers know about cognitive psychology tells us that emotional responses come prior to considered responses (Krosnick 1989, Morris et al. 2003, Mulligan et al. 2003, Lodge and Taber 2005) – people know how they *feel* about something before they know what they *think* about it. So, once people have established their feelings about someone or something, it's no problem for them to create facts in order to support those beliefs, and even easier for them to believe things that support those beliefs. For people who hate Bill Clinton, theories that he murdered Vince Foster to cover up the White House Travel Office scandal seem much more plausible than they would otherwise. After all, he's the sort of guy who *would* do that, and the more the individual dislikes him, the more prone they are to believe it.

The second is that the news sources Americans seek out in order to get more information about political conspiracies may not actually be interested in dispelling them. If individuals tend to turn to news sources that agree with what they already believe – liberals watching MSNBC, conservatives watching Fox – they're not going to get that sort of corrective information. Rather, they're likely to receive more information that tends to reinforce their feelings about the individuals implicated in the conspiracy. This means that they may wind up being *more* likely to believe the conspiracy: now, Bill Clinton sounds even more like the sort of person who would be involved in a murder cover-up. Of course, this problem could be resolved by having an agreed upon set of trusted bipartisan media sources – but in a polarized political landscape, bipartisan media sources will never by trusted by either side (Vallone et al. 1985, Morris 2007).

Belief in Political Conspiracy Theories

It's no surprise, then, that there are big partisan differences in how Americans evaluate modern political conspiracy theories. In a December 2012 survey, PublicMind asked registered voters nationwide to evaluate four different political conspiracy theories, asking whether each was "probably true" or "probably not true" or if they weren't sure. The theories the survey asked about were as follows:

- President Bush's supporters committed significant voter fraud in order to win Ohio in 2004.
- President Obama's supporters committed significant voter fraud in the 2012 Presidential election.
- President Bush knew about the 9/11 attacks before they happened.
- President Obama is hiding important information about his background and early life.

The first notable thing in the results is exactly how much Americans believe in these conspiracy theories: 63 percent of registered voters thought that at least one of these theories was "probably true," including 56 percent of Democrats and 75 percent of Republicans. The most popular of these theories was what's been referred to as "birtherism" – the belief that Obama is hiding important information about his birth and early life. Initially, these theories focused on the argument that Obama had actually been born in Kenya, and was therefore not eligible to be President of the United States, but by 2012, they had morphed into a number of theories about Obama holding foreign citizenship, using a stolen social security number, registering for college as a foreign student and so on. So, while the question was broad – asking respondents if Obama was "hiding important information" rather than if he was born in Kenya – it was still surprising when 36 percent of voters (and 64 percent of Republicans) thought it was probably true.

Obama isn't even the first President whose "natural birth" has been questioned – political opponents claimed that Chester Arthur was born in Canada, and even hired an attorney to investigate (Reeves 1970, Karabell 2004). This theory wasn't actually too far-fetched: Arthur was born in northern New York, well before definitive borders between the countries were enforced, and modern scholars think it plausible that he was born on the wrong side of the line. However, the attorney hired by Democrats, Arthur Hinman, came back with a report claiming that Arthur was actually born in Ireland and had not been brought to the US until he was 14 – a claim so improbable that it was promptly ignored (by the end, his theories included the idea that the real Arthur had died years before, and the person elected President was actually his brother). Once Obama responded to prodding by publicly producing his birth certificate, many thought that the conspiracy theories surrounding his birth would go the same way – but that certainly doesn't seem to have been the case. If anything, the birth certificate gave conspiracy theorists more ammunition, as they began to claim that it wasn't authentic, or had been digitally altered. Of course, the fact that conspiracies about Arthur hadn't panned out didn't stop his critics from continuing to pass them around either, even after they were largely debunked.

In addition, about one in four voters think it's probably true that Bush knew about the 9/11 attacks before they happened, coming very close to the "truther" movement, which holds that the truth about the 9/11 attacks is being hidden from the public. Either the planes never really crashed, or never really took off, or the whole thing was planned by Israel, or it was cruise missiles, or buildings don't collapse that way, or Bush let the attack happen as a way to justify war on Iraq. Whatever the explanation, it's been seen as a fringe conspiracy, but the results show that it's anything but. Moreover, people who were younger than 18 when the attacks happened are much more likely to believe in these theories. While belief is concentrated in a few demographics – young people and African-Americans, especially – there's enough of them to constitute a significant portion of the American electorate.

Theories about voter fraud also prove popular among American voters: 23 percent think that Bush committed voter fraud in order to steal the 2004 election, and 20 percent think that Obama stole the 2012 election. Now, there's nothing new about the perception of voter fraud in American elections. Andrew Jackson rebelled against the establishment Democrats over the very shady dealings that decided the 1824 Presidential election, and got his revenge when the winner, John Quincy Adams, sought re-election. At least one election – 1876 – was outright stolen, with the winner decided by a party line vote in Congress (Rehnquist 2007). It seems clear now that voter fraud was widespread in parts of the country, with areas like the border counties in Texas, Cook County, Illinois and the wards of Hudson County, New Jersey being delivered wholesale to the highest bidder by sometimes sophisticated political machinery. Before he became one of the most respected and feared leaders of the Senate in American history, Lyndon Johnson was known as "landslide Lyndon" after he won his first election by 87 votes, put over the top by a precinct that "discovered" a few hundred votes 2 days after the election, all of which had been cast in alphabetical order by people who swore that they hadn't been to the polls (Caro 1991). There were enough irregularities in the 1960 Presidential election that some of his partisans thought Richard Nixon could challenge the results, but some degree of chicanery was expected, and since both sides pursued it, it wasn't even considered illegitimate.

Since 1960, the decline of patronage, the rise in primary elections, and the computerization of records has eroded the ability of parties to steal elections outright in the way they previously had. Americans largely stopped worrying about the legitimacy of their elections, until the debacle of Florida in 2000 showed how badly the situation was broken. What Florida really demonstrated was that elections, like polls, have a margin of error, and if the results are within that margin of error, the results are up for grabs in a courtroom (Hasen 2005). Maybe we'd like to think that an election can be decided by one vote, but Florida may it clear that if it was, it wouldn't be until after all of the lawyers got involved.

Parties responded to this revelation in two ways. The first was by mobilizing to more effectively monitor the voting process. This isn't a bad thing – more eyes on voting booths may discourage fraud – but the parties' motives were more cynical. Rather than trying to prevent fraud, they were looking to find evidence of it in case they needed to go to court. The second was by paying closer attention to the returns than ever before, and sounding the alarm whenever there was any inkling that something might have gone wrong (Smith and Shortell 2007). Again, this isn't necessarily a bad thing, but it has led to a lot of false alarms, and in every election since 2000, the losing side has made well-publicized and widely believed claims that the election was stolen.

These perceptions of voter fraud are aided by polarization in political networks. While Americans in general have relatively heterogeneous political networks – they tend to know people from both sides of the spectrum – the more partisan people are, the less likely they are to talk about politics with people who disagree with them. So, while moderates – when they talk about politics at all – talk to both liberals and conservatives, people on the left and right tend to congregate together. This means that the people who feel the most strongly about the election simply may not know anyone who voted for the other candidate. If that's the case, it's no wonder they don't believe that the other candidate could have won. Charlie Webster, then chair of the Maine Republican Party, received widespread condemnation when he said in an interview with WCSH-TV after the 2012 election:

> In some parts of rural Maine, there were dozens, dozens of black people who came in and voted on Election Day. Everybody has a right to vote, but nobody in [these] towns knows anyone who's black. How did that happen? I don't know. We're going to find out.

Aside from any racist undertones, Webster had a point: in these small towns, residents had no idea that there were black people or Democrats in town. It goes the other way, too: in many urban African-American dominated precincts in Philadelphia and Chicago, Obama won 100 percent of the vote. This was taken by some as evidence of fraud, but it's really just a sign that there are whole neighborhoods where there aren't any Republicans. If someone doesn't know anyone who voted for the other guy, and he won, conspiracy theories about stolen elections don't seem so far-fetched.

Political Knowledge and Conspiracy Theories

The most striking thing in these results, though, is the relationship between belief in these conspiracy theories and how much people know about current events. Again, classic social psychology explanations for belief in conspiracies would tell us that more knowledge would lead to less belief: but that just doesn't seem to be the case here. Respondents in the survey were asked four questions about current events: about where drone strikes were taking place, about the unemployment rate, the party in control of the House of Representatives, and who the current Secretary of State was. The more of these questions respondents were able to answer (on average, respondents answered two of the four correctly; 10 percent missed them all, 18 percent answered them all correctly), the fewer of the conspiracy theories they believed. However, these results were contingent on the respondent's party. Among independents, each question answered correctly reduced the likelihood of believing in one or more of the conspiracy theories by about 2 points. Among Democrats, each question answered correctly reduced the likelihood of believing in one or more of them by 7 points. Among Republicans, though, better-informed respondents were actually *more* likely to believe in the conspiracies: each question answered correctly increased the likelihood that they'd believe in one or more of them by about 2 points. Results for all values of partisanship and political knowledge are shown in Figure 6.1, where it can be seen that higher levels of political knowledge increase the proportion who say that they believe in one or none of the conspiracies among Democrats, while having very little effect among independents, and actually increasing conspiracy beliefs among Republicans.

At first glance, this is a counter-intuitive result, and some pundits – like David Frum, or Jesse Walker at *Reason* – argued that it had to be due to the inclusion of the question about Obama's early life. After all, they argued, you didn't have to be a birther to believe that Obama was hiding something. However, the numbers simply don't bear this out: even when the Obama background item isn't

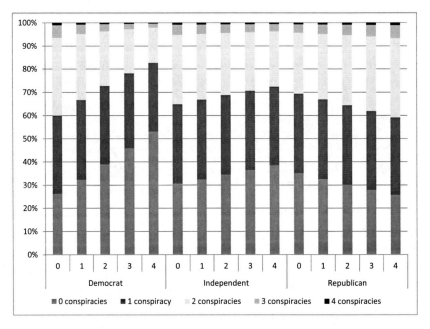

FIGURE 6.1   Number of Conspiracies Believed, by Party and Political Knowledge Score

included in the scale of conspiracy items, the interaction effect between party identification and political knowledge remains. Moreover, as seen in the analysis of the belief that weapons of mass destruction were found in Iraq, the same pattern holds up in other surveys, and on topics other than President Obama's background.

It seems likely that these results are being driven by motivated reasoning: partisans are much more likely than political independents to believe political conspiracy theories because they have reason to believe them. For instance, some of the most popular conspiracies in the December 2012 PublicMind survey involved accusations of voter fraud: 23 percent of Americans and 37 percent of Democrats say that President Bush "probably" committed significant voter fraud in order to win the 2004 Presidential election in Ohio. Similarly, 20 percent of Americans and 36 percent of Republicans say that President Obama "probably" committed significant voter fraud in the 2012 election. These are the sorts of beliefs that likely arise from motivated reasoning: partisans don't like the results of the election, and so seize on any evidence that the results aren't valid. Not surprisingly, for both of these beliefs, higher levels of political knowledge correspond with lower likelihoods of endorsing the theories.

However, not all of the beliefs are so easily explained, as increased levels of political knowledge don't universally reduce the rates at which individuals believe in them, and, among Republicans, increased information seems to lead to greater beliefs in conspiracy theories. These results indicate that there's something about the information Republicans are receiving that makes them more likely to believe in political conspiracies, and popular conservative news sources seem a likely culprit. When the results of this study were discussed on Fox News, for instance, the host, Megyn Kelly, discussed how strange it was that so many people believed in conspiracies. They then turned to commentator Tucker Carlson, who thought it was especially strange, given that the real question was why Obama had not yet released his college transcripts. Based on the partisan nature of the difference, and exchanges like this, it seems likely that differences in media sources play some role in the differences between how Republicans and Democrats evaluate certain conspiracy theories.

Birtherism

To address these sorts of issues, PublicMind carried out a second national survey measuring belief in conspiracy theories, political knowledge and media consumption in December 2014. Once again, an item asked respondents about their belief in "birther" theories, this time with a more specific item, asking whether they thought it was "definitely true, probably true, probably not true, or definitely not true that President Obama is not legally a citizen of the United States." The fact that this item uses different wording than was used in the previous survey is a strength: to the extent that the item is tapping into a real mental construct, the dynamics should be the same no matter what phrasing is used.

All told, 5 percent of Americans said that Obama was "definitely" not a citizen, and another 13 percent said that he "probably" wasn't, with the biggest group (41 percent) saying that it was definitely not true. While the more specific question led to lower levels of agreement, the partisan split remained enormous: 38 percent of Republicans said that Obama was definitely or probably not a citizen, compared with 23 percent of independents and just 8 percent of Democrats. In addition, 8 percent of Republicans said that they didn't know whether he was a citizen or not, in comparison with just 1 percent of independents and Democrats.

Higher levels of political knowledge also corresponded with a lower likelihood of saying that Obama wasn't a citizen: 21 percent of Americans who couldn't answer correctly any of the three political knowledge items on the survey said that he "probably" or "definitely" wasn't a citizen, compared with just 12 percent of those who were able to answer all of them correctly. Similarly, higher levels of education corresponded to lower levels of birther beliefs: 22 percent of Americans who never went to college thought Obama was likely not a citizen, compared with 16 percent of those with a college degree.

So far, this seems like a simple story: some Republicans who are opposed to Obama, who see him as illegitimate, are motivated to believe that he isn't a citizen, and that some shadowy conspiracy hid the facts about his birth in order to help him get elected. However, people who pay more attention to politics, and who have had more education, tend to discount such theories. Were this the case, it wouldn't be terribly surprising – or interesting, for that matter. What makes this important is the fact that effects of political knowledge differ based on the partisanship and media choices of the individual.

Using a logistic regression model to isolate the effects of individual factors, a few things become evident. First, even controlling for race, age, education and media choices, partisanship and political ideology still matter a great deal. All else equal, independents and Democrats are about equally likely to think that Obama isn't a citizen, but Republicans are 18 points more likely than either to think it.

Media choices matter, too: Americans who watch Fox are about 5 points more likely to think that Obama is probably not a citizen than those who don't. None of the other media indicators have a significant impact on the likelihood of believing that Obama isn't a citizen. Note that this is in addition to any indirect effects Fox viewership is likely having through changes in the levels of political knowledge among non-conservative Fox viewers (as discussed in Chapter 5). While Fox hosts haven't specifically endorsed birther views on the air in the past few years, they haven't dismissed them either. As Sean Hannity put it in a discussion about Obama's long-form birth certificate on April 27, 2011:

> The question has been raised. And I think you are very dismissive of people that I think have a legitimate – look, this is a constitutional requirement. No person except a natural born citizen or a citizen in the United States

at the time of the adoption of the Constitution is eligible to be President. It seemed to me like a legitimate question.

In discussions like this, Hannity makes sure to say that he thinks Obama is a citizen (largely based on the evidence of the birth announcements, rather than the actual birth certificate), but says that these are serious questions that should be dealt with. Even the fact that these issues are being discussed may be enough to drive some viewers to think that something is going on: where there's smoke, there must be fire.

Among Democrats, independents and Republicans who don't report watching Fox News, higher levels of political knowledge (measured through a set of three items described in methodology note 6.1) correspond with lower likelihoods of believing that President Obama isn't a citizen. Individuals at the highest level of political knowledge are 14 points less likely to think so than people at the lowest levels among Democrats, 12 points less likely among independents, and just 9 points less likely to think so among Republicans. This, by itself, is a sign of motivated reasoning at play: among Americans who are more motivated to believe that Obama is illegitimate, knowing more about politics and current events does less to convince them that he is, in fact, a citizen.

However, among independents and independents who lean towards the Republican Party and watch Fox News, higher levels of political knowledge correspond with *greater* likelihoods of thinking that Obama is not a citizen: an increase of 29 points among pure independents (who say that they don't lean towards either party), and an increase of 10 points among Republican leaners (see methodology note 6.1 for details). Interestingly, among Republicans, the story is a little more complicated. In this group, increases in political knowledge do tend to decrease the likelihood of saying that Obama is "probably" or "definitely" not a citizen, but the effects of political knowledge are much smaller among Republicans than among the other partisan groups. Also unlike the other groups, for Republicans, watching Fox News has little impact in the effect of political knowledge on the belief that Obama isn't a citizen.

The most likely explanation for the relative lack of an effect of Fox News among Republicans in their rates of believing that Obama is not a citizen comes from the higher base rates for this belief. Controlling for all other factors, Republicans are much more prone to say that Obama is likely not a citizen, so there's rather little room for the numbers to go up. This difference also highlights one of the reasons why Fox News is so influential: unlike MSNBC's, Fox News's reach means that its audience is fairly politically diverse. As such, there are enough independents and leaners watching for it to make a difference.

Even with a different, more specific wording, the general finding remains the same. Among Republicans, higher levels of political knowledge are less connected with the acceptance of birtherism. Americans who don't like Obama may be motivated to believe that his Presidency is illegitimate, and embrace conspiracy theories positing that he's not really a citizen, that he was born in Kenya, or some variant of birther theories about this issue. However, these beliefs are difficult to support in the face of overwhelming evidence to the contrary, so individuals who have higher levels of education or pay more attention to current events become less likely to embrace them. This effect of political knowledge in reducing the likelihood of believing a conspiracy theory falls apart, though, among those who consume a media source that raises doubts, or is at least ambiguous, about the verity of these birther conspiracy theories. For Americans consuming such a media source, with the motivation to believe that Obama is illegitimate and without existing high base rates of believing, knowing more about politics means being able to pick up on more cues that tend to support birther theories. It's not enough to say that ignorance or motivated reasoning alone lead to acceptance of these beliefs: the media is a necessary part of the equation as well.

Weapons of Mass Destruction in Iraq

The belief that American forces found an active program to produce weapons of mass destruction in Iraq after the 2003 invasion is one of the most popular conspiracy theories among the American public, likely because of the outsize political importance the search for such a program took on. As of December 2014, a PublicMind poll showed that 9 percent of the American public said that an active WMD program was "definitely" found; another 25 percent said that it was "probably" found; another 7 percent said that they didn't know. The question of WMD in Iraq is a fertile area for the sort of motivated reasoning previously discussed. While there were many justifications for the invasion of Iraq – human rights abuses carried out by Saddam Hussein, the protection of ethnic minorities within Iraq, long-term stability in the region through a democratization project, even enhancing the security of Israel – weapons of mass destruction were seized upon both by the Bush administration and by the public as the primary reason why the invasion needed to happen, and needed to happen now. In September 2008, then National Security Advisor Condoleezza Rice famously said that while no smoking gun of clear evidence for a WMD program had been found, "we don't want the smoking gun to be a mushroom cloud." While earlier research found that such elite rhetoric was influential at the time, it was thought that the effects would fade as "reality asserts itself" (Baum and Groeling 2010), but this does not seem to have been the case.

The importance of WMD for the war in Iraq is evident from contemporary polling results. Two months prior to the March 2003 invasion, a Gallup poll showed that 46 percent of Americans were "certain" that Iraq had facilities to create WMD, with another 49 percent saying that it was likely. Among Republicans, 58 percent were certain that WMD facilities existed. A month prior to the invasion, a CBS News poll found that 80 percent of the public (and 85 percent of Republicans) thought that Iraq currently had WMD. In polls carried out at the same time, this was viewed as a compelling justification for the invasion: a CNN/Harris poll carried out that month showed 41 percent of Americans thought that removing WMD from Iraq was a "very convincing" reason to go to war; another 31 percent thought that it was "fairly convincing."

During the invasion, polls showed that the American public was sure that WMD would be found: a Gallup poll carried out 10 days after the invasion began showed that 52 percent of Americans were "very confident" WMD would be found, and another 32 percent were "somewhat" confident. These groups included a staggering 94 percent of Republicans.

In a May 2003 CBS/*New York Times* poll, 27 percent of Americans said that WMD had been found, and by March 2004, a year after the invasion, that figure had increased (in a PIPA/Knowledge Networks poll) to 38 percent. Once public opinion on the war began to sour, though, a partisan split between Democrats and Republicans began to surface on the question of whether WMD had been found. By March 2006, 27 percent of Republicans said that WMD had been found, compared with 6 percent of Democrats. Five years later, about the same proportion of the American public thought that WMD had been found (16 percent in 2011 versus 18 percent in 2006), but the partisan split was even wider, with only 2 percent of Democrats thinking WMD had been uncovered.

At the time of the invasion, the absence of WMD was a major issue in the news and the political debate: it's difficult to imagine that someone could be well informed and believe that American forces had found the WMD. Some clues for how this happened can be found in a June 2003 poll carried out by the University of Maryland (see methodology note 6.3 for more information on the poll). The Maryland poll asked respondents about a number of items that aren't normally found in polls, including a six-item political knowledge battery that included a number of items about the Iraq war (for instance, asking respondents to give an approximation of the number of troops killed up until that point). What's striking about this is that there seems to be little or no connection between how much a respondent knows about politics and current events, and the likelihood of believing that WMD had been found in Iraq: 23 percent of individuals who weren't able to answer any of the questions correctly (17 percent of the sample) said that WMD had been found, but so did 16 percent of those who answered all of the questions correctly (a group which constituted 12 percent of the sample). Apparently, 16 percent of people who knew how many American troops had been killed, knew about how many European troops were fighting in Iraq and Afghanistan, knew which groups were controlling Afghanistan, who knew all of that, somehow missed one of the most widely reported facts about the war. How this is possible becomes clearer when the partisanship of respondents is taken into account: only 12 percent of Democrats said that WMD had been found, in comparison with 19 percent of independents, and 42 percent of Republicans.

Thus far, this looks like a fairly straightforward case of motivated reasoning: Republicans in particular wanted to believe that WMD had been found in order to bolster their support for the war in Iraq (in the same survey, 86 percent of Republicans said that they had become *more* supportive of the war effort since it had begun, in comparison with just 38 percent of Democrats). When the motivation to believe is strong enough, the facts follow, whether they're accurate or not. While the story might end there, it's missing a key component: the facts, or the ambiguity that may be interpreted as such, have to come from somewhere. In this case, it seems that Fox News was the likely culprit, especially when exposure to Fox was not coupled with corrective information from other news sources (Muddiman et al. 2014). Looking at coverage about the failure to find WMD in Iraq on Fox, it becomes clear why this might be the case. As Sean Hannity asked guest Karl Rove on September 12, 2013: "Why do I believe that Iraq's WMD were transported to Syria in the lead up to the war?" In April 2013, a guest on the same program, radio host David Webb, asserted that WMD had been found, saying:

> And to the issue of chemical weapons, by the way, let me refute something that's absolute fact. We found the ricin residue in Iraq. The WMDs were there. The 600,000 dead Kurds is proof and there were many Democrats from Madeleine Albright to Bill Clinton, Hillary Clinton who know this to be true and said so.

This assertion comes up frequently in the transcripts – that the chemical residue from Iraq's past chemical weapons programs was the WMD that had justified the war: as Bret Baier noted on his program on August 23, 2011: "People sitting at home may say how do we know the intelligence was right at the beginning that they had this stuff? Iraq, it didn't turn out that WMD was there in big numbers as suspected." In other cases, the issue of physical WMD is said to be beside the point. As host Greg Gutfeld said on *The Five* on March 19, 2013: "The WMD was [Saddam] Hussein himself."

Current Beliefs about WMD

After controlling for all of the relevant factors – gender, education, age, race, income and the like – a few factors remain significant predictors of whether or not the individual believes that WMD were found. Of course, partisanship matters a great deal: all else equal, independents are 10 points more likely to believe that WMD had been found than Democrats, and Republicans are 20 points more likely to believe it than independents. And while reported exposure to Fox News alone doesn't seem to matter, it has strong contingent effects, moderated by partisanship and political knowledge. All told, these effects tell a striking story. For nearly all of the groups, higher levels of political knowledge correspond with lower likelihoods of believing that WMD had been found. Among independents, for instance, someone at the top end (90th percentile) of the political knowledge scale was 12 points less likely to believe that WMD had been found than someone at the low end (10th percentile). Among Republicans, someone at the high end of the political knowledge scale was 22 points less likely to think that WMD had been found than someone at the low end – exactly as would be expected. However, this relationship breaks down among Republicans who reported getting their news from Fox, as shown in Figure 6.2. In that group, more political knowledge actually corresponds to a high likelihood of believing that WMD had been found: those at the high end of the political knowledge scale are 43 points *more* likely to have this false impression than those at the low end of the political knowledge scale.

The story here seems to be that while Republicans, in general, are motivated to believe that WMD had been found, it takes a confluence of factors to actually create that belief. Individuals who simply don't follow the news much (and therefore have low scores on the political knowledge scale) tend to think it might be the case, whether they're Republicans or Democrats. As these individuals learn more about current events, they become less likely to believe it, unless they're both motivated and consuming a media source that supplies them with sufficient ambiguity about the facts that they're able to maintain that belief in the face of all contrary evidence. In this case, higher levels of political knowledge would be a help in maintaining the false belief, as they allow individuals to

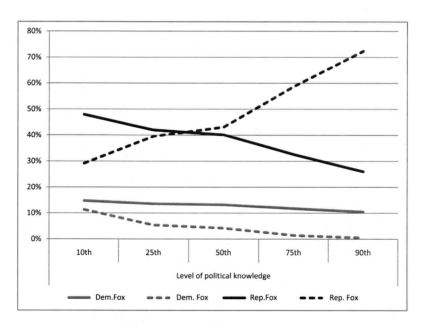

FIGURE 6.2 Likelihood of Believing That WMD Were Found in Iraq, by Party, Knowledge Level and Fox Viewership

better counter-argue information that's contrary to their desired beliefs, and find reasons to discard and information that would lead them to change their minds.

While this seems like a very cut-and-dried question, there has been increasing room for ambiguity about whether Iraq had a WMD program or not in the years since that 2003 survey. Before the invasion, there was some concern that Iraq could move any WMD outside the country, or transfer them to terrorist groups. As such, it's possible to reconcile the belief that Iraq had WMD at the time of, or just before, the invasion with the fact that no such program was found. Adding to the ambiguity is the fact that American forces did find some chemical weapons left over from the WMD program Iraq had been pursuing prior to the 1991 invasion, as many as 5,000 chemical warheads from that period, according to a *New York Times* report that centered on the health problems faced by Iraq War veterans. At the time, US News & World Report reported that this was seen as both a vindication for the proponents of the invasion and as evidence that the government had covered up the existence of the chemical weapons. The cover-up, to the extent that one occurred, was based on government denial of health claims from these veterans who may have been affected by exposure to these toxins, rather than a cover-up of the existence of a WMD program, but seeds of doubt had been sown. Between the post-invasion reports of the uncovering of small amounts of pre-war chemical weapons and the 2014 report on veterans' health that had the implication of a cover-up, it became even easier for individuals to believe that a WMD program had been found and, perhaps, simply not reported on in the mainstream media.

Because of the changing facts and the passage of time, it seems to have become easier to believe that an active WMD program actually was found in Iraq. In the previously cited December 2014 PublicMind poll, only 9 percent of Americans said that American forces had definitely found WMD in Iraq, but the figure was 15 percent among Republicans (another 37 percent of Republicans said that it's "probably true"). The motivation to believe that WMD were found may not be as strong as it was when this was a major issue in the political debate, but it remains nonetheless, and watching Fox still plays a significant role in maintaining that belief.

Watching Fox has a significant impact on the likelihood that respondents will say that American forces found an active WMD program in Iraq. All else equal, someone who watches Fox is about 11 points more likely to say that the predicted WMD program was found. However, everything is not equal: the effects of watching Fox on thinking that an active WMD program was found depend on people's partisanship, and how diverse their media diet is. In contrast to many of the other findings presented here, the effects of partisanship are not continuous: normally, it's assumed that being a Democrat is a little different from being an independent, which is a little different from being a Republican. In this case, though, it seems that the biggest difference is actually between Republicans and everyone else (what statisticians would call a "step effect"). All else equal, being a Republican makes someone 7 points more likely to believe that an active WMD program was found in Iraq, but this effect is amplified among those Republicans who say that their main source of information is Fox News (see methodology note 6.2 for more on this) – a group that includes 40 percent of all Republicans. Forty-five percent of Republicans say that their main source of news is cable programming, and half of Republicans say that they get their news from Fox. Among Republicans who get their news mostly from cable, watching Fox increases the likelihood of saying that American forces found an active WMD program by 27 points. In contrast, among independents who get most of their news from cable, watching Fox only increases the likelihood of believing that WMD was found by 4 points. The analysis suggests that Democrats who rely on (not just watch) Fox would also be much more likely to think that a WMD program had been found in Iraq, but there are simply too few Democrats in that category to draw any firm conclusions (see methodology note 6.4).

Non-Political Conspiracy Theories

Of course, not all conspiracy theories are inherently political. In recent years, issues on which there is broad scientific consensus have become subject to conspiracy theories that have been reported in the media, and cable news programming is fertile ground for anyone seeking to sow doubts about undesirable scientific findings. As discussed previously, journalists – for good reason – try very hard to be fair and show both sides of a controversy, but this sometimes serves to distort the truth. In circumstances under which there isn't really a serious debate within the scientific community, showing two sides doesn't necessarily serve to increase public understanding of an issue, and may well lead viewers to conclude that there's a scientific controversy when there really isn't. For instance, while there may be some debate about the extent to which humans are contributing to global climate change, there's really no question among climatologists that it's occurring. Similarly, while a lone British scientist did publish articles linking the early childhood measles, mumps and rubella (MMR) vaccine to the onset of autism, further scrutiny showed these findings to be falsified, the author was revealed to have had a financial interest in promoting alternative vaccination schemes, and the paper was retracted by the journal in which it was published. Since then, there has been enormous scientific inquiry about the link between vaccines and autism, universally showing that in the general public, there is no link between vaccinations and the onset of autism (Deer 2011, Godlee et al. 2011). In both cases, the consensus among scientists hasn't prevented cable news programs from presenting debates about such issues, with the autism debate being particularly attractive because of several minor celebrities who argue for the discredited link (Kata 2012).

These two beliefs – that autism is linked with vaccinations, and that global climate change isn't really occurring – are part of a distinct constellation of conspiracy theories, ones that hold that there's a conspiracy among scientists, rather than among government agencies, to withhold the truth from the public for some nefarious reason (to preserve sales of vaccines in one case, and to continue to receive grant money in the other). Both of these conspiracy theories have wide credence among the American public: in a national telephone poll PublicMind carried out in December 2014, 26 percent of Americans said that they believed that it was "definitely" or "probably" true that global warming is a myth propagated by scientists; 20 percent of the American public believed that it was "definitely" or "probably" true that early childhood vaccinations cause autism.

It may be possible to disregard some of the political conspiracy theories as being generally inconsequential: if someone thinks that the government is hiding the existence of aliens at Area 51, or that John F. Kennedy was killed by the CIA, it doesn't necessarily lead to any social or political consequences, or even lead to any policy preferences that are relevant to most elections. These sorts of non-political conspiracy theories, however, are different. If people strongly believe that early childhood vaccinations cause autism, they may delay necessary vaccinations, or even avoid them entirely. As a result of this, as well as some other contributing factors, the US and, to a lesser extent, the UK have seen enormous spikes in the number of children suffering from diseases that had basically been eradicated in the last 50 years (Jolley and Douglas 2014, Lynfield and Daum 2014). Worse, the decision not to vaccinate not only puts the children of the vaccination-skeptical parents at risk, but also the children they come into contact with. Even a small number of unvaccinated children can compromise what virologists call herd immunity, making infection more likely among all children, leading to sickness, or even death. This phenomenon first cropped up in the UK in the 1990s, leading sociologists there to create focus groups of parents (Evans et al. 2001) to try and find out why they were eschewing vaccines, and their results were troubling. Parents who chose not to vaccinate their children felt that their concerns weren't being taken seriously by their doctors, and because of this, they didn't have any trusted source with whom to discuss these issues. As a result, they often turned to websites and other not necessarily reputable sources to get information on the risks of vaccines. The false belief that vaccines were linked with autism not only put their children, and other children, in danger, but also served to shut down channels of communication with the people who otherwise would have been best situated to deal with the problem.

Belief in the legitimacy of global warming also has consequences. While beliefs about the John F. Kennedy assassination might not come up in modern elections very frequently, policies to mitigate the effects of global climate change, or to prevent worse effects in the future, do arise frequently. Gas taxes, energy tax credits, green energy subsidies and cap-and-trade programs are all common political footballs. While not every program to address climate change is necessarily worthwhile, individuals who don't believe that climate change is occurring in the first place are simply incapable of making the necessary cost–benefit analysis that would let them determine if the policies are a good idea.

For both of these beliefs, education is a huge driver of whether individuals accept the scientific consensus: 24 percent of Americans who never attended college say that there's likely a link between vaccinations and autism, a figure that drops to 14 percent of Americans who have a college degree. Similarly, 39 percent of those with only a high school education say that global warming is "definitely" or "probably" a myth propagated by scientists, compared with only 27 percent of those with a college degree.

While education matters, media choices also play a substantial role in how Americans view these scientific conspiracy theories: 22 percent of those who say that cable news is their primary source of information think it's likely that early childhood vaccinations cause autism, compared with 16 percent of those who get most of their news from network broadcasts. The best-informed group on this point are people who say that their primary source of news is political satire programs: only 12 percent of them think there's a link. Among the particular news sources which have enough viewers that conclusions can be fairly drawn, there's no clear pattern: CNN viewers are the most likely to see a link (25 percent saying that's it's "definitely" or "probably" there), along with 14 percent of Fox viewers, 10 percent of MSNBC viewers and 9 percent of those who watch *The Daily Show*. The spike among CNN viewers may well be due to a report on the network's user-generated news website that claimed that Center for Disease Control data had found a link between the age at which the MMR vaccine was given and the onset of autism among one racial subgroup. The report was quickly retracted after the researcher being quoted was found to have been recorded without his permission, and had dismissed the report as statistically invalid. Still, while there was no real news here, the issue was addressed repeatedly on CNN, as it explained why it had pulled the report from its website. It seems likely that even reporting on the controversy led some viewers to conclude that there was a serious debate.

Media consumption matters in beliefs about global climate change as well, though not quite in the same way. Unlike beliefs about vaccinations and autism, the policy implications arising from climate change mean that it has become enormously politicized – something that's evident in the data: 20 percent of Democrats (including independents who say that they "lean" toward the Democratic Party) say that global warming is "definitely" or "probably" a myth propagated by scientists, a figure that rises to 30 percent of political independents and 48 percent of Republicans. This seems to be a strong indication of motivated reasoning: Republicans would be expected to be more skeptical of the science behind climate change because they're opposed to most of the policy changes that have been suggested to deal with the problem. Opposition to the policies is easiest to justify if there's no problem in the first place – a view that nearly half of Republicans now hold.

Given the partisan split over climate change, it should come as no surprise that a similar split arises among audiences of ideological news sources. A majority – 54 percent – of Americans who say that they get their news from Fox say that global warming is likely a hoax, along with 23 percent of those watching CNN, 13 percent of those watching *The Daily Show* and just 7 percent of those watching MSNBC. As with the autism–vaccine link, Americans who get their news primarily from cable are the most likely to buy into the conspiracy theory: 39 percent of them say that global warming is a myth, compared with 31 percent of those who mostly get news from the networks and 9 percent of those who get news from political satire programs.

Still, it's not clear what the driving force is here. The audiences for these media sources are very different, and just looking at the topline numbers doesn't tell us what effect, if any, the media source is having on that audience. Controlling for education, race, partisanship and political knowledge, people who watch CNN are 8 points less likely to believe that global warming is a hoax, people who watch MSNBC are 17 points less likely to do so, and watching *The Daily Show* reduces the likelihood by 16 points (more details can be found in methodology note 6.5). The effects of watching Fox News are a bit more complicated, as they're contingent on the viewer's level of education (see Figure 6.3). Among people who never went to college, watching Fox has no real effect on the likelihood of ignoring the scientific consensus on climate change. Among those with some college education, watching Fox increases the likelihood by 9 points; for those with a college degree, Fox viewership increases the likelihood of doubting climate change by 21 points. Of course, people with higher levels of education are more likely to accept the scientific consensus in the first place, so the net effect is that watching Fox cancels out the effect of increased education. Among Americans who don't watch Fox, going to college reduces the likelihood of doubting global warming by 13 points, and receiving a college degree reduces it by another 11 points. For those who report watching Fox, however, increased education has no effect on the likelihood of accepting the scientific consensus on climate change. Such effects are well in line with past research showing the differences in how cable news channels cover climate change (Feldman et al. 2012): Fox coverage is generally more dismissive of climate change, and guests on Fox include a much greater proportion of climate change deniers than coverage on CNN and MSNBC.

Beliefs about the link between autism and vaccines are also impacted by media consumption, though the effects aren't contingent on political views as they are with climate change. Rather, the effects of the media differ based on the individual's education level, and the part that cable news, and CNN in particular, plays in their media diet. Age matters (older Americans are less skeptical about vaccines, perhaps because they remember the era before they were available), as does political ideology (conservatives are more likely to believe that vaccines are linked with autism than liberals), but the biggest effects come from media use (more

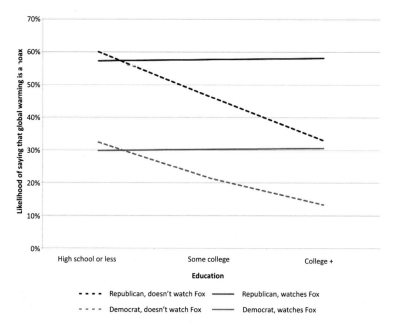

FIGURE 6.3   Likelihood of Saying That Global Warming Is a Hoax, by Party, Education and Fox Viewership

information is in methodology note 6.6). Controlling for all other factors, the fact that an individual watches CNN doesn't significantly increase the likelihood of believing in a link between vaccines and autism. However, among those who watch CNN and say that cable programming is their primary source of news, the results are rather different. In this group, and only in this group, increases in education lead to an increased likelihood of believing the vaccine–autism link. Among people who watch CNN, but don't primarily rely on cable programming for their news, those with college degrees are 10 points less likely to perceive a link than those with a high school education or less. Among those who mostly get their news from cable, but don't watch CNN, those with college degrees are 22 points less likely to perceive a link than those with a high school education or less. But for those who watch CNN and rely primarily on cable news, a college degree corresponds with an 11 point increase in the likelihood of thinking that vaccines and autism are linked compared to those who never attended college.

Certainly, much of what drives Americans to doubt the scientific consensus has nothing to do with the media. The analysis here suggests that most of what leads people to believe, or not believe, that autism is linked with childhood vaccines consists of factors that surveys just aren't measuring: social group pressure, trust in doctors, knowing someone with an autistic child, and so on. Personal experiences can be more persuasive than scientists, but that doesn't mean that the media isn't playing a role. People who rely on cable news for their information, and turn to CNN in particular, become rather more likely to believe that autism is linked with vaccinations. Similarly, much of what leads individuals to accept or reject the scientific consensus on climate change concerns their baseline political views: those who don't like the policies that are proposed to deal with climate change are likely to say that it isn't happening.

For beliefs about autism and climate change, the media has relatively modest main effects, but what's troubling here is the way in which the effects of the media interact with the education level of the viewer. In general, education tends to increase the likelihood that Americans accept the science on these issues, but these results show how certain patterns of media consumption can change that. Watching Fox News completely negates the effects of education on increasing acceptance of global warming; a media diet comprised primarily of cable news and CNN actually reverses the effects of education on rejection of the vaccine–autism link. It's generally thought that education will lead people to hold more rational views and accept scientific evidence, but this impact is contingent on the cooperation of the media. By questioning it, or seemingly even by giving airtime to skeptics, media coverage can neutralize, or even reverse, the effects of education in eliminating beliefs in scientific conspiracies.

Media, Political Knowledge and Conspiracy Theories

Belief in conspiracy theories is alive and well in America, and any account of why this is the case must incorporate media usage in general, and Fox News in particular, into the equation. Motivated reasoning – the search for beliefs to justify feelings – explains a great deal of this, but it fails to explain the seeming asymmetry in the rates at which Democrats and Republicans endorse conspiracy theories. Perhaps more importantly, it fails to explain why increases in the levels of political information, which should lead to a reduced likelihood of endorsing what are most likely false beliefs, don't always do so.

Reported Fox News viewership makes individuals more likely to say that Barack Obama is not a citizen, that global warming is a hoax and that WMD were found in Iraq. However, it doesn't make them more likely to endorse conspiracy theories or false beliefs that aren't featured on Fox, such as the discredited link between vaccines and autism. This is important because it cuts down, to some extent, the criticism that this is due to some sort of selection effect, in which Fox News viewers are simply different from everyone else in some unspecified way. Fox News viewers aren't simply more conspiracy-minded than other people – they're only more likely to endorse *some* conspiracies.

The idea that it's Fox viewership, and not some other factor, that's leading to the increased likelihood of endorsing conspiracy theories is bolstered by the fact that the major effect of Fox is through an interaction with political knowledge. It isn't just that people who watch Fox News are more likely to endorse such beliefs, but that people who report watching Fox and pay attention to the news are more likely to endorse them. Viewers who are paying attention to Fox, and are already motivated to believe these things, find their beliefs bolstered by that viewership.

When the first set of results from this chapter made the rounds in the media at the end of 2012, some took this as evidence that Republicans are just more prone to believe in conspiracy theories than Democrats. Science writer Chris Mooney, author of *The Republican Brain* (2012), contends that Republicans are more likely to believe in conspiracies because of differences in baseline personality traits, like a higher level of a characteristic called "need for closure." Need for closure is a personality trait that tends to lead people to be less accepting of ambiguity: good things have to be good, bad things have to be bad. While this might be the case, these sorts of differences aren't necessary to explain the difference: Republicans might simply be more motivated to like their side. The perceived difference between Republicans and Democrats is much greater among Republicans than it is among Democrats. Going back to the Eisenhower administration – as far back as reliable survey data goes – Republicans like Republican candidates more than Democrats like Democratic candidates. This is also visible in the rates of crossover voting: in almost every Presidential election, more Democrats vote for the Republican candidate than Democrats vote for the Republican candidate. This holds up even in lopsided elections like the one that brought Obama into power in 2008: 9 percent of Democrats voted for John McCain, while only 8 percent of Republicans voted for Obama. Of course, this difference could also be chalked up to differences in the ways in which Democrats and Republicans process information.

Another potential issue is that both of the PublicMind surveys used in this chapter were conducted during a period when the Democrats were in power. It's possible that surveys taken while the Republicans were in power would show opposite results: testing this means going back to archival data, to the extent that past surveys asked the questions that are needed. There aren't many of these – especially surveys that measured political knowledge, media use and belief in conspiracy theories – but the ones that exist tend to show the same pattern. For instance, the 2003 survey on the existence of WMD in Iraq took place while President Bush was near the peak of his popularity, and the results still show a degree of asymmetry in how partisans deal with false beliefs and conspiracy theories.

However, it seems possible to explain these partisan differences without having to find differences in the ways in which the brains of Republicans and Democrats function: this isn't to say that no such differences exist, simply that they aren't necessary to explain the asymmetry in the poll results, and in the effect of increased political knowledge. As the results here indicate, individual media sources can play an outsize role in fostering beliefs in these conspiracy theories: when CNN reports on a controversy about the link between vaccines and autism, more CNN viewers become likely to think that there is a controversy, and that, just maybe, there is a link. When Fox News hosts bring on guests that ask questions about President Obama's background, or raise doubts about the validity of scientific findings on climate change, viewers who are motivated to do so use the new information to bolster beliefs that otherwise might be discarded. Whatever their reasons for doing so, when these news sources present ambiguous or potentially misleading information, they tend to break down the connection between increased knowledge – either education or political knowledge, depending on the topic – and decreased belief in conspiracies. In extreme cases, such as with global warming, sufficient reliance on ideological media can even reverse the normal relationship between knowledge and belief in conspiracies, at least among a sufficiently motivated audience.

While differences in information processing between Republicans and Democrats provide a potential explanation for this, the differences in the media sources should first be evaluated. While MSNBC is sometimes thought of as the Fox News of the left, it differs from Fox in important ways. Most importantly, the data shows that it has a much smaller audience, and a much less diverse one. If it were the case that MSNBC viewership were as widespread as Fox viewership, and that independents and Republicans were as likely to view MSNBC as independents and Democrats were to watch Fox News, maybe a direct comparison would be appropriate. However, that's simply not the case, and until it is, there are simply too many confounding factors to allow the drawing of conclusions beyond media differences.

The conclusion here is clear: in many cases, ideological media sources are not only increasing the likelihood that their viewers will embrace conspiracy theories, but are serving to break down the expected relationship between conspiracy beliefs and information. It's tempting to treat these beliefs as a sideshow, but these conspiracy beliefs wind up having important policy implications: the belief that global warming is a hoax means that any steps taken to address it are unnecessary; the belief that vaccines cause autism or that birth control is a plot against African-Americans can literally lead to deaths. Until the media fully addresses the role it has in creating these beliefs, they're unlikely to ever go away.

7

THE MEDIA AND SOCIETY

Thus far, the focus has been on the effects of the media on politics: Presidential approval, campaign contributions, elections, belief in political conspiracies, and the like. However, the effects of media exposure and media content go well beyond politics. Just as, in the previous chapter, attitudes towards science can become politicized, beliefs and behaviors that have no obvious link to politics can be shaped by what's in the media. This chapter looks at three separate phenomena in which coverage on Fox News shapes the behaviors and attitudes of large portions of the American public. In the first, gun purchases, the analyses show that coverage of gun control on Fox News leads to more Americans attempting to buy firearms, with that coverage alone resulting in at least 2 million additional individuals seeking to buy guns. In the second, an issue that seems to have been created almost entirely by coverage on Fox, "The War on Christmas," has gained an enormous amount of acceptance in the American public, and individuals who report watching Fox News have markedly different attitudes about how Christmas should be celebrated as a result. Finally, coverage of what was a bi-partisan state-led effort to create unified education standards seems to have resulted in serious misconceptions about what is, and is not, included in the Common Core curriculum.

Firearm Background Checks

Much as with global warming, fights over policies regarding gun ownership have made it a political issue in a way that might not have been the case in the past, and this politicization means that firearm purchases are now being driven by media content in much the same way as attitudes about the President. Like partisanship, or views about important political issues, gun ownership is an important part of the social and political identities of many Americans (Dixon and Lizotte

1987, Seate et al. 2012, Littlefield 2013). As such, it makes sense for Americans to buy a firearm – or buy more firearms – when their political or social standing in some other arena is threatened. Indications of this can be found by looking at changes in gun purchases by Americans over time. While there's no central database in America listing how many firearms Americans own, or when they were bought, Americans who buy firearms from a licensed dealer are required to undergo a criminal background check to ensure that they are legally eligible to purchase a weapon. So, while there is no central record of how many firearms are being bought, there is a record of how many individuals initiated the process of buying a weapon through a licensed dealer. This measure necessarily misses a lot of gun sales – those that take place between individuals, those that take place at gun shows – and counts multiple gun purchases by one individual at one time as a single incident, thus undercounting the total number of firearms sold. There are also, of course, some individuals who are turned down after the background check and not allowed to purchase a weapon, meaning that the number of checks is also overcounted under some circumstances, but it's the best measure available.

In the 193 months the FBI has been reporting the number of background checks, there have been an average of a little more than 1 million checks per month, but that statistic hides a lot of the changes that have taken place over time. During the Clinton administration, the average was 760,000 checks per month, rising only to 800,000 during the Bush administration. However, as shown in Figure 7.1, after Obama won the 2008 Presidential election, the number of gun checks took off. In September 2012, the FBI reported 973,000 checks – a figure which increased to 1.2 million the following month, after Obama won the election, and 1.5 million for the following 2 months. Prior to Obama's election, the most background checks ever recorded in a month was a little less than 1.3 million (in December 2006); after Obama took office, the mean number of background checks per month was 1.5 million, with a peak of 2.8 million purchases in December 2012. While the mean number of purchases went up a little over time before Obama took office, the increase after he won the election is striking. Put another way, there were 86 million background checks during the 8 years of the Bush administration; under Obama, Americans surpassed that number by the end of his fifth year.

Of course, it isn't coincidence that a record number of individuals sought to purchase firearms in December 2012. As far back as the data goes, there has been a spike in attempted purchases every December, and December 2012 also saw the horrific shootings at Sandy Hook elementary school. While no federal gun control regulation ultimately passed, the shootings temporarily increased support for gun control measures, and apparently led prospective buyers to decide that if they wanted to purchase a weapon, they needed to do so immediately. In November 2012, there were just over 2 million background checks; in December, that rose to 2.8 million, and didn't go back below 2 million per month until the following April.

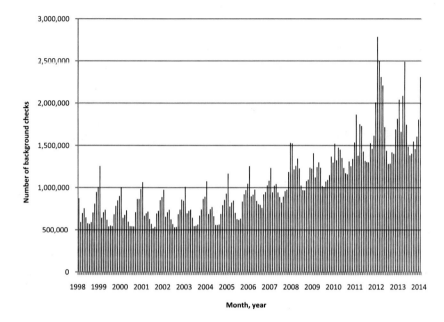

FIGURE 7.1   Background Checks by Month, 1998–2014

The spike after Obama's election makes it plausible that politics is playing some role in gun purchases, as does the spike after the Sandy Hook shootings, but it's not clear what role the media is playing here. One possibility is that some, or all, of the growth in gun sales after Obama took office is due to increases in media reporting about gun control. For example, this view would hold that the spike in gun purchases after Sandy Hook was not wholly due to an innate fear that personal security was at risk, or that gun control measures were imminent, but to increases in discussion of gun control in the media. It was these increases in media coverage that led to the increases in purchases.

Of course, there are factors aside from media coverage that lead to changes in the number of background checks. The most obvious is seasonality: on average, the number of background checks increases by 19 percent every September relative to the previous month, increases by 17 percent every December, and drops by 29 percent in January and another 14 percent in April. In addition, there are real events – like the shootings at Sandy Hook – that seem to have an impact on the number of people trying to buy a firearm. There also seems to be some pattern of year-to-year increases in the number of background checks that may have nothing to do with the media or politics, and that should be included as well. Finally, to the extent that gun purchases are being driven by a fear that President Obama will enact gun control legislation, it should be the case that Obama's approval for that month (which ranges from 41 to 53 percent over the period studied, with a mean of 45 percent) should have an impact.

Media Content and Gun Purchases

Of course, the factor of greatest interest here is the number of statements about gun control in the coded media sources. This data is limited by the fact that the Media Tenor dataset did not begin a separate coding for statements about gun control until the middle of 2011, limiting the ability to compare mentions of gun control under Obama with mentions under prior Presidents. Still, there are enough data points to allow for a meaningful analysis of the effect of statements in the media on the number of background checks in that month. In the 42-month period in question, Fox News had an average of twenty statements a month about gun control, and the networks averaged twenty-six statements per month. Of course, in many months, there were none at all, and at the peak of the debate over gun control after Sandy Hook, gun control was discussed 226 times in 1 month on Fox, and 321 times on the network evening news broadcasts. In addition to fear that Obama would restrict the ability to buy guns, individuals might also be purchasing weapons in order to protect themselves from shooters, so to isolate the effects of fears of gun control, it's also necessary to count the number of times mass shootings were mentioned. Such shootings weren't mentioned at all on coded broadcasts in half of the months being examined, but as would be expected, they were all over the news in certain months, peaking at 293 mentions in a single month, while the mean was only thirty-five mentions per month.

The results of the analysis (detailed in methodology note 7.1) again show the enormous effects media coverage can have on Americans' behavior. As would be expected, the Sandy Hook shootings led to an increase in the number of individuals seeking to buy firearms, with an estimated effect of increasing checks by 380,000 (though the size and significance of this effect depends on how the model controls for the average number of sales in a normal month, as December is normally the highest month for gun background checks). The number of times mass shootings were mentioned didn't have any effect (whether the total number of mentions was used, or the measure was simply whether or not any were mentioned that month), but statements about gun control did matter. While there is some general effect of the number of statements about gun control on the number of background checks, these effects seem to follow a threshold pattern: when there are a relatively low number of statements about gun control in a month – less than about ten – the effect is minimal. Once the number of statements exceeds that figure, though, there's an enormous impact, and one that's conditional on the media source and Obama's approval. Statements about gun control on the evening news broadcasts don't have any significant impact on the number of background checks, but statements about it on Fox News do. Controlling for the average change in the number of background checks for a given month, every 1 point increase in Obama's approval in the previous month increases the number of background checks by 31,000. When Obama's approval is at its lowest (41 percent), a large number of statements about gun control on Fox (anything more than ten) lead to a net increase of 878,000 more background checks than would occur if there was minimal coverage of gun control. That may seem like a lot, but if Obama's approval were at the high end it reached during the period studied (53 percent), the same number of statements about gun control on Fox would be expected to increase the number of background checks by 1.8 million.

These results show how much impact Fox News coverage has on the country as a whole, and how politicized the purchase of firearms has become. If it were the case that the specter of gun control was driving individuals to purchase guns now, as it might be more difficult to do so in the future, there wouldn't be any expected difference between the effects of coverage on Fox News and coverage on the networks. Significant amounts of coverage could be seen as a leading indicator of coming regulations, and purchases would increase in turn. However, coverage on the networks doesn't impact the number of background checks, indicating one of two things. First, it's possible that individuals who have a propensity to buy firearms are more disproportionately likely to get their news from Fox, or to weigh the information that they receive from Fox more heavily than they weigh information from the networks. Fox could be having a greater impact on gun purchasing behavior simply because of the differences between its audience and the wider audience viewing the network news broadcasts. Second, it's possible that the effects of coverage on Fox aren't due to the mere mention of gun control legislation, but rather to the politicization of that discussion. If – as seems likely – statements about gun control on Fox are more likely to include an appeal to political identity, they could have a disproportionate impact on the number of individuals seeking to buy weapons.

Discussions about gun control on Fox in the wake of the Sandy Hook shootings, for instance, often brought up examples of how gun control meant universal registration of firearms, or confiscation of all firearms. As Charles Krauthammer noted on *Special Report with Bret Baier* on February 4, 2013: "The only way you are going to make a difference [on gun violence] is to do what Australia did. You take away the existing guns." In the same broadcast, Tucker Carlson argued that universal background checks, which were a major part of the gun control legislation being pushed at the time, were equivalent to "universal registration" of guns, and a precursor to confiscation. Two weeks later, on *The Five* (February 15), one of the hosts likened gun control to apartheid in South Africa, stating that the problem in South Africa was that "law and order people had all of the guns, and they kept them away from everyone else who didn't like apartheid." The implication of these sorts of statements is clear: any gun control legislation is a precursor to confiscation of all firearms, and is a step towards a non-democratic government. In contrast, statements in the broadcast media focus on the polls and the politics of the issue, and there's no mention on those broadcasts of confiscation, Australia or South Africa in the context of gun control (the only mentions of Australia's gun policies on the networks during this period at all concern the lack of mass shootings in Australia).

The results indicate that discussions like these led viewers of Fox News to do more than change their attitudes about gun control legislation – it actually led them to go out and buy weapons, and not in small numbers. The combined estimated effects of Fox News coverage of gun control in the wake of Sandy Hook totaled near 2 million background checks that otherwise would not have happened. It's impossible to know how many new guns – probably more than 2 million – and how many new gun owners – probably far less than 2 million – this corresponds to, but it's a sign of how much impact the way media sources cover a story has on the lives of Americans.

"The War on Christmas"

By all indications, the idea of a "War on Christmas" has been almost entirely created by coverage on Fox News. The term first arose in writings of a British-born anti-immigration activist, Peter Brimelow, in 1999 (Altman 2008), and largely languished for several years. It wasn't mentioned on any primetime national American news broadcasts until October 2005, when Fox News host John Gibson appeared on *The O'Reilly Factor* to discuss his new book, *The War on Christmas: How the Liberal Plot to Ban the Sacred Christian Holiday Is Worse than You Thought* (Gibson did use the phrase on his own program a few hours before-hand, but only to tease his appearance on the higher-rated primetime *O'Reilly Factor*; in addition, Pat Buchanan mentioned the phrase during a morning show appearance on MSNBC a year earlier, though that didn't lead to additional coverage in the way that Gibson's appearances did). Like Brimelow, the main thrust of Gibson's (2005) argument is that state and local governments, as well as large corporations, in the United States are being overzealous in attempts to avoid offending non-Christians around the holiday season. For instance, Gibson points out that in 2004, Amazon.com wished its customers "Happy Holidays" rather than "Merry Christmas," that some schools listed a "Winter Break" rather than a "Christmas Break" on their calendars, and that the holiday stamps put out by the US Post Office that year featured a snowman rather than Santa Claus (though religious-themed stamps were also available). The net result of this, Gibson writes, is that Christians in America are prevented from openly practicing their religion, or afraid of doing so. This is, in Gibson's argument, part of a "secularist" plot that aims to, in the words of O'Reilly on November 18, 2005, "get religion out, [so] then you can pass secular progressive programs like legalization of narcotics, euthanasia, abortion at will and gay marriage." Moreover, it's not just the government that's threatening Christianity, but, potentially, your neighbors. As Gibson writes: "Every time a supermarket checker of store clerk greets you with those words ['Happy Holidays'] instead of 'Merry Christmas,' you have met another soldier in the war against Christmas." Saying "Merry Christmas," in this view, is not a personal act, but rather a political one, announcing your opposition to secular liberals in what Norton and Sommers (2011) categorize as a symbolic protest against a perceived loss of privilege.

This may seem like a contrived controversy, but it's received enormous coverage on Fox News. Between Gibson's initial appearance on *O'Reilly* to discuss his book and Christmas 2005, the phrase "War on Christmas" was uttered on ninety-nine separate programs on the channel, and twice on network broadcasts, both of which quickly dismissed it (in one, it was referred to as "a healthy fundraising mechanism" for Jerry Falwell; in the other, it was called an attempt by O'Reilly to get ratings). In the 9 years since, the term has been used a total of ten times on network news broadcasts (one of which, a CBS Sunday morning broadcast from December 3, 2006, included comedian Mo Rocca using the memorable phrase, "slogging through the nog of war"). On Fox News, "The War on Christmas" has been discussed on an average of seventeen programs each holiday season since 2005, fifteen times as much as on the networks, up to and including eleven times in the 2014 holiday season.

The fact that coverage of "The War on Christmas" is almost exclusively on Fox News, and has been ignored or dismissed by other news outlets, would seem to indicate that it isn't worthy of attention. It could be argued that the coverage on Fox began to help a Fox anchor peddle his book, and continued when it seemed to increase ratings, or received favorable comments from viewers. However, it would be wrong to dismiss "The War on Christmas" as nothing but a cynical ploy for sales or ratings, as it has quickly become accepted as fact by many Americans, well after the initial wave of coverage. In a December 2013 PublicMind poll, a national sample was asked several questions about the perceived war, and the results show how politicized and widespread these beliefs have become.

In the poll, 28 percent of Americans "agreed" or "strongly agreed" that "There has been a concerted effort by politicians to take 'Christ' out of Christmas." Forty percent of Republicans agreed with it (33 percent of Republicans agreed "strongly"), compared to only 16 percent of Democrats. While this item was designed to solicit attitudes about the perceived "War on Christmas," that specific phrase was avoided, to make sure that respondents wouldn't give unthinking responses upon hearing a phrase so closely associated with a particular media source. Frequent church goers (once a week or more) are more likely to think there's a "War on Christmas," with 35 percent agreeing, than those who seldom or never go to church, among whom only 21 percent agree. Fox News viewers are also more likely to agree that politicians are trying to secularize the holiday, but not by as much as might be imagined: 32 percent of Americans who say that they've watched Fox News agree with the statement (26 percent agree strongly), compared to 27 percent of MSNBC viewers (18 percent of whom agree strongly) and 30 percent of CNN viewers. The lack of a substantial difference between Fox News viewers and consumers of other cable news programs seems to imply that watching Fox News doesn't lead people to be more likely to believe that there's a "War on Christmas," but such a conclusion ignores the possibility that Fox News is having a disproportionate effect on some groups.

In most of the analyses presented in this book in which there have been conditional effects of media consumption, the conditionality has been on the basis of partisanship; in this case, though, it's conditional on how religious individuals are, as measured by their reported church attendance (the full analysis is in methodology note 7.2). Respondents in the survey were asked how often they attended religious services, aside from weddings and funerals: 37 percent said that they did so once a week or more, 31 percent said that they seldom or never did, and the remainder were in the middle. In general, individuals who go to church more are a bit more likely to say that politicians are trying to take Christ out of Christmas: people who report going more than once a week are about 5 points more likely to agree than those who seldom or never go to services. Watching Fox News has a significant effect in increasing the likelihood that individuals say that politicians are trying to take Christ out of Christmas – but only for people who don't actually go to church much in the first place. Among individuals who say that they seldom go to church, watching Fox News increases the likelihood of agreeing that there's a war on Christmas by 5 points; among those who say that they never go to church, the effect is 10 points.

The logic here is fairly clear: watching Fox News makes individuals more likely to say that politicians are engaging in a "War on Christmas," but only if religion isn't a particularly big part of their lives to begin with. People who go to church regularly are more likely to think that there's a "War on Christmas," indicating that religion and concerns about secularization are already part of their cultural identities. People who don't go to church very often adopt these concerns when they watch Fox News. It seems that the rhetorical strategy employed by Fox News commentators, as in the *O'Reilly Factor* quotes above, is working. By making "The War on Christmas" just one front in a more general political conflict, Fox News has made its viewers – even those who wouldn't normally be worried about religious issues – more likely to accept it.

Other items in the same survey asked respondents about agreement with specific policies criticized by proponents of "The War on Christmas." One asked respondents whether local governments should be allowed to put up manger scenes, even if doing so offended some people; the other asked whether schools should have non-religious holiday events rather than Christmas-themed pageants and displays (this last item was asked in such a way that agreement meant attitudes contrary to "The War on Christmas"). An overwhelming majority of Americans – 84 percent – agreed that "towns and cities should be able to put up manger scenes, even if it offends some people," with 68 percent of Americans agreeing strongly. A smaller group, but still a majority of 71 percent, disagreed that "schools should have non-religious holiday events."

These views were more common among respondents who said that they watch Fox News: 77 percent of Fox viewers didn't think schools should have non-religious holiday events, compared with 69 percent of MSNBC viewers and 70 percent of CNN viewers. While an overwhelming majority of Americans agreed that local governments should be allowed to put up manger scenes, that majority was even greater among Fox viewers: 91 percent agreed with the statement (75 percent of them agree strongly), compared with 82 percent of MSNBC viewers and 85 percent of CNN viewers. On both items, NPR listeners and people who reported watching *The Daily Show* were the most likely to prefer non-religious holiday events. Finally, the survey asked whether people preferred to say "Merry Christmas" or "Happy Holidays": 67 percent said that they preferred the religious-tinged "Merry Christmas," 18 percent preferred "Happy Holidays" and 15 percent said that it didn't matter to them either way. Seventy-four percent of Fox viewers said that they'd rather say "Merry Christmas," compared with 60 percent of MSNBC and CNN viewers, and 54 percent of those who watched *The Daily Show*.

Like the belief that politicians are trying to take Christ out of Christmas, belief that local governments should be allowed to put up manger scenes is driven by the interaction between church attendance and exposure to ideological media. In general, the less frequently Americans go to church, the less likely they are to think that towns and cities should be allowed to put up manger scenes, though a majority "agree strongly" in all categories. Among those Americans who go to church more than once a week, 84 percent agree strongly; this falls to 66 percent for those who go only a few times a year, and 59 percent for those who say that they never go to church.

However, the effect of going to church on support for public manger displays is conditional on exposure to Fox News (full results in methodology note 7.3). For Americans who go to church once or twice a week, exposure to Fox News has no effect on their support for manger displays. Among those who go to church a few times a year, Fox viewers are 4 points more likely to strongly support municipal manger displays. For those who seldom go to church, the effect is 11 points; for those who never do, it's 14 points. The pattern is the same: watching Fox News negates the effects of not going to church on the likelihood that someone "strongly agrees" that cities and towns should be able to put up manger displays. Among non-Fox viewers, Americans who go to church more than once a week are 23 points more likely to strongly agree with the statement than those who never go to church. Among Fox viewers, the difference is only 7 points.

Similarly, people who go to church less frequently are more likely to say that they prefer "Happy Holidays" to "Merry Christmas": 82 percent of Americans who go to church once a week or more say that they prefer "Merry Christmas," with only 10 percent saying that they prefer "Happy Holidays." At the opposite end of the spectrum, only 41 percent of Americans who never go to church say that they like the more religious greeting best, and while just 28 percent of them prefer "Happy Holidays," 31 percent say that it doesn't matter to them. As with the other questions relating to "The War on Christmas," Fox News viewership has a significant effect on the attitudes of less religious viewers that leads them to act much more like those who go to church frequently. Controlling for all other factors, individuals who never go to church are 16 points more likely to say that they prefer "Happy Holidays" than those who go to church more than once a week, but these effects are strongly mitigated by watching Fox News. For Americans who go to church once a week or more, watching Fox News has no substantial effect on the likelihood of preferring "Merry Christmas." It's not until religiosity decreases to the point of those who go to church only a few times a year that the effects of Fox News kick in, decreasing the likelihood that the individual prefers "Happy Holidays" by 6 points. For those who seldom to go to church, the effect is 10 points, and for those who say that they never go to church, watching Fox decreases the likelihood of saying that they prefer "Happy Holidays" by 16 points.

Regardless of why the notion of a "War on Christmas" became – and remains – so prevalent on Fox News, it has unquestionably made an impact on society. In a December 2005 Gallup poll, just 2 months after coverage began appearing on Fox, 41 percent of respondents said that they preferred that people say "Happy Holidays," with 56 percent saying that they'd rather hear "Merry Christmas." By a 2010 Marist poll, only 35 percent said that they preferred "Happy Holidays," while 61 percent preferred "Merry Christmas." By the time of our poll in December 2013 (the most recent available on this question), 67 percent of Americans said that they preferred "Merry Christmas," and only 18 percent would rather hear "Happy Holidays." There is certainly some variation between pollsters (a Fox News/Opinion Dynamics poll from 2005 showed a higher proportion favoring "Merry Christmas" than Gallup did), and based on the exact wording of the question, but the overall trend seems clear. Since the coverage on Fox began, up to a quarter of the American population changed their preference from "Happy Holidays" to "Merry Christmas." Based on the analyses presented here, this difference seems likely to be the result of a change in what leads Americans to prefer one holiday greeting to another, or to think that local governments should be able to put up holiday displays, or to say that politicians are conspiring to remove Christianity from the public discourse. In the absence of Fox News, it seems that these views, understandably, are closely linked to how often Americans attend church services. Among Fox News viewers, however, these views become divorced from religious beliefs, leading individuals who don't go to church often, or ever, to behave like Americans who go to church frequently (see methodology note 7.4). While the data can't tell us why this link exists, the rhetoric used by Fox News hosts in discussing why these moves towards secularization are important gives one explanation. In their discussions, Fox News hosts and guests argue that moves towards secularization are part of a larger liberal agenda. As frequent guest Sarah Palin put it during a

December 2013 broadcast of *The O'Reilly Factor.* "The War on Christmas is the tip of the spear that really translates into a war on religious freedom" – an agenda that, according to O'Reilly, also includes such non-religious issues as drug legalization and universal healthcare. The results suggest that these rhetorical links have been successful in persuading viewers that these secularization issues are universal, rather than just of concern to individuals who are already religious.

Interestingly, while the broadcast networks have not given much airtime to "The War on Christmas," the other major ideological cable channel, MSNBC, has. Since Fox News began its coverage in October 2005, MSNBC has used the phrase on 131 programs, far more than any of the networks, and second only to Fox News. Almost all of this coverage, though, is mocking in tone, making the case that the controversy is overblown – as host Keith Olbermann put it during a December 2005 broadcast: "Run for you lives! The War on Christmas is coming to Capitol Hill!" However, this counter-offensive doesn't seem to have been particularly effective: in the three analyses presented here, MSNBC viewership had a significant effect only on the question of whether or not towns and cities should be allowed to put up manger scenes despite the objections of some residents. In that case, the effect was such that it decreased the likelihood of believing that cities and towns should be able to put up manger scenes – but only among individuals who frequently attended church to begin with. Among individuals who didn't go to church often, the effect was minimal. In this case, at least, the idea that two media sources with opposed ideological viewpoints could balance each other out on an issue seems to be false.

Common Core

While the American government has been infringing on the traditional state and local roles of education since at least 1965 (Manna 2006), the role of the federal government in education has become more contested since the 2001 passage of the No Child Left Behind Act (Peterson and West 2003, Fusarelli 2004, Hess 2006, Hursh 2007), with its mandated standardized tests and consequences for schools that failed to bring students up to standards determined from the outside. This controversy simmered, and boiled over with the inter-state adoption of educational standards known as Common Core (Jacobsen and Saultz 2012). The Common Core standards were created by a consortium of states, and include detailed standards for what students should be taught at each grade level. While this was not a federal initiative, the controversy over it tapped into many of the same attitudes about local control of education that were raised earlier by No Child Left Behind. In a Gallup poll in September 2014, 35 percent of Americans said that they had "negative" or "very negative" views of Common Core; 33 percent had positive views. Some of this seems to be driven by misconceptions about what Common Core is: in an NBC/*Wall Street Journal* poll from around the same time, support for Common Core was at 59 percent. But that item, unlike most, also gave a detailed explanation of what Common Core is before asking respondents whether they supported it or not.

Between the earliest coverage of the Common Core standards in national broadcast media in 2009 and the start of 2015, it was mentioned on thirty-eight network news broadcasts, on fifty-six CNN programs, sixty-one MSNBC programs and eighty-five Fox News programs. While the difference between coverage on Fox and coverage in other broadcast media sources isn't as great as for "The War on Christmas," the difference in the volume of coverage is striking. While much of this coverage is about the politics of the issue – especially with regard to Republican governors retreating from their initial support – there is also a great deal of rhetoric about the symbolic importance of the Common Core that recalls the discussion of "The War on Christmas." As George Will put it on *Special Report with Bret Baier* on May 5, 2014: "This [Common Core] is the thin edge of an enormous wedge of federal power that will be wielded for the constant progressive purpose of concentrating power in Washington so that it can impose continental solutions to problems nationwide." As he goes on to explain, adherence to Common Core might be voluntary, but so many states have signed on that it will inevitably become a national curriculum that "disregards . . . federalism." The argument here is familiar: rhetoric on Fox News takes what is otherwise a non-political issue, and links it to existing partisan beliefs – in this case, about the importance of federalism and the expansion of centralized government. There are no signs in the transcripts of actual misinformation about what's in the standards being reported, but the strong anti-Common Core cues being given seem to have led viewers to hold both negative attitudes and misconceptions about what Common Core actually includes.

Even with the significant amounts of coverage the Common Core controversy has received, Americans generally say that they don't know much about it. In a December 2014 PublicMind poll, a national sample of Americans were asked about their views about education policy in general, and their knowledge about Common Core in particular. Forty-seven percent said that they'd heard "some" or "a lot" about them, leaving the majority to say that they'd heard "just a little" or "nothing at all." However, Fox viewers said that they were better informed on the subject: 30 percent said that they'd heard "a lot" about Common Core, compared to 21 percent of CNN viewers and 17 percent of MSNBC viewers, and far more than the 22 percent of Americans overall who said the same.

As such, it isn't surprising that opinions about Common Core are linked to media choices. Overall, 11 percent of respondents said that the federal government should take the lead in establishing education policy, with 23 percent saying that it should be the role of the states, and the largest group, 39 percent, saying that educational policy should be set by teachers and principals at individual schools. However, individuals who said that they watched Fox were 6 points less likely to say that the federal government should take the lead, and 7 points more likely to put the onus on local governments.

Specifically with regard to Common Core, Fox News viewers were more likely to disapprove of the standards: viewers were 14 points more likely to disapprove of Common Core than Americans overall. Viewers of CNN (48 percent), *The Daily Show* (49 percent) and MSNBC (62 percent) were all more likely to support the standards.

However, higher levels of self-reported knowledge and more negative opinions among Fox viewers did not translate into greater actual knowledge about the Common Core standards. Overall, 34 percent of Americans (mistakenly) said that Common Core includes teaching about sexual education, when, in reality, Common Core only includes standards for math and English. Forty-three percent said that evolution is included in the standards, the same proportion that said that global warming is part of the standards. A larger group – 48 percent – said that the American Revolution (something individuals politically opposed to standards in general might want taught) is included. On many of these items, Fox viewers were more likely to mistakenly believe that the topic in question is included in Common Core: 19 points more likely than Americans overall on sexual education, 9 points more likely on global warming, and 5 points more likely on the American Revolution. However, these beliefs also linked with ideology (conservatives were more likely to think they're included), partisanship (Republicans were more likely as well) and political knowledge, meaning that it's unclear from the direct comparisons whether the differences are being caused by the coverage on Fox or characteristics of the audience.

The regression analysis shows that the effects are complicated, but consumption of ideological media plays a huge role (the full analyses are in methodology note 7.5). Approval of Common Core is fairly straightforward: all else equal, Fox viewers are 10 points less likely to approve than non-viewers. When it comes to beliefs about what's included in Common Core, though, the results are more nuanced. For instance, conservatives are more likely than moderates or liberals to think that sexual education is included in Common Core, but the difference between conservatives and other ideological groups is heightened among those who watch Fox News. Among Americans who don't watch Fox, conservatives are about 10 points more likely to think sexual education is part of Common Core than liberals; among Fox viewers, conservatives are 30 points more likely to think so. These effects are also conditional on education, such that the effect of Fox News is greatest on those individuals who have the least amount of education themselves. The sum of these effects is that conservatives who watch Fox News and have little education are the most likely to think that Common Core includes sexual education, and less-educated liberals are the least likely to think so. Similar effects pertain for the belief that global warming is part of Common Core, with Fox News viewership having the biggest effects on individuals with higher levels of education.

In the Spring of 2014, the increasing controversy over the Common Core standards led three states – Oklahoma, Indiana and South Carolina – to withdraw from the Common Core standards project, with more Republican-governed states backing away without withdrawing (yet). The project has become controversial enough that one of the main topics of discussion in media reports about Common Core is whether a Republican who supports the curriculum standards, like Jeb Bush, could possibly win the Republican Presidential nomination. These moves – which will impact the education of millions of school children – have been fueled by the growing unpopularity of Common Core, and the results here show that the unpopularity is driven, in part, by misconceptions about what's included in the curriculum, especially the belief that it includes sexual education. While there's no evidence that these perceptions are directly the result of false statements in ideological media, exposure to Fox News among certain groups – especially conservatives – makes these beliefs much more prevalent. As with the effects of coverage on gun buying behavior, what's said on ideological media, and the effect it has, go far beyond the individuals who consume it, impacting the lives of all Americans.

Conclusions

The effects of Fox News coverage go well beyond obviously political outcomes, such as voting, contributions and the endorsement of political conspiracy theories. The evidence in this chapter indicates that the mere mention of gun control measures on Fox – though not on the networks – leads Americans to buy far more guns than they would have otherwise. In other areas, like the belief that Christianity is under attack in America as part of a "War on Christmas," Fox viewership seems to politicize a belief that's otherwise based on religion. Finally, with regard to beliefs about the Common Core curriculum, Fox viewers are less likely to approve, but conservatives who watch Fox news wind up being much more likely to hold false views about an educational initiative that they might otherwise favor.

Combined with Chapter 6, these results show that Fox News content and viewership have the general effect of politicizing issues that might otherwise be outside the realm of partisan politics, like belief in global warming, support for the Common Core curriculum, and perceived conflict between religion and politics. It seems merely the fact that the issues are discussed in a setting which presents so many subjects as issues of partisan conflict leads anything under discussion to be perceived in these terms. What's especially interesting is how viewership interacts with other attributes, such as general political ideology, in these cases. This implies that the coverage on Fox is leading individuals to link existing political views with new issue areas. This means that, in some ways, Fox News is fulfilling the role political scientists have thought that political ideology should: providing a framework that allows individuals to hold consistent attitudes across issues, and in relation to new issues. To the extent that the lack of consistent political attitudes – and, really, consistent ideology – is a concern, Fox News is therefore fulfilling a valuable function.

8

CONCLUSION

In the relatively short time it's been in existence, Fox News has made an enormous impact on American politics and society. Despite the fact that it's viewed by far fewer people than the network evening news broadcasts, Fox has been shown to have a much greater impact on American politics than the networks. President Obama's approval rating, for instance, is responsive to coverage on both the network broadcasts and Fox News – but the coverage given to him on Fox has a much greater effect. Similarly, once Fox News became widely available on American cable services, it began having a significant effect on President George W. Bush's approval ratings, indicating that the effects are not simply due to the fact that Fox has been acting as the voice of opposition during a Democratic Presidency. Rather than simply reflecting what's happening in the world, the tone of coverage of Obama has a direct impact on his approval ratings a few days down the line. These media effects are made even more important by the fact that the actual events often thought to drive Presidential approval rarely make any difference at all. Rather, it's generally the coverage of these events that drives Americans to approve or disapprove of the job the President is doing.

Of course, the effects of Fox on Presidential approval aren't spread equally across the entire electorate. Fox coverage matters more to Republicans than to Democrats, and more to wealthy Americans than to poorer ones. Some individual topics of coverage seem to help Obama's approval ratings – like discussions of his personal life – but these are rarely covered on Fox. Coverage of other topics, like healthcare and political scandals, hurts Obama's approval ratings, and these topics are mentioned on Fox rather more frequently.

While the media in general, and Fox News in particular, have significant effects on Presidential approval, they seem to have an even greater impact during Presidential elections. Most of the coverage on Fox and the networks is pure horserace, detailing who's currently winning and why, what the polls are saying and so on. There's very little in this coverage that actually gives voters any idea of why people are supporting, or not supporting, a particular candidate, but the amount of horserace coverage, at least, does seem to be related to a candidate's electoral prospects, with leading candidates receiving a greater amount of substantive coverage. Fox had particularly large effects during the volatile 2012 Republican primary election, in which candidate after candidate overtook front-runner Mitt Romney in the polls, only to quickly fade out, while Romney came back stronger from each challenge. The frequent ups and downs of the candidates in the race seems to have been driven, to some extent, by shifts in coverage on Fox. When Romney's opponents were rising in the polls, Fox coverage turned strongly positive, accelerating their rise by as much as half a point per day. Once the poll numbers for the challenger started to decrease, however, the coverage on Fox tended to make them fall even faster than they otherwise would have.

In addition, Fox coverage had a huge impact on contributions to the candidates, especially candidates in the lower tier. Jon Huntsman, one of the few candidates in the race who didn't make a run to the top of the polls at some point, can thank the small amount of coverage he received on Fox for about one-third of all of the money donated to him over the course of the campaign. Interestingly, coverage on Fox had a much greater effect on the behavior of small donors than large ones. These small donors seemed to be using positive coverage on Fox News as a signal that a candidate was ideologically acceptable, and their donations were likely meant to be a statement of solidarity with a candidate, rather than an attempt to bolster a candidate's chances of winning. The large donors, on the other hand, responded to coverage on the networks, which may be a better indication of whether a candidate has a chance of actually winning the election. They were also much more rational in how they structured their donations. For instance, small donors gave money to candidates based on their current standing in the polls, regardless of whether they were currently going up or down, meaning that small donors wound up throwing money at candidates who were already on their way down. In contrast, large donors were responsive not only to the current standing of the candidates, but also the trajectory of the poll numbers, giving more money when a candidate was on the way up. This irrationality is perhaps one of the reasons why small donors are less influential in the system than large donors, and coverage on Fox, which serves to push these small donors towards ideologically acceptable candidates who don't have much of a chance of winning, is part of the issue as well.

Most likely because of the importance of partisan cues during a general election campaign, Fox coverage doesn't have as much impact during the general election as it does during a primary. Just as with Presidential approval, events generally don't have much of an impact on the course of the election – but coverage of those events in the media does matter. The first debate between Obama and Romney, for instance, impacted Obama's poll numbers not because he did badly, but rather because coverage of Obama turned so strongly negative after the debate. The tone of media coverage of the candidates has a significant impact on their relative standing in the polls, with positive coverage tending to push their numbers up, and negative coverage pushing it down, though this is strongly contingent on the current state of the race.

Outside the electoral context, Fox News viewership has a substantial impact on the attitudes and behaviors of individual viewers. Non-conservatives who report watching Fox News – a surprisingly large group – wind up less able to answer general questions about current events and politics than otherwise similar individuals who get their news from other sources, or even no sources at all. The negative effects of Fox are likely due to a combination of reduced attention on Fox to some of these issues and the cognitive effort required for individuals when trying to process information that's at odds with their existing political views.

Fox viewers are also more likely to endorse conspiracy theories and false claims, like the belief that Obama isn't a citizen, or that global warming is a hoax per-petrated by scientists. What's especially interesting about how Fox impacts these beliefs is that it seems to negate effects that otherwise tend to reduce the likelihood of these beliefs. For instance, higher levels of education generally lead people to be less likely to say that global warming is a hoax – but among Fox News viewers, education has no effect at all. In some cases, effects are even reversed: higher levels of political knowledge generally lead people to be less likely to believe that Obama isn't really a citizen. Among Republicans watching Fox, however, higher levels of political knowledge correspond with a greater likelihood of thinking that Obama isn't legally a citizen. Such effects indicate that for some viewers, Fox News serves as a framework that can be used to understand unfamiliar issues, replacing the ways they'd normally be evaluated. For instance, more strongly religious Americans are generally more likely to think that politicians are trying to "take Christ out of Christmas," but among Fox viewers, this belief is predicted by political views.

Perhaps the most striking example of how Fox coverage politicizes behavior comes from coverage of gun control. Discussions of potential gun control meas-ures on Fox lead Americans to buy far more guns than they otherwise would, even controlling for the threat represented by coverage of mass shootings. An event like the shootings at Sandy Hook led to a large number of gun sales – but frequent discussions of gun control measures led to far more, with coverage on Fox leading to millions of firearms being sold. There's nothing necessarily politi-cal about mass shootings, but the coverage on Fox spurred viewers to action, to buy guns as a symbolic act, or even just to do so before the gun control legisla-tion that never actually came.

What's New about These Findings?

Some of the findings presented in the previous chapters are novel just because they haven't been closely examined before, such as the relationship between media coverage and campaign contributions in primary elections, or the connection between Fox News coverage of gun control proposals and actual gun sales. In other cases, the methodology of the analyses and the richness of the newly available datasets allow for the uncovering of effects that might otherwise be too subtle to find. For instance, while the effects of news coverage on Presidential approval and the standing of candidates in an election are significant, they're only visible with a very detailed content analysis of the results, as found in the Media Tenor data, and with surveys updated daily. The data to carry out these analyses simply hasn't been around long enough for scholars to be able to fully scrutinize it before now.

In a broader sense, these results upend some of what scholars have thought about the way the media impacts American politics. The scholarly consensus has been that media content works mainly through changing perceptual frames, and that the increased ability of Americans to choose their own news sources means that they aren't being confronted by information that would serve to change their minds. Much of the research cited in the previous chapters deals with how well Americans are able to dispense with information that disagrees with their existing beliefs about candidates and issues, so media coverage shouldn't really be having an effect. What makes these analyses different is the recognition that while individuals are often motivated to avoid new information, not everyone is putting in the effort to do so. Maintaining attitudes in the face of disconfirming information requires effort, and it seems that some individuals, when passively watching Fox News, just aren't putting that effort in. Even in areas in which Americans have very crystallized attitudes – evaluations of President Obama, for instance – coverage on Fox and other media sources has the potential to move the public.

The data and methodology used in these analyses are part of the reason why these findings are different, but there's also a difference in the focus. Many of the studies of media effects make use of experimental designs in order to better isolate the exact causes of observed changes – what researchers refer to as "internal validity." The studies presented here, on the other hand, are more concerned with understanding how the effects play out in the real world – or external validity. The distinction is important: people often behave differently in the lab, so things that happen in a well-controlled experiment may, or may not, happen in the real world. In addition, very subtle effects, like many of those discussed in the previous chapters, may only be significant when they're aggregated over a very large number of cases. This isn't a problem for the analyses here, but it may be impossible for many research designs to uncover.

How the Findings Fit into the Existing Literature

The findings presented here show many of the ways in which media coverage has an impact on American politics and society, but such findings have not been universal. The most careful recent studies of media effects have come to somewhat different conclusions, and it's important to try and understand why this is. Markus Prior's *Post-Broadcast Democracy* (2007) was the first major work to document how media practices changed since the widespread availability of ideological news channels: he showed that politically interested partisans are now able to consume far more news, leading them to become more informed, and more likely to participate. However, the ghettoization of political content onto a few channels in a universe of increasing choice means that people who don't care much about politics are better able to avoid it altogether, leading to less participation among moderates, and, on the whole, a more polarized electorate. Prior's work argues that media consumption tends to make viewers more active – though not more partisan – but doesn't do much to change attitudes.

Arceneaux and Johnson's (2013) series of laboratory-based studies on media effects has three main findings: the first is that exposure to incongruent information tends to strengthen, not weaken, existing attitudes. In line with the motivated reasoning effects discussed throughout the previous chapters, conservatives who see liberal messages, or liberals who see conservative messages, tend to stick more strongly to their existing attitudes afterwards. Second, ideological media sources have an enormous potential to change attitudes among people who don't pay much attention to politics. Third, in their study, this potential to change attitudes remains just that – potential – as people who aren't seeking information about politics rarely, if ever, happen to come across it. Ideological media, in their view, doesn't have much of an effect on the public, simply because the people that it could impact aren't watching it.

Finally, Matthew Levendusky's *How Partisan Media Polarize America* (2013) argues that exposure to ideological media does, in fact, change the attitudes of viewers who seek it out, making them more ideologically extreme, and more consequentially, less willing to negotiate with the opposition. More importantly, he argues, ideological media empowers certain extreme elements in the electorate, giving them much greater control over the political agenda and what the mainstream media winds up covering.

Some of the findings presented here are well in line with what Prior, Arceneaux and Johnson, and Levendusky have found. The research presented here confirms the findings that exposure to congruent media sources tends to increase political knowledge: when conservatives watch Fox News and liberals watch MSNBC, they get something out of it. Exposure to ideological media also tends to change beliefs and attitudes to be more in line with the individual's party, even when those beliefs – like the existence of WMD in Iraq or the rejection of scientific evidence on climate change – are false.

In other ways, the findings here show the conditionality of some of the arguments made by other researchers. For instance, ideological media does tend to increase participation, at least in terms of campaign contributions, but those contributions go to certain candidates, especially those who get positive coverage on ideological media.

Finally, there are some ways in which the findings here are at odds with those presented by other research. Some of these effects are due to measurement issues: while the number of Americans who say that they're regular viewers of particular ideological media programs is fairly small (Prior 2009, Dilliplane et al. 2013, Prior 2013), and Nielsen ratings seem to confirm this, in surveys such as those presented here, large portions of the American electorate say that they get news from these sources. This disconnect means one of two things. Either lots of people are lying when they say they get news from these sources, or, more likely, they're getting news from these sources in ways that aren't picked up by Nielsen. This could be in a waiting room, or a friend's house, or in clips shared via social media. These avenues for casual exposure to ideological media greatly increase the potential audience for them, and therefore their potential impact. Such avenues for casual exposure are likely the result of the agenda-setting capacity Levendusky (2013) points to: when ideological media is dictating what gets traction in the media more generally, it's going to be seen by people outside the regular audience. It is this casual audience that gives ideological media the potential to shift Presidential approval and vote choice figures among the American public as a whole to the extent shown in the results presented here.

Another potential reason why the findings of this book differ from other recent works on the effects of ideological media – Arceneaux and Johnson (2013) and Levendusky (2013) in particular – is that the biggest effects of ideological media on changing the views of voters when it comes to vote choice and Presidential approval are contextual. Analyses throughout this book have shown how the effect of media coverage on these attitude changes is mediated by the current political climate, measured here by the direction of the polls. The effects of the media, especially during the general election, are generally counter-cyclical, increasing support for candidates when that support has been falling, and decreasing it when it has been increasing. The most obvious explanation for this is that there is a "normal" level of support for a candidate in the polls (as in Converse 1966), with current events temporarily pushing support back towards the normal level. However, the endogenous factors in the analysis – especially the fractional integration – already control for the return of the series towards the natural level. This means that the counter-cyclical influence of the media on poll numbers in Presidential elections is the result of some real change in how the public is evaluating the candidates, driven by coverage in the media (and especially on Fox News). As such, the most likely explanation is one based on motivated reasoning: when a candidate is doing badly, his or her supporters seek out more good news, and attach greater weight to it. When the candidate is doing well, opponents of the candidate do the opposite. Media coverage – and especially biased media coverage – therefore tends to exacerbate shifts in support, something seen most clearly during the 2012 Republican Presidential primary campaign. The dramatic swings in support from one candidate to another were, to a great extent, based on coverage those candidates were receiving in ideological media. In the absence of such coverage, insurgent candidates would not have risen so high in the polls so rapidly, nor would they have fallen so quickly. Perhaps more importantly, in the absence of Fox News, the lower-tier candidates would not have been able to stay in the race nearly as long as they did, as coverage on Fox was responsible for much of their ability to raise money.

Framing or Direct Effects?

One of the recurring issues in these analyses has been the distinction between direct media effects and indirect effects of media coverage, most likely through framing. Fox is having an impact on the views and behaviors of Americans either way, but in many of the analyses, it isn't clear whether this effect is happening because it's actually changing viewers' minds about something, or if it's simply making some issues more relevant to the evaluation at hand. There have been, however, a few cases in which the evidence is more consistent with a direct effects model. One area in which this is clear is the effect of horserace coverage, which, despite having no real content, had significant effects on support for candidates in the 2012 primary and general elections. Horserace coverage is as close to a pure affective expression as is likely to air on the news: simply saying that a candidate is doing well or doing poorly seems to make more or fewer voters want to back that candidate, and it isn't clear what new framing could be resulting from such statements.

Further evidence for direct effects comes from the various ways in which actual behaviors have been linked to Fox coverage. Positive coverage of candidates on Fox spurs viewers to give money to candidates, and coverage of gun control proposals leads them to actually go out and purchase firearms. Now, it's unlikely that Fox coverage would lead someone who had no intention of giving to any candidate to donate, or that it would lead someone who had no interest in guns to go out and buy one. However, even pushing people with certain predispositions over the line into concrete behaviors is a much greater effect than simply changing an attitude, and if Fox coverage can lead to behavioral changes, small shifts in attitudes don't seem beyond the realm of possibility.

None of this is to say that Fox is not reframing issues as well: the evidence on how Fox viewership leads to individuals replacing one framework, like religion, or education, with a partisan framework in how they understand certain issues is almost certainly evidence of framing. For non-Fox viewers, saying "Merry Christmas" instead of "Happy Holidays" is a religious matter; for Fox viewers, it's a partisan one. For most Americans, distrust in science is reduced by education; for Fox viewers, it's not. Framing and direct effects are both happening, and there's no reason why one should preclude the other.

Media Responsibility

Fox News wields enormous power in shaping the American political environment. The biggest predictor of how the public's approval of the President changes on a day-by-day basis is the tone of the coverage, especially on Fox

News: more positive coverage of the President leads to higher approval ratings, and more negative coverage leads to lower ones. In the years since Fox's ascendance as a major source of news, a cottage industry has grown up criticizing its coverage, with websites like Media Matters dissecting every segment, and popular programs like *The Daily Show* devoting themselves almost entirely to what the host sees as failures of the media, and Fox in particular. *The Daily Show*'s longtime companion program, *The Colbert Report*, was itself a long-form parody of Bill O'Reilly. Making Fox an object of ridicule tends to miss the point: Fox is an enormously powerful force in American politics. Treating it as a joke, or an object of contempt, makes it seem like it's not worth taking seriously. Rather, as the results have shown, it has a huge impact on American politics and society in a variety of areas, and has done for some time.

While the data may not be as complete as it is for Obama, analyses indicate that Fox News had a similarly outsize effect on perceptions of George W. Bush as well. While the data doesn't allow for any conclusions about when Fox News reached its current levels of importance, it's possible to say when networks became less important – some time around 2004, a period that corresponds to a Presidential election and increasing political tensions over the invasion of Iraq.

During the Republican primary, coverage of the candidates on Fox exaggerated the swings in support that characterized the 2012 primary race, making the highs of insurgent candidates higher, and their drop-offs more severe. Perhaps more importantly, though, coverage of the Republican candidates on Fox was a major source of campaign fundraising. For all of the candidates except Romney – who had the benefit of having won the invisible primary of fundraising, and had the support of the party establishment behind him – positive coverage on Fox led to substantial increases in the amount of money they were able to raise from small donors. Candidates at the lowest levels of support – like Jon Huntsman – benefited even from negative coverage on Fox: it seems that merely being mentioned was enough to drive some small donors to open their wallets. This seems entirely rational: Fox News is a trusted information source for Republicans (Turner 2007), so positive coverage seems like it could be a cue for small donors. However, this also means that decisions about coverage made by the network can have an enormous impact on the race: if it were the case that the network wanted to support the candidacy of a particular candidate, it seems likely that it would be able to do so.

Coverage on ideological media isn't limited to political outcomes either. As shown in Chapter 7, the topics that are covered in the media, and the ways in which those topics are framed, have enormous consequences for American society as a whole. The number of Americans saying "Happy Holidays" is way down, the number of guns is up, and state-initiated attempts to standardize curricula across the country are in trouble. When politically expedient, science is questioned in ways that could have serious consequences.

There's a heated academic debate about the effects of broadcast media generally, and ideological media more specifically, on the American political system and American society, and while that debate is being carried out by professors, it's far from academic. It's easy to think of ideological media as little more than entertainment: if MSNBC makes fun of Republicans for not understanding science, or Fox News keeps bringing up scandals that don't appear to have much basis in facts, it's not high journalism, but it's not any worse than the reality shows that litter the television landscape. Ideological media, in this view, is preaching to the choir, and since it's just telling people what they already know, or reinforcing existing views, it's unpleasant, but safely ignored. However, the goal of this book has been to show the various ways in which ideological media coverage impacts the American political system and American society, and the sum of these effects is such that it can't simply be ignored: ideological media has enormous power, and with that power must come the responsibility to use it wisely.

9

METHODOLOGY NOTES

Note 1.1

The tone of coverage for individual political figures is calculated by taking the number of positive statements, minus the number of negative statements, divided by the total volume of statements about that figure over the desired period. Therefore, if all of the statements about an individual are negative, the tone would be −1; if all are positive, the tone would be +1. Importantly, this calculation takes into account neutral statements (which constitute most of the statements on news broadcasts), as they tend to push the tone towards neutral (0). However, this calculation isn't useful when there are a relatively small number of statements being aggregated, as the values can be easily pushed very high, or very low, by a small number of positive or negative statements. Since neutral statements constitute most of the statements made on news broadcasts, and push the tone scores towards zero, figures that receive a lot of coverage tend to have scores closer to zero than those that receive less coverage. For individuals like Hillary Clinton or Barack Obama, who receive a great deal of coverage, this isn't much of a problem; for others, it would be.

Note 1.2

The degree of bias for a given news source is calculated by separately measuring the bias for or against members of a given party, then summing the two. First, the coverage for members of each party is aggregated separately for each media source and each year, giving a separate score for Republicans and Democrats. The Republican score is coded such that positive values represent more positive coverage, and the Democratic score such that positive values represent more

$$Bias_{Source} = \left(\frac{Pos_{Rep} - Neg_{Rep}}{Volume_{Rep}} \right) + \left(\frac{Neg_{Dem} - Pos_{Dem}}{Volume_{Dem}} \right)$$

FIGURE 9.1 Equation for Calculating Degree of Pro-Republican Bias in Media Sources

negative coverage. These scores are then summed (possible because they're coded in the same direction – in favor of Republicans is the same as against Democrats), giving the final bias score (see Figure 9.1).

Note 2.1

The daily approval data is the 3-day rolling average released by Gallup, from January 22, 2009 through March 13, 2014. Gallup didn't release figures for some days during that period, mostly over holidays, amounting to a total of fourteen gaps (one as long as 4 days), which were filled with mean values of the existing data above and below. Perhaps because there's very little in the news about the President in the news during those periods, the artificial stability during the gaps introduced by the imputation doesn't appear to be out of line with the averages provided by Pollster or other aggregators during this time. Essentially, the gaps weren't numerous or large, and nothing was happening during the series on the days when there were gaps.

The problem with using a time series with a very high frequency – like the approval series used here – is that the measurements at one point in time aren't unrelated to the measurements at the next point in time. Indeed, the best predictor of the President's approval on any given day is probably the President's approval yesterday. This complicates the analysis, because teasing out the effects of media coverage on the President's approval means first statistically correcting for the degree to which the data points in the series are related to each other. If it were the case that the data points were related to each other, but the overall trajectory of the data points weren't (essentially, that every day the President's approval rating moves up or down relative to yesterday's approval, but that whether it moves up or down is unrelated to whether it moved up or down yesterday), it would be trivial to correct, as just taking the difference would be sufficient. Things get more complicated when there's some degree of fractional integration in the model. Fractional integration means that the series "remembers," to some extent, where it has been in the past, so the effects of exogenous shocks to the series fade after a time. Think about the successful raid on Osama bin Laden's compound in May 2011. That raid led to a significant increase in President Obama's approval ratings: but it isn't as though his approval ratings were forever after that point several points higher than they would have been otherwise. Rather, the size of the bin Laden bump began to decrease over time, eventually returning Obama's approval to where it would have been anyway.

Past research (Lebo and Cassino 2007) has shown this sort of fractional integration to be present in Presidential approval, so it makes sense to test for its presence, and to correct for it if necessary.

Statistical tests created for this purpose indicate that the Obama approval series has strong properties of fractional integration (see Table 9.1). The Portmanteau test for white noise has a Q statistic of 1931.5 (1163.1 with 10 lags), both giving chi-square probabilities of less than 0.0001, and indicating strong serial correlation. The Durbin-Watson d-statistic is 0.34, and the alternative Durbin-Watson test gives a chi-square of 386.6 (df 1), rejecting the null hypothesis of no serial correlation. Similarly, Breusch-Godfrey gives a chi-square of 115.3 (df 1), rejecting the null of no serial correlation. Robinson's estimate of fractional integration (at power = 0.9) is 0.69 (standard error of 0.05) and a t-statistic of 14.8. The Geweke-Porter-Hudak (GPH) and Lo's tests (all of the tests were carried out in *Stata* using the packages created by Christopher Baum) both confirm the existence of a fractionally integrated series (though in Lo's test, that means that the test statistic of 1.7 failed to reject the null hypothesis of no fractional integration), though the GPH estimate of the degree of fractional integration (0.95, standard error of 0.08) is slightly higher than that given by Robinson's test. Robinson's estimate of 0.79 was used to correct for the fractional integration, and tests for stationarity afterwards confirm that the corrected series is indistinguishable from a stationary series.

TABLE 9.1 Correlogram for Approval Series after Correction of Fractional Integration at d = 0.79

Lag	AC	PAC	Q	Prob.>Q	-1	0	1	-1	0	1
					(Autocorrelation)			*(Partial autocorrelation)*		
1	0.0674	0.0674	0.69958	0.4029						
2	0.2236	0.2239	8.4541	0.0146						
3	0.0600	0.0621	9.0153	0.0291						
4	0.1218	0.1004	11.346	0.0229						
5	0.0587	0.0581	11.892	0.0363						
6	−0.0716	−0.1063	12.707	0.0479						
7	0.0659	0.0518	13.404	0.0629						
8	0.0894	0.1361	14.694	0.0654						
9	0.0606	0.0632	15.291	0.0832						
10	0.0373	0.0219	15.518	0.1143						
11	−0.0447	−0. 0758	15.848	0.1469						
12	−0.0463	−0.0983	16.204	0.1821						
13	−0.0484	−0.0395	16.597	0.2184						
14	−0.0780	−0.0294	17.622	0.2245						
15	0.0206	0.0703	17.694	0.2791						

Dickey-Fuller tests, and augmented Dickey-Fuller tests for a unit root, confirm the lack of a unit root or cointegration. Note that these results are for Presidential approval as measured on a daily level; when it's measured on a weekly or higher level, the results are rather different.

Note 2.2

There are several ways in which it's possible to operationalize the tone of the coverage. Past researchers have often looked at the percentage of the coverage which is positive (or negative), but this can lead to the problem of having very large figures on days when there's very little coverage. For instance, a single day on which there's one negative item about the President, and no positive items, would be coded as the same as a day on which there are ten negative items about the President, and no positive ones, when it makes more sense to suppose that the latter day would have a greater impact on approval. Other analyses in this book separate out the number of positive and negative statements about Obama as separate predictors, but doing so is only really appropriate when there's a hypothesis of strongly asymmetrical effects of positive and negative news coverage, and enough data that the increased number of predictors (which also interact with other factors) isn't a problem. The compromise measure used in this analysis is a net positivity measure, which simply subtracts the number of negative statements from the number of positive statements, resulting in a figure which is theoretically unbounded. This figure also has the desirable characteristic of encapsulating both the volume of statements about the President made on a given day and their positivity or negativity in a single measure. The only information lost in doing so is the difference between days when there are a small, but approximately equal, number of positive and negative statements and days when there's a large, but approximately equal, number of positive and negative statements: both days would give about the same values.

Note 2.3

In the daily approval model, the approval series (once corrected for fractional integration, as described in Note 2.1), was used in Granger causality Wald tests, testing for prediction against positive and negative statements made on Fox and the network broadcasts over the previous 5 days. The results indicate that positive statements on Fox (chi-square of 24.3, 10 df), and negative stories on Fox (chi-square of 19.3, 10 df), Granger-cause the corrected approval series. The network broadcasts (chi-square of 13.0 and 10.2, both with 10 df), in this analysis, appear to be unrelated to the corrected approval series (as will be seen in the regression analysis). Interestingly, there is some indication of reciprocal causation: positive statements on Fox Granger-cause changes in approval, and changes in approval seem to have some effect on the number of positive statements on Fox about the President. Most likely, this indicates reporting on Fox about changes in the approval rating: when it goes up or down, it gets mentioned on Fox (and is rarely mentioned on the less politically focused network broadcasts), slightly increasing the amount of positive or negative coverage of Obama on Fox in the following days. If the media coverage on just the previous day is used as a predictor, the results vary only slightly: positive statements on Fox are still a significant predictor of changes in approval (chi-square of 16.5, 10 df), though negative statements on Fox drop out of significance (chi-square of 14.0, 10 df), and the reciprocal causation is still significant (chi-square of 23.2, 10 df).

Note 2.4

The regression uses the corrected approval rating as the dependent variable (mean of 0.06, standard deviation of 1.3; range from −4.0 to 5.2). The predictors are the number of positive items on Fox in the 5 days prior to the approval day, and the same for negative items on Fox, as well as positive and negative items on the networks. In addition, the predictors include the 1-week trend (the difference in approval from 8 days to 1 day prior to the approval date), and the four significant events (other events that proved to have no significant effect on the approval rating were excluded from the analysis). OLS regression was used (as the dependent variable is both continuous and theoretically unbounded), with a sample size of 1,764 and an r^2 of 0.03 (adjusted to 0.03) (see Table 9.2).

The low r^2 of the analysis is likely due to two factors: the number of media sources that aren't included and are likely having an impact as well, and the sampling error in the daily approval estimates. Much of the fluctuation in approval ratings is almost certainly random error, and this will necessarily drive down to r^2, though it's not expected to bias the results.

TABLE 9.2 OLS Regression Model for Daily Changes in Presidential Approval

Predictor	B	Std. error	t
Positive statements on Fox	0.011	0.005	1.97
Positive statements on networks	0.007	0.005	1.34
Negative statements on Fox	−0.002	0.002	−0.91
Negative statements on networks	0.002	0.003	0.48
1-week trend	−0.072	0.014	−5.3
Nobel Prize	2.481	1.290	1.92
Fiscal deal	3.049	1.291	2.36
bin Laden	3.656	1.292	2.83
Boston Marathon bombing	2.073	1.291	1.61
Constant	−0.039	0.052	−0.75

TABLE 9.3 OLS Regression Model for Daily Changes in Obama Approval

	Main effects			Interacted with neutral trend in approval			Interacted with positive trend in approval		
	B	Std. error	t	B	Std. error	t	B	Std. error	t
Fox: positive statements in past 5 days	0.019	0.008	2.32	−0.032	0.017	−1.91	−0.012	0.012	−1.06
Fox: negative statements in past 5 days	−0.007	0.003	−2.45	0.017	0.006	2.7	0.009	0.004	2.07
Network: positive statements in past 5 days	0.013	0.009	1.5	−0.006	0.014	−0.39	−0.009	0.012	−0.74
Network: negative statements in past 5 days	0.005	0.005	0.99	−0.008	0.010	−0.77	−0.008	0.008	−1.09
Neutral trend in approval over past week	−0.487	0.148	−3.28						
Positive trend in approval over past week	−0.423	0.114	−3.71						
Constant	0.209	0.078	2.67						
Events									
Nobel prize	2.556	1.287	1.99						
Extends Bush tax cuts	3.077	1.288	2.39						
Raid on bin Laden	3.564	1.287	2.77						
Boston Marathon bombing	2.313	1.291	1.79						

Note 2.5

The main predictor variables in the model predicting daily changes in Presidential approval are the numbers of positive and negative stories about the President on Fox News and on the networks for 1,764 days of Obama's presidency. The media coverage is used as a lagged indicator, from 1 to 5 days behind the Presidential approval day being predicted. Also included is the trend (positive, negative or neutral: the direction, rather than the degree, of the trend was used, as these effects are expected to be the result of media avoidance or engagement, depending on the direction of approval) of the President's approval numbers as separate indicators (negative trend was used as the baseline category). To determine the trend, the President's approval 8 days before the day being predicted was subtracted from the President's approval 1 day prior to the day being predicted, resulting in a positive figure if the President's approval had increased in the week prior to the day being measured, and a negative figure if it had decreased. The trend was negative in 44 percent of the cases, neutral in 17 percent of the cases, and positive in 40 percent of the cases (see Table 9.3).

The regression model also included the events that had been found to have a significant effect on approval. The overall r^2 of the model was 0.04 (adjusted to 0.03).

Note 2.6

Unlike the series of overall approval, the disaggregated series (by party and ideology, race, and income group) don't show characteristics of fractional integration. This is most likely because fractional integration in the aggregate series is thought to be the result of differential behavioral patterns being aggregated into a single series (Granger 1980, Box-Steffensmeier and Smith 1996, 1998). As such, to the extent that these series disaggregate the combined series into meaningful groups, there should be less fractional integration. Tests for fractional integration in these series come up negative, though the correlograms do reveal that, in their base forms, endogenous factors are still present. Using the correlograms as a guide, the best specified ARIMA models for these variables appear to be (0,1,1): differenced, with a single moving average component. In all of the models described, the moving average component is significant.

For conservative Republicans, approval has a mean value of 6.8 (1.6). For moderate Republicans (a series which includes the small number of liberal Republicans), it's 21.8 (3.7), and for moderate Democrats, it's 78.2 (5.5). Mean approval is highest among liberal Democrats, at 86.1 (standard deviation of 4.3) (see Table 9.4).

The weekly positivity measure has a mean value of −13.4 (standard deviation 9.3, ranging between −34 and 12) on Fox, and −3.9 (standard deviation of 6.0, ranging between −22 and 33) for the networks. Volume has a mean value of 59.5 (standard deviation 28.8, ranging between 2 and 167).

TABLE 9.4 ARIMA Analysis of Changes in Approval Series, by Ideological and Partisan Group

Predictor	B	Std. error	Z
Conservative Republicans			
Network positivity	0.014	0.009	1.51
Fox positivity	**0.010**	**0.006**	**1.73**
Volume of coverage	0.004	0.002	1.87
Constant	−0.046	0.085	−0.54
Moving average	−0.869	0.052	−16.76
Moderate Republicans			
Network positivity	0.030	0.023	1.3
Fox positivity	**0.042**	**0.017**	**2.51**
Volume of coverage	0.013	0.005	2.69
Constant	−0.118	0.242	−0.49
Moving average	−0.769	0.062	−12.37
Moderate Democrats			
Network positivity	0.034	0.025	1.36
Fox positivity	−0.026	0.016	−1.61
Volume of coverage	−0.001	0.005	−0.16
Constant	−0.179	0.259	−0.69
Moving average	−0.668	0.079	−8.48
Liberal Democrats			
Network positivity	0.035	0.023	1.47
Fox positivity	−0.024	0.017	−1.41
Volume of coverage	−0.002	0.005	−0.33
Constant	−0.089	0.219	−0.41
Moving average	−0.694	0.069	−10.06

Note 2.7

The approval series by income and racial group are from Gallup's weekly detailed Presidential approval series. In each of the disaggregated models, the predictors are the same: the positivity (see Note 2.2) of coverage on Fox and the networks in the previous week, and the total volume of coverage on all of them in the previous week (as well as the moving average component). The inclusion of volume is meant to control for the total number of statements made about Obama during the week, compensating, in part, for the inability of the positivity measures to distinguish between fairly balanced coverage when there's a large number of statements, and fairly balanced coverage when there's a low number of statements. The simpler models, with positivity rather than separate indicators for positive and negative coverage, are necessitated by the smaller number of data points present in the weekly series compared to the daily series.

TABLE 9.5 ARIMA Analysis of Changes in Approval Series, by Racial Group

Predictor	B	Std. error	Z
Whites			
Network positivity	0.043	0.019	2.29
Fox positivity	−0.006	0.012	−0.5
Volume of coverage	0.002	0.003	0.48
Constant	−0.045	0.177	−0.25
Moving average	−0.569	0.083	−6.83
Non-whites			
Network positivity	0.023	0.025	0.93
Fox positivity	0.006	0.017	0.36
Volume of coverage	0.010	0.005	1.92
Constant	−0.452	0.251	−1.8
Moving average	−0.673	0.068	−9.97

The racial disaggregations compare white and all non-white Americans, though the results are substantially the same if African-Americans are used instead of non-whites. Mean approval among whites is 35.8 (3.3), among non-whites it's 70.3 (5.7), and among African-Americans it's 86.4 (3.5) (see Table 9.5).

The analysis of the income groups (see Table 9.6) is carried out with the same predictors. In the lowest income group, Group I, mean approval is 51.9 (5.9); in Group II, mean approval is 45.3 (3.9), dropping to 43.6 (3.9) in Group III, and rebounding to 44.2 (3.7) in the wealthiest income group, Group IV. While the overall approval ratings for these groups are correlated at a reasonably high level (rs range between 0.57 and 0.75), changes in the series are not, with rs ranging between 0.18 (between Groups II and IV), and −0.18 (between Groups II and III).

Note 2.8

The initial coding done by Media Tenor contains more than 3,000 topics, and tens of thousands of protagonists (the individuals, groups, governments or companies that are making the news: everything from the National Football League to individual members of Congress to swimmer Diana Nyad). These categories are extremely specific, distinguishing between things like "Price of Gas/Diesel," and "Fossil Energy/Crude Oil." To create a more manageable set of topics, these were grouped into eighty-seven larger topics (such as "Performance/Fine Art" and "Financial Regulation"), based on the extent to which the low-level topics appeared together. Topics that appeared in reference to the same protagonist on the same day more than 80 percent of the time were considered to be in reference to the same general area. The resulting set of eighty-seven categories

TABLE 9.6 ARIMA Analysis of Changes in Approval Series, by Income Group

Predictor	B	Std. error	Z
Income Group I			
Network positivity	0.155	0.072	2.17
Fox positivity	0.140	0.055	2.54
Volume of coverage	0.081	0.021	3.77
Constant	49.662	1.106	44.9
Moving average	0.435	0.093	4.67
Income Group II			
Network positivity	0.081	0.044	1.82
Fox positivity	0.033	0.033	0.98
Volume of coverage	0.058	0.011	5.08
Constant	42.598	0.724	58.86
Moving average	0.320	0.079	4.05
Income Group III			
Network positivity	0.064	0.059	1.09
Fox positivity	0.097	0.043	2.29
Volume of coverage	0.054	0.016	3.46
Constant	41.973	0.785	53.49
Moving average	0.294	0.091	3.23
Income Group IV			
Network positivity	0.070	0.049	1.44
Fox positivity	0.100	0.042	2.37
Volume of coverage	0.049	0.016	3.04
Constant	42.970	0.901	47.67
Moving average	0.312	0.087	3.6

was still unwieldy, and iterating the process, again with an 80 percent threshold, resulted in the smaller set of topics presented here.

Positivity and negativity of the statement in the Media Tenor data is based on two dimensions of analysis: explicit and implicit positivity and negativity. Explicitly positive statements praise a protagonist, or point to a success of that protagonist, in terms that are unambiguously positive: "President Obama won re-election," for instance. Implicitly positive or negative statements are textually neutral, but carry positive or negative implications – as in the Benghazi example cited in Chapter 1 (the full criteria for coding are dozens of pages long, but this hopefully gives the basic idea). In analyses throughout this book, statements are considered positive or negative if they have either implicit or explicit positive or negative coding; still, most of the statements are considered to be neutral.

Note 2.9

While most of the coverage is coded as being neutral, there's still enough affectively loaded content in the coverage to require that analyses of the effects of individual issues include the positivity of coverage (on Fox and the networks) as a control (however, it should be noted that they're generally not significant predictors in the weekly data). All of the regressions were (0,1,1) ARIMA models, with significant moving average components, and no additional significant endogenous effects. For both the overall approval model (Table 9.7) and the approval by ideological-partisan group (Table 9.8), the sample size was 144.

Gallup divided its sample into six ideological-partisan groups, and the results here were carried out for four of them (their categories of "pure independent" and "conservative Democrats" show much greater volatility than the other categories, most likely because they're rather smaller than the other categories). There were few enough liberal Republicans that Gallup folded them into the "moderate Republican" category.

Note 2.10

The ARIMA regression analyses for the effect of horserace/election coverage on Obama approval (see Table 9.9) used the same (0,1,1) endogenous model as the previously discussed models, and all included significant moving average components. They didn't include other controls, such as network and Fox positivity, as they weren't intended to provide comprehensive models of what caused approval to change in these groups: rather, they were simply intended to

TABLE 9.7 ARIMA Regression for Change in Overall Approval, Based on News Coverage in Previous Week

	B	Std. error	Z
Positivity on Fox	0.00	0.01	−0.32
Positivity on networks	0.01	0.02	0.72
Constant	−0.09	0.14	−0.66
Topics			
Education	−0.11	0.10	−1.08
Crime	0.16	0.05	2.84
Guns	−0.02	0.03	−0.81
Women's/LGBTQ issues	−0.05	0.05	−0.99
Terrorism	0.01	0.02	0.32
Scandals	−0.01	0.03	−0.35
Personal matters	0.10	0.04	2.64
Healthcare	−0.01	0.02	−0.77
Budget and taxes	−0.02	0.01	−1.72

TABLE 9.8 ARIMA Regression for Change in Approval by Political Group, Based on News Coverage in Previous Week

	Conservative Republicans			Moderate Republicans		
	B	Std. error	Z	B	Std. error	Z
Positivity on Fox	0.01	0.01	1.03	0.04	0.02	1.9
Positivity on networks	0.00	0.01	0.25	0.04	0.04	1.09
Constant	0.06	0.07	0.8	−0.05	0.26	−0.18
Topics						
Education	−0.01	0.09	−0.15	−0.08	0.21	−0.38
Crime	0.05	0.05	1.06	0.06	0.13	0.48
Guns	−0.01	0.01	−0.8	−0.03	0.03	−1.14
Women's/LGBTQ issues	−0.04	0.02	−1.8	0.05	0.08	0.71
Terrorism	0.02	0.01	1.29	0.03	0.04	0.71
Scandals	**−0.02**	**0.01**	**−1.79**	0.03	0.03	0.95
Personal matters	**0.04**	**0.02**	**1.92**	**0.15**	**0.07**	**2.12**
Healthcare	**−0.02**	**0.01**	**−2.23**	0.02	0.03	0.68
Budget and taxes	0.00	0.01	0.43	0.01	0.02	0.39

	Liberal Democrats			Moderate Democrats		
	B	Std. error	Z	B	Std. error	Z
Positivity on Fox	−0.02	0.02	−1.11	0.02	0.01	1.16
Positivity on networks	0.01	0.02	0.32	−0.03	0.03	−1.34
Constant	−0.01	0.16	−0.05	−0.03	0.12	−0.25
Topics						
Education	0.09	0.21	0.45	−0.25	0.19	−1.31
Crime	0.10	0.12	0.86	0.04	0.11	0.32
Guns	−0.02	0.03	−0.61	**−0.05**	**0.02**	**−2.55**
Women's/LGBTQ issues	**−0.11**	**0.04**	**−2.48**	−0.06	0.05	−1.36
Terrorism	0.00	0.05	−0.1	−0.03	0.03	−0.82
Scandals	**−0.06**	**0.03**	**−2.48**	−0.01	0.03	−0.34
Personal matters	0.08	0.05	1.5	**0.22**	**0.05**	**4.2**
Healthcare	−0.02	0.02	−1.21	**−0.05**	**0.02**	**−2.96**
Budget and taxes	−0.01	0.01	−1.01	−0.01	0.01	−0.71

TABLE 9.9 Effect of Previous Week's Horserace Coverage on Obama Approval, Overall and by Ideological-Partisan Group

	Overall	Conservative Republicans	Moderate Republicans	Moderate Democrats	Liberal Democrats
B	0.016	0.003	0.009	0.023	0.017
Std. error	0.008	0.004	0.011	0.008	0.009
Z	2.03	0.74	0.84	2.87	1.93

demonstrate that content which fails to activate any relevant concerns can still have an impact on changes in approval during the following week.

Note 2.11

The series of Bush's approval rating was created by combining approval items taken during his Presidency from Gallup (288 polls), Pew (102), CNN/NORC (47), Fox/Opinion Dynamics (143), ABC/*Washington Post* (108) and NBC/*Wall Street Journal* (53), amounting to a total of 741 polls, excluding those which used a registered voter or a likely voter sample (almost all of which were taken around the time of the 2004 Presidential election). Only one of these, Gallup, always reported partisan breakdowns, so partisan data is available only for the Gallup polls. In weeks (Sunday–Saturday) in which more than one poll was reported, the mean of all of the reported polls was used (there was just one survey in 37 percent of the weeks, two in 34 percent, three in 19 percent, and four or more in 10 percent, including one week, during the invasion of Iraq, in which eight surveys were taken: NBC was in the field twice). Even so, there was still no survey data available for 61 weeks (15 percent) of Bush's term in office, with no gaps of more than 2 weeks. These weeks were filled in with the mean of the prior and next values. Whether the analysis is carried out with these imputed values included or not doesn't change the reported coefficients for the variables.

Note 2.12

Interestingly, unlike the weekly series of Obama's approval, the weekly series of Bush's approval does appear to be fractionally integrated. The Geweke-Porter-Hudak test (carried out on the differenced version of the approval) gives an estimated d value of 0.2 (indicating a value in the non-differenced series of 0.8); Robinson's test estimates a d value of 0.79. Lo's test gives a test statistic of 1.32 against a critical value range of 0.8 to 1.9 (in Lo's test, the null hypothesis is a lack of fractional integration). Based on these results, the overall series of approval was corrected for a fractional integration level of 0.79 (though the results aren't much different if the ARIMA (0,1,1) model used for the weekly Obama series

TABLE 9.10 OLS Regression Results for Fractionally Integrated Bush Approval Series

Predictor	B	Std. error	t
Positive statements	0.014	0.005	3.0
Negative statements	-0.011	0.004	-3.0
9/11 attacks	31.168	2.377	13.1
Iraq invasion	9.106	2.378	3.8
Constant	0.092	0.155	0.6

is used here as well). Tests carried out after the fractional integration correction indicate that the fractionally integrated version of the series is stationary.

The fractionally corrected series is used as the dependent variable in an OLS regression model (see Table 9.10) which includes as predictors the number of positive and negative statements in the media about Bush during the previous week, along with event indicators (dummy variables, coded as 0 in all weeks except the week in which the event happened) for the 9/11 attacks and the invasion of Iraq in 2003 (other events were tested, but didn't prove to be significant predictors of the corrected Bush approval series). The model had a total sample size of 411 weeks, with an r^2 of 0.33 (corrected to 0.32).

A second model (see Table 9.11), differentiating between Fox News and network coverage, was also specified, though it had the disadvantage of a more limited dependent variable, as there is no extant coding for Fox News programming prior to 2004 (a total of 206 weeks in the analysis). The r^2 for this analysis is 0.02, corrected to 0.01.

The large difference in the r^2 between the two models is likely due to the inclusion of the event dummy variables, which, because of the time frame covered, simply aren't applicable in the second analysis. As noted in the text, an analysis was also carried out on just the effect of network coverage, before and after 2004, in order to establish the cause of the decline in the effect of network coverage (see Table 9.12). This analysis comprised two separate OLS regressions (with sample sizes of 197 and 214, respectively), for the 2001–2004 period, and the 2005–2009 period. The first had an r^2 of 0.45, the second 0.00.

TABLE 9.11 OLS Regression Results for Fractionally Integrated Bush Approval Series, 2004–9

Predictor	B	Std. error	t
Network positivity	-0.004	0.008	-0.5
Fox positivity	0.014	0.008	1.7
Constant	-0.020	0.178	-0.1

TABLE 9.12 OLS Regression Results for Fractionally Integrated Bush Approval Series, 2004–9

Predictor	2001–4			2005–9		
	B	Std. error	t	B	Std. error	t
Network positivity	0.028147	0.007697	3.66	−0.00217	0.007854	−0.28
9/11 attacks	31.19661	2.655778	11.75			
Iraq invasion	8.878015	2.653663	3.35			
Constant	0.479525	0.199805	2.4	−0.25013	0.158135	−1.58

Note 3.1

Statements were counted as being about the Republican primary if they referenced one of the candidates by name, electoral results for a nominating contest, or were coded as concerning the Republican Party in general during the primary election (which might include statements that didn't directly reference election results, but certainly bore on the primary). Statements were coded as being about the Obama administration or the White House if the statement was coded as having President Obama, a cabinet-level secretary, "The White House" or a cabinet-level agency as the main protagonist of the statement.

Note 3.2

Statements were counted as being about the horserace if the topic of the statement was an electoral result for one of the named candidates or the Republican Party in general, predictions of the likely results of an election, coverage of advertising from one of the candidates, candidate strategy, or polls regarding the candidates or the Republican Party in general. "Personal Qualities" of the candidates included discussion of the candidate's personal history, spouse, leadership capacity or style (the most common of these), awards or honors given to the candidate, or non-political activities pursued by a candidate (attending a funeral, going on vacation and so on). Domestic policy includes all statements about cultural and political issues within the US, including tax policy, policies towards women, LGBTQ issues, general references to culture, and a myriad of other issues (but not including statements about healthcare and healthcare reform, which were so numerous as to be broken out into a separate category). A statement was coded as being about foreign policy if it touched on any country other than the US, terrorism or terrorist activities, or military and defense policies. Statements were only counted as being about healthcare if they specifically touched on healthcare reform in the US, healthcare systems in the US or abroad, or the Affordable Care Act.

Note 3.3

To determine the effects of news coverage on candidates in the 2012 Republican primary, the numbers of positive and negative stories for both Fox and non-Fox sources (ABC, NBC and CBS evening news broadcasts) were aggregated over the 3 days prior. These four variables (number of Fox positive stories over the previous 3 days, number of non-Fox positive stories over the previous 3 days, and so on) were used as predictors in a regression analysis where the dependent variable was the change in the aggregate poll result for that day. It should be noted that on most days, there was no change in the polling for most of the candidates: while the polling, taken in the aggregate, updated frequently, wasn't on the level of the daily updates seen in the Obama approval and Obama/Romney general election series.

The number of statements for each candidate (see Table 9.13) includes an overabundance of zeroes: days on which there were no statements about the candidate from a particular source. Aggregating the non-Fox sources into one indicator helps with that (as each of them has less coverage than Fox, the scale of the Fox and non-Fox indicators is approximately the same: 1.2 statements per candidate per day on Fox, and 1.4 statements per candidate per day on the rest combined), but doesn't solve it entirely. Even with the aggregation, there's no statement about a particular candidate on Fox on a particular day in 60 percent of cases, and in 64 percent of cases for the aggregated non-Fox broadcasts.

In addition, because of the pooling of several candidates (Santorum, Paul, Gingrich, Cain, Perry and Huntsman; Bachmann was excluded because her poll numbers were near or at zero for the entire run of the series), the analysis was carried out in a slightly different way than most of the other analyses here. Most

TABLE 9.13 Number of Coded Statements by Day, across All Candidates, July 2011– April 2012

No. of statements	Fox frequency	% Fox	Non-Fox frequency	% Non-Fox
0	1,122	60.23	1,187	63.68
1	215	11.54	179	9.6
2	160	8.59	108	5.79
3	128	6.87	130	6.97
4	92	4.94	53	2.84
5	58	3.11	42	2.25
6	33	1.77	48	2.58
7	26	1.4	29	1.56
8	11	0.59	16	0.86
9	9	0.48	26	1.39
10 or more	9	0.49	46	2.46

importantly, the data was structured to treat all of the candidates (except for Romney, who was treated differently, as described in the text) as fungible for the purposes of the analysis, meaning that there were six (seven, if Romney is counted) observations for each date in the data series. Clustering techniques were used to correct for the artificially high number of observations created by this data structure. For example, there were a total of 1,581 cases used in the calculation of beta values estimating the effect of news coverage on the non-Romney candidates, but the standard errors were calculated for a sample size of just 271.

Because this was essentially a time-series analysis (though ARIMA modeling wasn't used), it's important to note that differencing the series used here was found to be sufficient to provide stationarity. Tests for fractional integration were negative, and no significant auto-regressive or moving average components were found in the series once the differencing was carried out. This puts these series at odds with the general approval series, but means that they seem to be similar to the general election electoral support series, which makes sense. As will come up again, this could be driven by the fact that these series don't update on a daily basis: so, when differenced, the days of no new polls show as zero, making them appear to be more of a unit root series than they might appear if daily-level data was available.

The dependent variable in these analyses was the change in the aggregated poll numbers between the previous day and the current day, first for all of the non-Romney candidates, then, separately, for Romney.

For the candidates other than Romney (see Table 9.14), only statements on Fox had a significant impact on the change in the poll numbers, with p values of less than 0.05 (one-tailed; positive for positive statements, negative for negative statements). Coefficients for the non-Fox statements are in the expected direction, and have smaller standard errors than those for the Fox statements, but are much smaller in magnitude, putting them outside traditional bounds of statistical significance. Overall r^2 is 0.04, though this is surely magnified by the overabundance of no change in the dependent variable dataset, as polls weren't carried out every day.

TABLE 9.14 Effect of Media Statements over Past 3 Days on Change in the Aggregated Poll Numbers for Non-Romney Candidates

Predictor	B	Std. error	t	P
Non-Fox positive statements	0.0138	0.0235	0.58	0.280
Non-Fox negative statements	−0.0418	0.0274	−1.53	0.064
Fox positive statements	0.0675	0.0375	1.8	0.037
Fox negative statements	−0.0524	0.0309	−1.7	0.046
Constant	0.0250	0.0198	1.26	0.104

TABLE 9.15 Effect of Media Statements over Past 3 Days on Change in the Aggregated Poll Numbers for Romney

Predictor	B	Std. error	t	P
Non-Fox positive statements	0.0146	0.0190	0.77	0.222
Non-Fox negative statements	−0.0408	0.0251	−1.63	0.052
Fox positive statements	0.0133	0.0262	0.51	0.307
Fox negative statements	0.0949	0.0507	1.87	0.031
Constant	−0.0478	0.1408	−0.34	0.367

For Romney (see Table 9.15), the coefficients on the non-Fox sources were of about the same magnitude as for the other candidates, and with slightly smaller standard errors, but this wasn't enough to make them significant. The only significant predictor was negative statements on Fox, which had a fairly strong positive effect. Overall r^2 for Romney was 0.03.

As with all time-series analyses, it's important to look at causation. In this case, we're positing that media coverage on days 1, 2 and 3 resulted in a change in the polls on day 4. It would be difficult to make a convincing case that a change in the polls led to better coverage in the prior days (as opposed to absolute performance in the polls: a candidate doing well in the polls could easily lead to that candidate getting more favorable coverage in previous days), and Granger causality tests bear this out: the number of positive and negative statements on Fox for both Romney and non-Romney candidates did significantly impact changes in poll numbers, but the opposite isn't the case ($p<0.05$, 15 lags).

Note 3.4

"Horserace" coverage was calculated in the same way as in note 3.2. "Non-horserace" coverage includes all statements in which Romney was the main protagonist that didn't meet the definition of "horserace" coverage.

Note 3.5

It's theoretically possible to link bundled contributions by noting contributions given at the same time by donors who share certain characteristics, such as occupation and geographical area. However, this isn't necessary for our analysis, as we're using the total amount of money given in donations of a certain size per day. As such, if a number of large donations were bundled together, they would all enter the dataset together anyway, as long as they were all reported by the campaign on the same day. Bundling, in effect, may make the data a bit "lumpier," especially with regard to candidates who don't get these sorts of contributions often, but doesn't pose a serious threat to the data validity.

Note 3.6

Because the movement in the polls for a certain candidate on a certain day is theoretically unbounded, and can be either negative or positive (even though there are some constraints on the observed changes in the data), we were able to use simple OLS regression. Contributions, however, don't play by the same rules: the number of contributions, and their amount, can't go below zero for a given candidate on a given day (there are some refunds and givebacks recorded in the data, but they were removed prior to the analysis). As such, OLS regression results would be biased, with the extent of the bias dependent on the number of days on which the contributions for a candidate were at zero, which is fairly large in this case, since we're dividing contributions up into several categories based on the size of the individual donations (there were no contributions of $250 or less on 23 percent of candidate days, no contributions of $251–1,750 in 23 percent, no contributions of $1,751–2499 in 67 percent, and no contributions of $2,500 or more on 43 percent of candidate days). To correct for this bias, we used Tobit regression, a technique which assumes that some values of the dependent variable are actually below the observation threshold. Essentially, it's assuming that some candidates would have received negative contributions on some days, but we can only see days on which contributions are zero or greater. While necessary, the use of Tobit regression does tend to complicate the interpretation of expected values. In OLS regression, we could calculate the total amount of expected contributions for a candidate on a given day, given a certain level in the polls and a degree of media coverage. When we use Tobit regression, however, many of these expected values will be negative. While this isn't a statistical problem, it does lead to some odd interpretations. As such, in the text, we talk only about the marginal effects of changes in poll standing and media statements, not about the total expected values resulting from them.

In addition to removing returned funds from the data, we also eliminated from the data all donations candidates made to themselves (including Huntsman's $5 million to himself, and Santorum's small, frequent contributions of $300–700 to himself), as well as all listed contributions of $0. There are sixty-six of them in the data: why they're there is anyone's guess – credit card charges that didn't go through, or contributions that were returned to the contributor before being processed in the first place? Who knows?

The four categories of contributions are a little uneven, but are that way for a reason. Contributions of $250 or less (referred to as "small contributions" in the text) constitute 51 percent of all donations, and have the additional distinguishing feature that not all of them may be reported in the FEC data, depending on the circumstances of the contribution. The largest contributions – $2,500 or more (referred to as "large contributions" in the text) – are substantively different than other contributions in that they represent a donor maxing out contributions for that candidate in that cycle. In 2012, an individual could give a maximum of $2,500 to a candidate for the primary election cycle, and another $2,500 for the general election. The middle two categories – $251–1,749 and $1,751–2,499 – are distinguished by the frequency with which they're made. There are, quite simply, a lot more contributions of $500 and $1,000 than there are contributions of $2,000: but the bigger contributions are a larger proportion of a candidate's budget. The dividing line between the two categories was based on the point at which the percentage of money brought in by the contributions outpaced the percentage of contributions of that size. While there are many ways the line could be drawn, it doesn't wind up being terribly important for our results, as most of the discussion is based on the patterns of small and large contributions.

Note 3.7

For the Tobit regression modeling of the effect of media statements on the number of contributions given to candidates, predictors were the candidate's standing in the aggregate polling, the trend of that standing (running from 8 days ago to 1 day ago), and the statements in the media about that candidate over the past 3 days. For non-Romney candidates (sample size 1,573), with the standard errors adjusted via clustering to 267, pseudo r^2 was 0.02 (see Table 9.16).

As with most of these analyses, the negative constant reflects the high number of days on which there are no observed contributions to a particular candidate. In this analysis and throughout all of the analyses of contributions, a candidate's standing in the polls is the most important predictor, though media effects still have a significant impact. In this case, positive statements about the candidate on Fox drive contributions, as do negative statements on the non-Fox broadcasts. As will be evident from later analyses, the effects of media statements and poll standing strongly interact. For Romney (see Table 9.17), none of the predictors except poll standing had a significant effect: pseudo r^2 was 0.003, with 262 observations.

TABLE 9.16 Effect of Media Statements over Past 3 Days on Number of Contributions for Non-Romney Candidates

Predictor	B	Std. error	t	P
7-day trend in polls	−0.02	1.35	−0.02	0.49
Aggregate poll standing	7.86	0.93	8.47	0.00
Non-Fox positive statements	2.68	3.05	0.88	0.19
Non-Fox negative statements	−5.73	1.79	−3.19	0.00
Fox positive statements	16.92	7.65	2.21	0.01
Fox negative statements	1.46	3.43	0.43	0.34
Constant	−57.86	12.91	−4.48	0.00

TABLE 9.17 Effect of Media Statements over Past 3 Days on Number of Contributions for Romney

Predictor	B	Std. error	t	P
7-day trend in polls	−2.60	5.29	−0.49	0.62
Aggregate poll standing	12.35	4.00	3.09	0.00
Non-Fox positive statements	3.19	7.03	0.45	0.65
Non-Fox negative statements	−3.68	5.97	−0.62	0.54
Fox positive statements	−4.65	9.06	−0.51	0.61
Fox negative statements	−1.36	11.28	−0.12	0.90
Constant	2.00	82.22	0.02	0.98

Note 3.8

The dependent variable for this analysis is the total amount of money raised by the candidate on a given day; predictors are how well the candidate is doing in the polls on that day, the difference between how well they were doing 8 days ago and yesterday, and media coverage in the previous 3 days. Total sample size was 1,573, with standard errors adjusted to 267 clusters. Pseudo r^2 for the analysis was 0.01.

As Table 9.18 shows, both positive and negative statements on Fox had a significant effect (one-tailed, $p<.05$), as did negative non-Fox statements. As will become evident from later analyses, the positive effect of negative Fox statements is almost entirely driven by small donors responding positively to any coverage for candidates who are struggling in the polls (and there are more struggling candidates at any time than successful ones).

Sample size for Romney was 267, pseudo r^2 was 0.003. For Romney, as Table 9.19 shows, media effects on overall contributions are rather smaller, and the directions of the effects don't make much sense. In later analyses, we'll see that they're strongly conditional on standing in the polls, but these results help to

TABLE 9.18 Effect of Media Statements over Past 3 Days on Total Contributions for Non-Romney Candidates

Predictor	B	Std. error	t	P
7-day trend in polls	883.93	1708.26	0.52	0.30
Aggregate poll standing	7104.51	1133.63	6.27	0.00
Non-Fox positive statements	368.69	1741.56	0.21	0.42
Non-Fox negative statements	−6924.75	2444.35	−2.83	0.00
Fox positive statements	4683.66	2838.58	1.65	0.05
Fox negative statements	7360.22	4489.38	1.64	0.05
Constant	−54705.09	12404.27	−4.41	0.00

TABLE 9.19 Effect of Media Statements over Past 3 Days on Total Contributions to Romney

Predictor	B	Std. error	t	P
7-day trend in polls	−6195.95	3498.49	−1.77	0.04
Aggregate poll standing	7532.55	1857.97	4.05	0.00
Non-Fox positive statements	4409.14	3453.57	1.28	0.10
Non-Fox negative statements	581.33	3130.11	0.19	0.43
Fox positive statements	−7352.30	4563.79	−1.61	0.05
Fox negative statements	412.97	5846.73	0.07	0.47
Constant	−25900.65	38255.07	−0.68	0.25

demonstrate why a simple model like this probably isn't the best representation of what's going on here.

Note 3.9

For these analyses, we used eight separate Tobit regressions: one for each of the four contribution categories, where the dependent variable is the total amount of money raised through contributions in that category (see Note 3.6 for a discussion of the categories). As in previous sets of analyses, the non-Romney candidates were aggregated, and analyzed separately from Romney. The predictors in each of these models were the candidate's standing in the aggregate poll measure as of that day, the trend from 8 days ago to the previous day), the number of positive and negative statements about the candidate over the previous 3 days on Fox and the non-Fox media sources, and the interaction between each of these media statement indicators and the candidate's standing in the polls.

For small contributions to non-Romney candidates (see Table 9.20), sample size was 1,573, clustered to 267. Pseudo r^2 was 0.01. Both the main and interaction effects for coverage on Fox were significant predictors of small contributions, though it should be cautioned that they can't be reasonably interpreted in isolation from one another. For the contributions of $251–1,749, sample size was the same, with pseudo r^2 at 0.02. For this category, positive statements on Fox had the most consistent effects, with significant main and interaction effects.

For both regressions, the total sample size was 1,573, clustered to 267 for the calculation of standard errors. Pseudo r^2 was 0.03 for contributions of $1,750–2,499, and 0.02 for contributions of $2,500 or more (see Table 9.21). Standing in the polls was still the strongest predictor of contributions at all levels for the non-Romney candidates, but the interaction effects were strong, and had significant effects nearly throughout. The large negative constants reflect the large number of days on which total contributions of that size for the candidate were zero.

TABLE 9.20 Effect of Media Statements over Past 3 Days on Small and Moderate Contributions to Non-Romney Candidates

Predictor	Contributions of $250 or less				Contributions of $251–$1,749			
	B	Std. error	t	P	B	Std. error	t	P
7-day trend in polls	40.55	159.02	0.25	0.40	492.08	320.49	1.54	0.06
Aggregate poll standing	1379.69	239.29	5.77	0.00	2006.81	223.56	8.98	0.00
Non-Fox positive statements	541.49	541.49	0.59	0.28	1174.39	1041.55	1.13	0.13
Non-Fox negative statements	−374.49	567.66	−0.66	0.26	1017.31	759.10	1.34	0.09
Fox positive statements	5384.58	2560.94	2.10	0.02	5391.49	2556.62	2.11	0.02
Fox negative statements	2203.94	1034.65	2.13	0.02	−726.01	1402.05	−0.52	0.30
Interactions with aggregate standing in polls								
Non-Fox positive statements	−10.68	34.12	−0.31	0.38	−23.71	46.58	−0.51	0.31
Non-Fox negative statements	−5.39	25.55	−0.21	0.42	−80.35	43.90	−1.83	0.03
Fox positive statements	−175.59	94.04	−1.87	0.03	−167.74	109.54	−1.53	0.06
Fox negative statements	−150.28	46.93	−3.20	0.00	67.84	93.65	0.72	0.23
Constant	−13629.71	3399.05	−4.01	0.00	−16066.57	2876.51	−5.59	0.00

TABLE 9.21 Effect of Media Statements over Past 3 Days on Large and Very Large Contributions to Non-Romney Candidates

Predictor	Contributions of $1,750–2,499				Contributions of $2,500 or more			
	B	Std. error	t	P	B	Std. error	t	P
7-day trend in polls	−39.13	92.53	−0.42	0.67	2266.83	1711.02	1.32	0.09
Aggregate poll standing	493.21	48.02	10.27	0.00	8218.21	1643.90	5.00	0.00
Non-Fox positive statements	92.80	204.54	0.45	0.65	7516.66	2697.71	2.79	0.00
Non-Fox negative statements	794.75	278.87	2.85	0.00	6468.83	3527.78	1.83	0.03
Fox positive statements	1134.12	416.28	2.72	0.01	4860.98	4275.89	1.14	0.13
Fox negative statements	−1219.97	556.33	−2.19	0.03	−7942.27	6534.70	−1.22	0.11
Interactions with aggregate standing in polls								
Non-Fox positive statements	−3.34	9.87	−0.34	0.74	−515.15	177.56	−2.90	0.00
Non-Fox negative statements	−46.60	14.81	−3.15	0.00	−697.55	261.69	−2.67	0.00
Fox positive statements	−49.69	18.79	−2.64	0.01	−450.67	232.12	−1.94	0.03
Fox negative statements	64.86	30.36	2.14	0.03	927.49	494.93	1.87	0.03
Constant	−10316.68	1053.48	−9.79	0.00	−117150.70	25881.54	−4.53	0.00

Note 4.1

The first step in removing the endogenous portions of the series is to determine the degree, if any, of fractional integration in the series (in this case, the combined series measuring the difference between the two candidates; since Obama led for the entire general election, the series is the size of Obama's lead at any given time).

The Geweke-Porter-Hudak test for fractional integration gives estimated fractional integration values slightly above 1 (a fully integrated series with permanent memory), and estimates of the value of d (representing the degree of fractional integration) of 1.14 to 1.53, depending on the power used in the analysis (see Table 9.22).

Results for the Robinson's fractional integration test (see Table 9.23) are similar, with estimated levels of fractional integration running between 1.06 and 1.44 (though the highest levels of power in Robinson's test are probably untenable because of the amount of data used in the estimate relative to the total sample size of the dataset).

The final test used, the modified Lo's test, works a bit differently, providing a test value against the null hypothesis of no fractional integration. The test statistic in this case was 2.08, against test values of 1.86 for 95 percent confidence and 2.10 for 99 percent confidence. Since the test statistic was greater than the test values, Lo's test rejected the null hypothesis of no fractional integration.

TABLE 9.22 Results of GPH Fractional Integration Test for Difference between Candidates

Power	ords.	Est. d	Std. err.	t(HO: d=0)	P>|t|	Asy. Std. err.	z(HO: d=0)	P>|z|
.5	15	1.13662	.2603	4.3667	0.001	.2304	4.9338	0.000
.55	19	1.3824	.2254	6.1330	0.000	.1948	7.0975	0.000
.6	25	1.49853	.1905	7.8657	0.000	.1621	9.2433	0.000
.65	33	1.41523	.1474	9.6044	0.000	.1361	10.3953	0.000
.7	42	1.4644	.1292	11.3323	0.000	.118	12.4112	0.000
.75	55	1.52754	.104	14.6899	0.000	.1016	15.0366	0.000

TABLE 9.23 Results of Robinson's Fractional Integration Test for Difference between Candidates

Power	ords.	Est. d	Std. err.	t(HO: d=0)	P>|t|
.65	33	1.386222	.1410092	9.8307	0.000
.7	41	1.439454	.1264073	11.3874	0.000
.75	55	1.4827	.0980918	15.1154	0.000
.8	71	1.442104	.0886953	16.2591	0.000
.85	93	1.343558	.0761847	17.6355	0.000
.9	121	1.247549	.0686593	18.1701	0.000
.95	159	1.059699	.0639603	16.5681	0.000

Combined, these results provided strong evidence for fractional integration in the series, with a d value of somewhere between 1.1 and 1.5. Such a d value is itself somewhat interesting for what it says about the dynamics of the race on a day-to-day basis (as the values are very different when measured on a different time scale), but its main function here is to allow for the removal of this endogeneity. To do so, it's necessary to settle on a point value for d. To determine which of these values within the ranges of the GPH and Robinson's tests worked best, correlogram analysis was used to determine which values minimized autocorrelation within the series (see Table 9.24). In this case, the degree of partial autocorrelation between values was minimized at a value of d = 1.5.

This correlogram shows a small degree of remaining autocorrelation at 2 lags, but not enough to make for a significant moving average or autoregressive function. The next step was to test for stationarity in the now corrected series using the Kwiatkowski-Phillips-Schmidt-Shin test (see Figure 9.2). This test has a null hypothesis of stationarity, so if the test value exceeds the critical value, we can conclude that the series isn't stationary. In the original (non-differenced) series, the critical value was 0.146 (for p = 0.05), against a test statistic ranging of 0.953 at 0 lags, declining as the number of lags increased, and not going below the critical value until six lags out. In the corrected series, the critical value was the same, but the test statistics were stable at around 0.04, allowing the conclusion that while the original series wasn't stationary, the corrected series was (note that the first 12 days of the corrected series are missing, as there was insufficient data before that point to accurately correct for the fractional integration).

TABLE 9.24 Correlogram for Difference between Candidates, at d=1.5

Lag	AC	PAC	Q	Prob.>Q	−1	0	1	−1	0	1
					(Autocorrelation)			(Partial autocorrelation)		
1	−0.0340	−0.0340	.23003	0.6315						
2	0.1426	0.1446	4.2974	0.1166						
3	0.0752	0.0870	5.4358	0.1425						
4	0.0235	0.0109	5.5473	0.2356						
5	−0.0123	−0.0407	5.5783	0.3494						
6	0.0182	−0.0020	5.6462	0.4640						
7	0.0439	0.0462	6.0413	0.5349						
8	−0.0655	−0.0652	6.9258	0.5447						
9	−0.0419	−0.0666	7.2897	0.6070						
10	−0.0516	−0.0586	7.846	0.6439						
11	−0.0943	−0.0850	9.7096	0.5567						
12	−0.1225	−0.1164	12.876	0.3781						
13	0.0039	0.0276	12.879	0.4572						
14	−0.0082	0.0416	12.894	0.5349						
15	−0.0146	0.0117	12.939	0.6070						

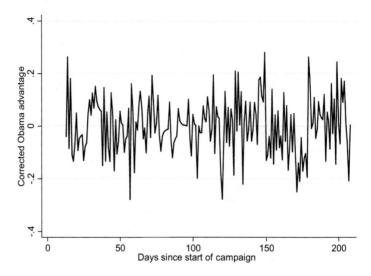

FIGURE 9.2   Corrected Obama Advantage

Note 4.2

The models predicting changes in the fractionally integrated series of Obama's advantage in the general election include all of the media coverage on the previous day (positive and negative coverage on Fox, and the aggregated non-Fox broadcasts), the 2-week trend in Obama's advantage (running from 15 days previous to 1 day previous), and the interaction of that 2-week trend with each of the media coverage predictors.

For the initial model (see Table 9.25), these predictors were used to model daily changes in the corrected series throughout the course of the general election campaign (a total of 197 days of data – there were no pre-election polls in the Pollster aggregation in the last few days before the election). The r^2 of the model is 0.16, with a corrected r^2 of 0.08.

In the analysis of the last 2 months of the campaign (see Table 9.26), there was obviously less data – 60 days' worth – but the r^2 was much higher: 0.56 (adjusted to 0.39).

Note 4.3

The naïve model for the effects of campaign events (see Table 9.27) used the day-to-day change in Obama's margin in the polls (not the corrected margin with the fractional integration corrected, but a 0,1,0 model) as the dependent variable, and only the campaign events as the independent variables (coding for these variables is described in the main regression model for these effects: see Note 4.4).

TABLE 9.25 Regression Model for Corrected Obama Advantage, Whole Campaign

Predictor	B	Std. error	t
2-week trend	−0.022	0.012	−1.84
Statements in media			
Romney non-Fox positive	−0.014	0.010	−1.4
Romney non-Fox negative	−0.009	0.006	−1.48
Romney Fox positive	**0.013**	**0.007**	**2.03**
Romney Fox negative	**−0.010**	**0.004**	**−2.43**
Obama non-Fox positive	**0.017**	**0.008**	**1.95**
Obama non-Fox negative	−0.009	0.007	−1.4
Obama Fox positive	**−0.024**	**0.010**	**−2.34**
Obama Fox negative	0.003	0.003	0.9
Interactions with 2-week trend			
Romney non-Fox positive	−0.008	0.005	−1.67
Romney non-Fox negative	0.007	0.006	1.23
Romney Fox positive	−0.001	0.005	−0.31
Romney Fox negative	−0.001	0.005	−0.18
Obama non-Fox positive	**−0.013**	**0.006**	**−2.35**
Obama non-Fox negative	0.006	0.004	1.48
Obama Fox positive	0.011	0.008	1.31
Obama Fox negative	0.003	0.003	0.97
Constant	0.010	0.013	0.8

This model (which used changes over the entirety of the campaign) had an r^2 of 0.18 (adjusted to 0.15).

Note 4.4

To model the effects of campaign events, we added separate dummy variables to the media models representing each of the events: the announcement of Vice-Presidential nominee Paul Ryan (August 11), the Republican Convention (August 27–30), the Democratic Convention (September 3–6), the Presidential debates (October 3, 16 and 22), the Vice-Presidential debate (October 11) and the landfall of Hurricane (later "Superstorm") Sandy (October 29).

Because several of these events took place in the evening (the debates, Hurricane Sandy's landfall), they were unlikely to show up in changes in the polls for that day; as a result, the dummy variable (set to 0 for the entire series except the day of the event, when it takes a value of 1) was set to the following day. For the conventions, which took place over 4 days, the dummy variable was set to 1 for all 4 days. Once these variables were added into the existing media models, the coefficients essentially revealed the independent effects of

TABLE 9.26 Regression Model for Corrected Obama Advantage, Last 2 Months of Campaign

Predictor	B	Std. error	t
2-week trend	−0.023	0.014	−1.58
Statements in media			
Romney non-Fox positive	**−0.033**	**0.012**	**−2.64**
Romney non-Fox negative	**−0.017**	**0.008**	**−2.25**
Romney Fox positive	0.016	0.011	1.43
Romney Fox negative	**−0.037**	**0.012**	**−3.14**
Obama non-Fox positive	**0.028**	**0.010**	**2.78**
Obama non-Fox negative	0.002	0.010	0.16
Obama Fox positive	−0.023	0.015	−1.56
Obama Fox negative	**0.013**	**0.006**	**2.14**
Interactions with 2-week trend			
Romney non-Fox positive	**−0.014**	**0.005**	**−2.70**
Romney non-Fox negative	0.012	0.006	1.90
Romney Fox positive	−0.007	0.006	−1.25
Romney Fox negative	−0.015	0.008	−1.90
Obama non-Fox positive	**−0.020**	**0.006**	**−3.47**
Obama non-Fox negative	0.008	0.005	1.82
Obama Fox positive	**0.022**	**0.010**	**2.27**
Obama Fox negative	**0.012**	**0.004**	**2.81**
Constant	−0.005	0.024	−0.22

the events themselves, in terms of changes in Obama's margin not otherwise explained by endogenous effects or media coverage (see Table 9.28).

There was no estimated effect of the Ryan announcement or the Republican Convention on Obama's margin during the last 2 months of the campaign because these events took place before the last 60 days of the race. Of the campaign events listed, only one – the Democratic National Convention – had a significant impact on Obama's margin in the polls, controlling for the content of media coverage. During the 4 days of the convention, Obama's margin increased by 0.23 points per day. Of the other events, only the Vice-Presidential debate came close to statistical significance.

The inclusion of these events in the media coverage model does have some impact on the estimated effects of media coverage, mostly by increasing the strength of the conditionality effects. When the events are included in the model estimating effects for the whole campaign, the 2-week trend variable becomes more significant as a main effect, as well as in interaction with one more of the media coverage variables, than in the model without the events. In the model for the last 2 months of the campaign, the inclusion of the events

TABLE 9.27 Naïve Regression Model for Differenced Obama Advantage, Campaign
Events Only

Predictor	B	Std. error	t
Ryan announcement	−0.091	0.130	−0.7
Republican Convention	0.059	0.066	0.9
Democratic Convention	**0.359**	**0.066**	**5.48**
1st debate	**−0.391**	**0.130**	**−3**
2nd debate	0.109	0.130	0.84
3rd debate	0.009	0.130	0.07
VP debate	−0.091	0.130	−0.7
Sandy	0.209	0.130	1.61
Constant	−0.009	0.009	−0.99

pushes several of the main effects of coverage of Obama out of significance,
but makes all of the interaction effects of the 2-week trend with the coverage
significant. However, as is evident from the low t-values on most of the event
indicators in both models, the inclusion of these events doesn't explain much
of the variance in the corrected Obama margin series: the r^2 of the model for
the whole campaign increases only slightly, to 0.23 (adjusted to 0.12; up from
0.16/0.08), and to 0.63 (adjusted to 0.40; up from 0.56/0.39). The most likely
explanation for these changes is that some of the variance that had previously
been attributed to coverage of Obama was actually driven by the Democratic
National Convention. However, none of these results fundamentally change
the way we understand the effects of media on the campaign: media coverage
still has significant direct effects, many of which are contingent on the dynamics
of the race, and coverage of Romney matters more than coverage of Obama.
Perhaps more importantly, the direction and magnitude of the effects is about
the same between the models with and without campaign events.

Note 5.1

The item asking respondents to name the Vice-President has been used by
several organizations over the past 25 years. Fifty-nine percent were able to
name Joe Biden as the Vice-President in a May 2010 Pew Survey – one of the
lower figures for recent Vice-Presidents. More were able to name Dick Cheney
as Vice-President during his tenure (61 percent in an April 2002 Pew survey,
and 67 percent in a November 2001 Pew survey), and by the end of his term
(when Gore was running for President), as much as 90 percent of the American
public were able to name him (90 percent in a January 2000 Gallup poll;
69 percent in a June 1996 Gallup poll; 65 percent in a July 1994 *Times Mirror*
poll and 70 percent in a January 1994 *Times Mirror* poll).

TABLE 9.28 Regression Model for Corrected Obama Advantage, Including Events, Full Campaign and Last 2 Months of Campaign

Full campaign

Predictor	B	Std. error	t
2-week trend	**−0.028**	**0.012**	**−2.34**
Statements in media			
Romney non-Fox positive	−0.014	0.010	−1.43
Romney non-Fox negative	−0.007	0.006	−1.07
Romney Fox positive	**0.014**	**0.007**	**1.97**
Romney Fox negative	**−0.009**	**0.004**	**−2.28**
Obama non-Fox positive	0.011	0.009	1.27
Obama non-Fox negative	−0.008	0.006	−1.23
Obama Fox positive	**−0.024**	**0.010**	**−2.39**
Obama Fox negative	0.002	0.003	0.75
Interactions with 2-week trend			
Romney non-Fox positive	−0.007	0.005	−1.5
Romney non-Fox negative	0.009	0.006	1.44
Romney Fox positive	−0.003	0.005	−0.62
Romney Fox negative	−0.001	0.005	−0.11
Obama non-Fox positive	**−0.012**	**0.006**	**−1.98**
Obama non-Fox negative	**0.008**	**0.004**	**2.04**
Obama Fox positive	0.011	0.008	1.37
Obama Fox negative	0.003	0.004	0.81
Events			
Ryan announcment	−0.027	0.103	−0.26
Republican Convention	0.029	0.057	0.51
Democratic Convention	**0.197**	**0.053**	**3.72**
1st debate	−0.075	0.108	−0.69
2nd debate	0.088	0.123	0.72
3rd debate	−0.044	0.107	−0.41
VP debate	0.082	0.126	0.65
Sandy	0.062	0.102	0.61
Constant	0.005	0.013	0.36

Last 2 Months

Predictor	B	Std. error	t
2-week trend	−0.027	0.014	−1.91
Statements in media			
Romney non-Fox positive	**−0.028**	**0.012**	**−2.25**
Romney non-Fox negative	−0.015	0.008	−1.91

Romney Fox positive	0.027	0.013	2.04
Romney Fox negative	−0.036	0.011	−3.16
Obama non Fox positive	0.021	0.011	1.81
Obama non-Fox negative	−0.001	0.010	−0.10
Obama Fox positive	−0.019	0.014	−1.38
Obama Fox negative	0.009	0.006	1.49
Interactions with 2-week trend			
Romney non-Fox positive	−0.012	0.005	−2.50
Romney non-Fox negative	0.014	0.006	2.19
Romney Fox positive	−0.015	0.007	−2.29
Romney Fox negative	−0.016	0.008	−2.00
Obama non-Fox positive	−0.021	0.007	−3.10
Obama non-Fox negative	0.012	0.005	2.58
Obama Fox positive	0.021	0.009	2.37
Obama Fox negative	0.015	0.005	3.26
Events			
Ryan announcement			
Republican Convention			
Democratic Convention	0.228	0.109	2.09
1st debate	0.059	0.108	0.54
2nd debate	0.042	0.124	0.34
3rd debate	−0.097	0.111	−0.88
VP debate	0.240	0.128	1.88
Sandy	0.013	0.096	0.14
Constant	−0.012	0.024	−0.5

Note 5.2

The issue of how best to measure consumption of media sources is contentious. In most of the PublicMind polls described here (one, from December 2014, used a different methodology, explained in Note 6.3), respondents are asked: "Americans have more ways than ever to get their news these days. Which of the following news sources have you used in the past week?" This is followed by a list of channels (CNN, MSNBC, Fox News), types of programs (Sunday morning talk shows, network evening news broadcasts, local evening news broadcasts), specific programs (*The Daily Show with Jon Stewart*) and non-broadcast news sources (national newspapers, local newspapers, talk radio, political websites) in a randomly determined order, shuffled for each respondent.

In the past, researchers used relatively basic measures, such as asking how many nights each week respondents watched "the news" or "programs about the campaign" (Dilliplane et al. 2013). Today, such measures are obsolete, for several reasons: they fail to capture the difference between news sources, they rely on the respondent to decide what is and what isn't news or campaign programming, and they fail to recognize that some of the viewing may not be done in the traditional manner of sitting down in front of a television, and may include time spent multi-tasking. They're also difficult to answer (Schwarz and Oyserman 2001), leading respondents to rely on heuristic processes in their response (Prior 2009). Dilliplane et al. (2013) make use of a program list format, in which respondents (via an online modality, so the items are presented visually) have a list of programs, and indicate which ones they watch regularly, finding that these measures are stable over time and that higher reported levels of exposure result in increased political knowledge.

However, Prior (2013) argues that while such a measure is an improvement, it's still inadequate, as it fails to measure exactly how much news content respondents are getting. For instance, he points out that (as in our data) far more people report watching Fox News than are counted as doing so in Nielsen data (though Dilliplane et al. 2013 aren't convinced of the validity of the Nielsen data in the first place), and suggests that the likely reason is that many people are watching the channel for only a few minutes. As such, a program list format lumps together individuals who watch a program or channel a great deal with those who rarely watch it. He suggests that the real problem isn't with Dilliplane et al.'s specific items, but with self-reported items in general, and that the solution is automatic monitoring of media choices (incidentally, the same approach adopted by Nielsen in recent years). While such an approach might be better than any question, it carries its own ethical, financial and logistical issues, though Goldman et al. (2013) argue that it's still the best approach available to researchers today.

As such, the PublicMind surveys make use of a modified program list format, in which the respondent is asked about exposure to specific channels and programs; in the 2014 survey discussed in Chapter 6, this format is modified to ask respondents about which programs and channels they rely on most, in an effort to overcome the over-reporting problem identified by Prior (2009, 2013).

Note 5.3

The analysis of the eight-item PublicMind political knowledge scale (see Table 9.29) includes a number of demographic factors, the complete set of media indicators and the interactions of the ideological media sources with political ideology as predictors. The major control variables are party identification (5-point scale), ideology (3-point scale) and education (5-point scale, with higher values indicating more education). The pseudo r^2 for the ordered logit model is 0.11, with a sample size of 809.

Cut points are at -0.78, 0.29, 1.25, 1.95, 2.61, 3.25, 4.34 and 6.00. There is no theoretical reason to believe that reported exposure to the other news sources would have a significant interaction with ideology, and their inclusion doesn't reach statistical significance or substantively change the presented results.

TABLE 9.29 Ordered Logit Analysis of Number of Political Knowledge Items Answered Correctly, PublicMind Data

Predictor	B	Std. error	Z
Party identification	0.034	0.049	0.7
Education	0.498	0.064	7.8
Age	0.449	0.077	5.8
Ideology	−0.333	0.162	−2.1
Gender	−1.085	0.132	−8.2
Media sources (coded as 1 is yes, 2 is no)			
NPR	0.881	0.168	5.2
Daily Show	0.469	0.204	2.3
CNN	0.098	0.137	0.7
MSNBC	1.299	0.415	3.1
Evening news	0.008	0.0140	0.1
Talk radio	−0.338	0.434	−0.8
Local TV news	0.112	0.162	0.7
Sunday morning show	0.430	0.139	3.1
Local newspaper	0.164	0.146	1.1
National newspaper	0.217	0.154	1.4
Political website	0.540	0.154	3.5
Fox News	−2.113	0.443	−4.8
Interactions of media source with ideology			
Fox News	0.850	0.185	4.6
MSNBC	−0.649	0.172	−3.8
Talk radio	0.358	0.177	2.0

Note 5.4

The analysis of the ANES data (see Table 9.30) is almost identical to that of the PublicMind data. The biggest differences are in the coding of the media variables (0 for non-viewers, 1 for viewers). Additionally, the more general category of "talk radio" has been replaced by a particular program (*The Rush Limbaugh Show*). This also corresponds to the one major difference in the results between the ANES and PublicMind results, with *Rush Limbaugh* failing to show the interaction effect with ideology demonstrated by "talk radio" in the PublicMind data.

Note 6.1

The December 2014 PublicMind poll used a three-item political knowledge scale, asking respondents to name the three branches of the federal government (61 percent answered correctly), which party currently controlled the House

TABLE 9.30 Ordered Logit Analysis of Number of Political Knowledge Items Answered Correctly, 2010 ANES Data

Predictor	B	Std. error	Z
White	0.257	0.135	1.9
Male?	0.293	0.104	2.8
Ideology	−0.033	0.055	−0.6
Party ID	0.034	0.033	1.0
Education	0.479	0.058	8.3
Media sources			
Fox News	−1.432	0.358	-4.0
MSNBC	0.765	0.391	2.0
NPR	0.755	0.164	4.6
Sunday morning programs	0.419	0.147	2.8
Daily Show	0.592	0.187	3.2
Rush Limbaugh	0.899	0.912	1.0
Interactions of media sources with ideology			
Fox News	0.348	0.079	4.4
MSNBC	−0.078	0.095	−0.8
Rush Limbaugh	−0.064	0.163	−0.4

of Representatives (74 percent answered correctly) and the name of the Chief Justice of the Supreme Court (24 percent answered correctly). All told, 32 percent of the sample were unable to answer any of the items, 24 percent answered just one correctly, 28 percent answered two correctly, and 16 percent answered all three items correctly. There were no significant differences between scores by partisanship: Democrats (not including leaners) had a mean score of 1.34 correct, Republicans (also not including leaners) had a mean score of 1.29 correct.

The logit regression analysis (see Table 9.31) used a collapsed version of the "Barack Obama is not a legal citizen of the United States" item, as described in Note 6.5. Predictors included the respondent's education, age, whether or not the respondent was African-American, party identification (on a 5-point scale), ideology, age, whether or not cable was listed as the primary source of news, whether or not the respondent was a Republican, and dummy variables for the individual media sources with sufficient sample sizes to warrant their inclusion (CNN, MSNBC, Fox, evening news programs and *The Daily Show*). Also included was the three-way interaction of Fox viewership, party identification and score on the political knowledge scale, along with all of the necessary two-way interaction effects. Of these, only the three-way interaction and the interaction of Fox viewership with political knowledge were significant. Interestingly, the results imply that Fox News viewership has the greatest impact, increasing the likelihood of believing that Obama isn't a citizen among (non-leaner) Democrats; however, the group of Fox-watching strong

TABLE 9.31 Logit Regression Model for Likelihood of Saying That President Obama Is "Probably" or "Definitely" Not a Citizen, December 2014

Predictor	B	Std. error	Z
Education	−0.182	0.163	−1.1
Black?	−0.628	0.573	−1.1
Party ID	0.111	0.195	0.6
Political knowledge	−0.547	0.356	−1.5
Fox?	−3.298	2.165	−1.5
CNN?	−0.353	0.335	−1.1
Daily Show?	0.315	0.477	0.7
Evening news?	−0.107	0.372	−0.3
MSNBC?	−0.458	0.606	−0.8
Ideology	0.244	0.183	1.3
Age	−0.073	0.123	−0.6
Republican?	0.824	0.445	1.9
Cable as main source	0.050	0.299	0.2
Knowledge × Fox	2.435	1.122	2.2
Knowledge × party ID	0.082	0.100	0.8
Fox × party ID	0.624	0.479	1.3
Knowledge × Fox × party ID	−0.493	0.251	−2.0
Constant	−1.197	0.881	−1.4

Democrats is small enough that drawing conclusions about it is problematic. The takeaway from this, instead, seems to be that Fox viewership has a greater effect on increasing the likelihood of thinking Obama isn't a citizen among independents, and independents who lean towards the Republican Party – a conclusion that makes sense given the lower base rates in these groups. The total sample size for the model was 487, with a pseudo r^2 of 0.14.

Note 6.2

The survey was carried out through Knowledge Networks on a national probability sample size of 1,051, and the results were retrieved from the Roper iPoll service. While Knowledge Networks is an online-based survey platform, the results of its polls are more reliable than those of other online platforms, largely because it begins with a national non-online probability sample, and when it comes across a respondent who doesn't have internet access (and therefore would be excluded from normal online surveys), it simply provides the respondent with internet access for the duration of the individual's term on the Knowledge Networks panel. As such, the normal sampling bias that comes along with online surveys (namely, the fact that not everyone in the US, especially as of 2003, had internet access) isn't an issue.

TABLE 9.32 Logit Regression Model for Likelihood of Saying That WMD Had Been Found, June 2003

Predictor	B	Std. error	Z
Political knowledge scale	−0.256	1.052	−0.2
Party ID	0.425	0.161	2.6
Female?	0.248	0.221	1.1
Household income	−0.046	0.031	−1.5
Education	−0.088	0.122	−0.7
Black?	−0.024	0.447	−0.1
Age	−0.125	0.070	−1.8
MSNBC?	−0.259	0.463	−0.6
Fox News?	−0.182	1.355	−0.1
Knowledge × party ID	−0.146	0.305	−0.5
Fox × party ID	−0.128	0.346	−0.4
Fox × knowledge × party ID	1.428	0.766	1.9
Constant	−1.126	0.714	−1.6

The regression model described here (see Table 9.32) is a logit model in which the dependent variable is whether the respondent believes that WMD were found in Iraq or not (22 percent said that it had been found). Respondents who said that they didn't know or refused to answer the question weren't included in the analysis. Predictors in the model were the number of political knowledge items answered correctly (reduced to a 0–1 scale, with a mean value of 0.44), a 5-point partisanship scale, gender, reported household income (a 19-point scale with a mean value of 10.1), a 4-point education scale, whether or not the respondent was black (a 0 or 1 dummy variable), age (on a 1–7 scale), whether the respondent reported watching MSNBC and whether the respondent reported watching Fox. Also included was a three-way interaction effect (with all necessary two-way components) of partisanship, watching Fox and political knowledge. Because not every respondent was asked about every item, the total sample size for the analysis was 505, with a pseudo r^2 of 0.08.

Note 6.3

In the December 2014 PublicMind survey used in this chapter, respondents were asked a series of items to determine their media usage. They were first asked whether they got information from a certain kind of media source (cable news channels, network news broadcasts and political comedy programs), and if they did, they were asked to say which program or channel they used most. Finally, they were asked which of these categories was their primary source of news (35 percent said cable news, 39 percent network news, 5 percent political satire/comedy and 18 percent said that it was a combination).

Individuals were coded as having Fox News as their primary news source if they said that they got news from cable news programming, named Fox News as their preferred channel, and said that cable news was their primary source of information. This group constituted half of everyone who said that cable news was their primary source: 12 percent of the overall sample. The partisan breakdown of the audience is clear from this measure: only 3 percent of Democrats and those leaning Democrat were coded as having Fox as their main source, along with 9 percent of independents, 30 percent of those who leaned Republican, and 40 percent of Republicans.

Note 6.4

As described in Note 6.5, the dependent variable in this model was the dichotomized version of the conspiracy theory item. Respondents were coded as 0 if they said that American forces "probably" or "definitely" hadn't found an active WMD program in Iraq, and 1 if they said that American forces "probably" or "definitely" had found one (refused and "don't know" responses were excluded from the analysis). All told (in the unweighted data), 45 percent were coded as 1, and 55 percent were coded as 0. Because of the large number of predictors used in the model, the total sample size was smaller than usual, at 481.

The analysis included education, age, ideology, party identification, score on the political knowledge scale and age as control variables, as well as the full set of media variables: reported viewing of Fox, CNN, MSNBC, network evening news and *The Daily Show*. In addition, the analysis also included indicators for the stated primary source of news: cable or political comedy/satire (leaving network news and combinations as the baseline category). Finally, two sets of interaction effects were included: the first interacted whether or not the respondent was a Republican with whether or not their main source of news was cable, and whether they watched Fox (so a respondent would be scored as 1 only if they were a Republican – not including leaners – who said that they watched Fox and cable was their primary source of news; all others would be coded as 0). The second interaction looked at the variable effect of having satire/political comedy as their primary information source by age.

Note 6.5

All of the data in this section comes from a PublicMind poll carried out in December 2014, with a mixed sample of landline and cell phone calls. The total sample size for the items used here was 987 (the total sample size for the survey was 1,247, but some segments of the survey were assigned randomly to participants).

In the model predicting beliefs about climate change (see Table 9.33), responses were pooled into two categories: those who said that global warming

TABLE 9.33 Logit Regression Model for Likelihood of Saying That Global Warming Is "Probably" or "Definitely" a Hoax

Predictor	B	Std. error	t	P
Education	−0.579	0.143	−4.05	0.00
Black?	0.225	0.326	0.69	0.49
Party ID	0.297	0.066	4.5	0.00
Fox News?	−0.717	0.614	−1.17	0.24
Education × Fox News	0.597	0.253	2.36	0.02
Political knowledge	0.035	0.105	0.33	0.74
CNN?	−0.464	0.249	−1.87	0.06
Daily Show?	−0.855	0.444	−1.93	0.05
Evening news?	−0.125	0.224	−0.56	0.58
MSNBC	−1.018	0.512	−1.99	0.05
Constant	−0.205	0.416	−0.49	0.62

was "probably" or "definitely" a hoax, and those who said that it "probably" or "definitely" wasn't (those who gave a "don't know" response, or refused to answer the question, weren't included in the analysis).

Predictors in the model included dummy variables for media choices and whether or not the respondent was African-American, as well as partisanship (coded 1–5, with 1 representing Democrats, 2 leaning Democrats, 3 independents, 4 leaning Republicans and 5 Republicans), education level (1 representing those who never went past high school, 2 for those with some college credit or a sub-bachelor's degree, and 3 for those with a bachelor's degree or more), and score on that survey's political knowledge scale. The political knowledge scale described in Note 6.1 was included as well. The pseudo r^2 for the logit model was 0.13.

Note 6.6

Data on the effects of media usage on beliefs about the autism–vaccine link is drawn from the same survey described in Note 6.5. The regression model in Table 9.34 (a logit model, in which the four possible responses were collapsed into two categories, as described in Note 6.1) included all of the same predictors as the model for beliefs about global warming, as well as some additional controls: whether or not the respondent was a parent (a dummy variable, in which 0 represented individuals who weren't parents, and 1 represented individuals who were), age (coded 1–4, with higher values representing older individuals), political ideology (1 conservative, 2 moderate and 3 liberal), and whether or not the respondent said that cable programming was their primary source of news (another 0–1 dummy variable). The contingent effect of watching CNN, having cable as a primary news source, and education was represented as a three-way interaction effect. The pseudo r^2 for the logit model was 0.07.

TABLE 9.34 Logit Regression Model for Likelihood of Saying That Autism Is "Probably" or "Definitely" Caused by Early Childhood Vaccinations

Predictor	B	Std. error	t	P
Education	−0.075	0.281	−0.27	0.79
Black?	−0.062	0.437	−0.14	0.89
Party ID	0.028	0.102	0.27	0.79
Political knowledge	−0.148	0.157	−0.94	0.35
Parent?	−0.035	0.351	−0.10	0.92
Age	−0.389	0.144	−2.70	0.01
Cable as primary source?	1.719	1.016	1.69	0.09
CNN?	0.663	1.085	0.61	0.54
Daily Show?	−0.158	0.538	−0.29	0.77
MSNBC?	0.535	0.562	0.95	0.34
Fox News?	−0.059	0.441	−0.13	0.89
Political ideology	0.439	0.215	2.04	0.04
Cable primary × CNN	−2.740	1.629	−1.68	0.09
Cable primary × education	−0.819	0.444	−1.84	0.07
CNN × education	−0.306	0.487	−0.63	0.53
Cable primary × CNN × education	1.544	0.718	2.15	0.03
Constant	−1.311	0.904	−1.45	0.15

Note 7.1

The number of background checks reported by the FBI for a given month varied widely in the dataset, from a low of 1.15 million to a high of 2.8 million (mean of 1.7 million, median 1.5 million, standard deviation of 391,000). Much of this variation, though, follows a seasonal pattern, with sales peaking in December, and falling to their lowest point in June. Several methods were used to control for this seasonal trend, but the simplest (including each month as a dummy variable in the regression model) proved the most effective, despite concerns that the inclusion of eleven dummy variables (with January as the excluded baseline) would eat up too many degrees of freedom in a relatively limited dataset. The alternative, using the average change for that month as a predictor, failed to reach significance when included, but the results (see Table 9.36) are otherwise substantively the same (with the significance and size of the Sandy Hook variable seeing the biggest change; if the average monthly change is used in the model, the Sandy Hook indicator is about twice as large, and reaches statistical significance). The sample size for the model was 41 months (though the mean change variable was calculated using the whole dataset), and has an r^2 of 0.91 (adjusted to 0.84). The high r^2 is largely a function of the enormous predictive power of the seasonality and year indicators.

TABLE 9.35 OLS Regression Model for Number of Background Checks in a Given Month

Predictor	B	Std. error	t
Average monthly change			
February	204850.3	130083.3	1.57
March	291003.7	138110	2.11
April	−149790	136745	−1.1
May	−398134	133041.6	−2.99
June	−488273	133041.6	−3.67
July	−365152	142522.1	−2.56
August	−229001	128681.6	−1.78
September	−108816	147477.4	−0.74
October	−83899.2	128915.8	−0.65
November	133593.6	129999	1.03
December	466682.8	137007	3.41
Lagged approval	30778.05	13874.09	2.22
Year	141003.2	46297.27	3.05
Sandy Hook?	375593.9	227897.7	1.65
Shooting coverage	−16140.3	112147.6	−0.14
Gun control statements (10+) on Fox	−2368522	1218461	−1.94
Gun control statements (10+) on networks	43028.83	76206.44	0.56
Fox statements × lagged approval	48406.35	26321.08	1.84
Constant	−2.83E+08	9.31E+07	−3.04

The greatly skewed nature of the distribution of the number of statements about gun control (on both Fox and the networks) led to the operationalization of the statements as a dummy threshold variable (coded as 0 if the number of statements was less than ten for a source in a given month, and 1 if it was more than ten; ten was the median number of statements, and seemed an appropriate cut point, though the results didn't differ if a higher threshold of twenty was used instead). Simply using the raw number of statements would mean that the predictor would expect 300 times the effect in some months compared to others, which seems utterly unrealistic. Moreover, from a theoretical perspective, the difference would seem to be between a great deal of coverage of gun control – which might make it seem like a realistic possibility – and little enough coverage that it could be ignored. A similar process tested various operationalizations of the number of statements about mass shootings in a month, but none of the operationalizations yielded a predictor with a significant effect on the number of background checks, controlling for statements about gun control.

The general increasing trend in the number of background checks – which may or may not have anything to do with Obama's election – was controlled for through the use of the year as a predictor, which proved to be significant (with an estimated increase of 141,000 background checks per month per year).

Interestingly, the negative coefficient of the threshold based dummy for the number of statements on Fox News implies that, when Obama's approval is sufficiently low, statements about gun control on Fox will actually decrease the number of background checks carried out in a given month. However, the much larger and positive coefficient for approval, added to the positive coefficient for the interaction effect of Fox coverage and approval, means that this cut point is very low, around 29 percent approval. This is far lower than the lowest approval rating in the dataset (41 percent), and so remains in the realm of hypotheticals.

An interaction between network coverage and Obama's approval was also tested, though there's no theoretical reason to believe that such an interaction would exist. Its inclusion doesn't substantially impact the coefficient for the Fox coverage indicators and interaction, though it does increase the standard error attached to the Fox interaction effect, as would be expected, dropping the t-value below the threshold for statistical significance.

Note 7.2

The analysis of the December 2013 PublicMind poll has a sample size of 812. The dependent variable is the collapsed form of the item "Do you strongly agree, agree somewhat, disagree somewhat, or strongly disagree with the statement: There has been a concerted effort by politicians to take 'Christ' out of Christmas." Half the respondents heard the item in this order; the other half heard "disagree" options first. The collapsed version turned the four response categories (in the original, 58 percent disagreed strongly, 12 percent disagreed somewhat, 8 percent agreed somewhat, and 22 percent agreed strongly) into two categories, coded as 1 if the respondent agreed somewhat or strongly, and 0 if the respondent disagreed somewhat or strongly. The main predictors of interest in the model were consumption of cable news sources (Fox News, *The Daily Show* and MSNBC were included as dummy variables, though the coding was strange: 1 if they reported using the source, 2 if they didn't; as such, the coefficients were reversed from their intuitive interpretation. To ameliorate this problem, the dummy variable for Fox was recoded as a 0–1 variable, with 1 representing Fox viewers) and reported church attendance (on a 1–6 scale, in which higher values indicated less church attendance; respondents who said that they attended more than once a week were coded as 1, those who said that they never went to church services were coded as 6). Also included were variables for race (dummy variables for white and black, leaving neither white nor black as the excluded baseline group), gender, age (in four categories, with higher values indicating older respondents), education, party identification (on the same 5-point scale used elsewhere), and a 3-point ideology scale (running from liberal to conservative). Also included was the interaction of church attendance with consumption of the ideological media sources (MSNBC and Fox News).

TABLE 9.36 Logit Model for Agreeing That "Politicians Are Trying to Take 'Christ' Out of Christmas"

Predictor	B	Std. error	Z
Age	−0.172	0.084	−2.05
Male?	−0.003	0.163	−0.02
White?	1.165	0.496	2.35
Black?	1.180	0.552	2.14
Church attendance	−0.201	0.111	−1.81
Education	−0.021	0.073	−0.29
Fox?	−1.140	0.382	−2.98
MSNBC?	0.193	0.396	0.49
Daily Show?	0.043	0.228	0.19
Party ID	0.199	0.065	3.04
Ideology	0.167	0.135	1.23
Fox × church attendance	0.275	0.101	2.72
MSNBC × church attendance	−0.023	0.107	−0.21
Constant	−1.627	0.839	−1.94

The effect of the interaction of MSNBC and church attendance wasn't a significant predictor, and the results didn't change substantially if it wasn't included (see Table 9.36). The pseudo r^2 for the logit model was 0.05.

Note 7.3

In most respects, including the predictive variables used, the analysis for the "Towns and cities should be allowed to put up manger scenes, even if it offends some people" agree/disagree item was the same as that discussed in Note 7.2. The only notable difference comes from the fact that the dependent variable used here wasn't a collapsed version, as in almost all of the other analyses of agree/disagree items. The decision not to use a collapsed version was made because the majority agreeing with the statement was so high that most of the variance in the model comes from whether or not individuals "strongly agree" with the item, rather than whether or not they agree (this is also why the discussion in the main text is based on the rate at which people "strongly agree," rather than just "agree"). Because of this, an ordered logit model was used to estimate the full range of responses to the variable, from strongly disagree (1) to strongly agree (4) (see Table 9.37). The sample size was 842, with a pseudo r^2 of 0.15.

Note 7.4

The predictors in the model for whether respondents preferred "Happy Holidays" instead of "Merry Christmas" (or saying that it doesn't matter to

TABLE 9.37 Ordered Logit Regression for Agreement with "Towns and Cities Should Be Allowed to Put Up Manger Scenes"

Predictor	B	Std. error	Z
Age	0.068	0.086	0.79
Male?	0.043	0.173	0.25
White?	0.496	0.343	1.45
Black?	−0.119	0.407	−0.29
Church attendance	−0.408	0.112	−3.64
Education	−0.344	0.080	−4.32
Fox?	−0.327	0.442	−0.74
MSNBC?	−1.031	0.473	−2.18
Daily Show?	0.896	0.195	4.59
Party ID	0.346	0.072	4.82
Ideology	0.359	0.134	2.68
Fox × church attendance	0.183	0.109	1.68
MSNBC × church attendance	0.205	0.113	1.82
Cut points			
1	−1.860	0.772	
2	−1.057	0.765	
3	0.242	0.763	

them) were the same as for the previous two models. Like the analysis of the item asking respondents whether or not politicians were trying to "take Christ out of Christmas," and unlike the previous analysis, the model used a collapsed version of the item (set to 1 if the respondent preferred "Happy Holidays," and 0 otherwise), and so made use of a dichotomous logit, rather than an ordered logit, model. All told, 150 respondents (18 percent of the sample) said that they preferred "Happy Holidays." As in the other models, the interaction of MSNBC viewership and church attendance wasn't a significant predictor of preferences, and was included only for the sake of comparison. Removing it doesn't substantially change the outcome of the analysis shown in Table 9.38 (the coefficient on the Fox News by church attendance interaction changes from -0.2619 to -0.2610; the standard error is the same in both cases). Note that the direction of the coefficients is reversed from the other analyses, as here the dependent variable is coded such that a value of 1 indicates disagreement with "War on Christmas" ideas.

Note 7.5

The first analysis (see Table 9.39) looked at whether or not individuals approved of Common Core in a logit model, grouping together those who didn't approve

TABLE 9.38 Logit Model for Preferring "Happy Holidays" over "Merry Christmas"

Predictor	B	Std. error	Z
Age	−0.122	0.109	−1.12
Male?	−0.249	0.224	−1.11
White?	−0.639	0.411	−1.56
Black?	0.703	0.471	1.49
Church attendance	0.416	0.138	3.02
Education	0.005	0.101	0.05
Fox?	0.590	0.588	1
MSNBC?	−0.352	0.576	−0.61
Daily Show?	−0.082	0.269	−0.31
Party ID	−0.211	0.089	−2.36
Ideology	−0.482	0.172	−2.8
Fox × church attendance	−0.262	0.146	−1.8
MSNBC × church attendance	−0.008	0.142	−0.06
Constant	−0.078	0.960	−0.08

and those who said that they didn't know whether or not they approved into a single category (excluding the small group of respondents who refused to answer the question), and contrasting them with those who said that they approved. Predictors included 0/1 dummy variables for media use, whether or not the respondent had school-age children in the household, race, as well as party identification, ideology and score on the survey's political knowledge scale. The total sample size for the analysis was 576 (not all respondents in the survey were given all of the sections, so the portion that received both the media series and the Common Core series consisted of about half of the overall sample, randomly selected), with a pseudo r^2 of 0.08.

TABLE 9.39 Logit Model for Approving of Common Core

Predictor	B	Std. error	Z
Education	0.179	0.164	1.1
Age	−0.064	0.119	−0.54
African-American?	0.474	0.332	1.43
Daily Show	−0.115	0.374	−0.31
MSNBC	−0.003	0.422	−0.01
Party ID	−0.296	0.089	−3.32
Fox News	−0.793	0.353	−2.24
Political knowledge	0.183	0.131	1.4
Ideology	0.017	0.175	0.09
Parent?	−0.068	0.286	−0.24
Constant	−1.052	0.633	−1.66

Models for the belief that specific elements are included in Common Core (see Table 9.40) were more complicated, involving interaction effects between media use, education and ideology. The sample size for this model was 579, with a pseudo r^2 of 0.02.

TABLE 9.40 Logit Model for Believing That Sex Education Is Included in Common Core

Predictor	B	Std. error	Z
Education	−0.474	0.418	−1.13
Age	−0.051	0.085	−0.61
African-American?	−0.114	0.306	−0.37
Daily Show	0.185	0.313	0.59
MSNBC	−1.368	2.780	−0.49
Party ID	−0.076	0.067	−1.12
Fox News	−6.738	3.153	−2.14
Ideology	−0.232	0.435	−0.53
Ideology × education	0.202	0.186	1.09
MSNBC × ideology	0.635	1.576	0.4
Fox × ideology	2.496	1.148	2.17
MSNBC × education	0.610	1.165	0.52
Fox × education	2.799	1.220	2.29
MSNBC × ideology × education	−0.242	0.681	−0.36
Fox × ideology × education	−0.998	0.450	−2.22
Constant	0.713	1.053	0.68

REFERENCES

Abramowitz, Alan I. 1995. "It's Abortion, Stupid: Policy Voting in the 1992 Presidential Election." *Journal of Politics* 57: 176–86.

Aldrich, John H. 1980. *Before the Convention: Strategies and Choices in Presidential Nomination Campaigns*. Chicago, IL: University of Chicago Press.

Alesina, Alberto. 1988. "Credibility and Policy Convergence in a Two-Party System with Rational Voters." *The American Economic Review* 78: 796–805.

Altman, Alex. 2008. "A Brief History of the War on Christmas." *Time* (December 24).

Ansolabehere, Stephen and Shanto Iyengar. 1995. *Going Negative: How Attack Ads Shrink and Polarize the Electorate*. New York: Free Press.

Ansolabehere, Stephen, Shanto Iyengar and Adam Simon. 1999. "Replicating Experiments Using Aggregate and Survey Data: The Case of Negative Advertising and Turnout." *American Political Science Review* 93: 901–9.

Ansolabehere, Stephen, Shanto Iyengar, Adam Simon and Nicholas Valentino. 1994. "Does Attack Advertising Demobilize the Electorate?" *American Political Science Review* 88: 829–38.

Arceneaux, Kevin and Martin Johnson. 2013. *Changing Minds or Changing Channels? Partisan News in an Age of Choice. Chicago Studies in American Politics*, ed. Benjamin I. Page, Susan Herbst, Lawrence R. Jacobs and Adam Berinsky. Chicago, IL: University of Chicago Press.

Arceneaux, Kevin, Martin Johnson and Chad Murphy. 2012. "Polarized Political Communication, Oppositional Media Hostility, and Selective Exposure." *Journal of Politics* 74: 174–86.

Bader, Christopher D., F. Carson Mencken and Paul Froese. 2007. "American Piety 2005: Content and Methods of the Baylor Religion Survey." *Journal for the Scientific Study of Religion* 46: 447–63.

Barilleaux, Ryan J. and Randall E. Adkins. 1992. "The Nomination: Process and Patterns." In *The Elections of 1992*, ed. Michael Nelson, 21–56. Washington, DC: CQ Press.

Barrett, Andrew W. and Matthew Eshbaugh-Soha. 2007. "Presidential Success on the Substance of Legislation." *Political Research Quarterly* 60: 100–112.

Bartels, Larry M. 1993. "Messages Received: The Political Impact of Media Exposure." *American Political Science Review* 87: 267–85.

Baum, Matthew A. 2002. "The Constituent Foundations of the Rally Round-the-Flag Phenomenon." *International Studies Quarterly* 46: 263–98.

Baum, Matthew A. and Tim Groeling. 2010. "Reality Asserts Itself: Public Opinion on Iraq and the Elasticity of Reality." *International Organization* 64: 443–79.

Beck, James W., Alison E. Carr and Philip T. Walmsley. 2012. "What Have You Done for Me Lately? Charisma Attenuates the Decline in US Presidential Approval over Time." *The Leadership Quarterly* 23: 934–42.

Beckman, Matthew N. and Joseph Godfrey. 2007. "The Policy Opportunities in Presidential Honeymoons." *Political Research Quarterly* 60: 250–62.

Bennett, W. Lance and Shanto Iyengar. 2008. "A New Era of Minimal Effects? The Changing Foundations of Political Communication." *Journal of Communication* 58: 707–31.

Berggren, Jason D. 2007. "Two Parties, Two Types of Nominees, Two Paths to Winning a Presidential Nomination, 1972–2004." *Presidential Studies Quarterly* 37: 203–27.

Birdsong, Daniel, Nate Ramsey and Misook Gwon. 2014. "Cable News: Audience Autonomy and Political Polarization." Paper presented at the APSA Annual Meeting, Washington, DC.

Bolsen, Toby and Thomas J. Leeper. 2013. "Self-Interest and Attention to News among Issue Publics." *Political Communication* 30: 329–48.

Box-Steffensmeier, Janet and Renee M. Smith. 1996. "The Dynamics of Aggregate Partisanship." *American Political Science Review* 90: 567–80.

Box-Steffensmeier, Janet and Renee M. Smith. 1998. "Investigating Political Dynamics Using Fractional Integration Methods." *American Journal of Political Science* 42: 661–89.

Brace, Paul and Barbara Hinckley. 1991. "The Structure of Presidential Approval: Constraints within and across Presidencies." *Journal of Politics* 53: 993–1,017.

Buell, Emmett H., Jr. 1987. "'Locals' and 'Cosmopolitans': State Newspaper Coverage of the New Hampshire Primary." In *Media and Momentum: The New Hampshire Primary and Nomination Politics*, ed. Gary R. Orren and Nelson W. Polsby, 60–103. Chatham, NJ: Chatham House.

Canes-Wrone, Brandice and Scott De Marchi. 2002. "Presidential Approval and Legislative Success." *Journal of Politics* 64: 491–509.

Carmines, Edward G. and James A. Stimson. 1980. "The Two Faces of Issue Voting." *American Political Science Review* 74: 78–91.

Caro, Robert. 1991. *Means of Ascent, The Years of Lyndon Johnson*. New York: Vintage.

Cassino, Dan, Charles S. Taber and Milton Lodge. 2007. "Information Processing and Public Opinion." *Politische Vierteljahresschrift* 48: 205–20.

Christenson, Dino P. and Corwin D. Smidt. 2012. "Still Part of the Conversation: Iowa and New Hampshire's Say within the Invisible Primary." *Presidential Studies Quarterly* 42: 597–621.

Cohen, Marty, David Karol, Hans Noel and John Zaller. 2008. *The Party Decides: Presidential Nominations before and after Reform*. Chicago, IL: University of Chicago Press.

Converse, Phillip E. 1966. "The Concept of a Normal Vote." In *Elections and the Political Order*, 9–39. New York: Wiley.

Deer, Brian. 2011. "How the Case against the MMR Vaccine Was Fixed." *BMJ* 342: 77–82.

DellaVigna, Stefano and Ethan Kaplan. 2007. "The Fox News Effect: Media Bias and Voting." *Quarterly Journal of Economics* 122: 1,187–234.

Delli Carpini, Michael X. and Scott Keeter. 1991. "Stability and Change in the US Public's Knowledge of Politics." *Public Opinion Quarterly* 55: 583–612.

Delli Carpini, Michael X. and Scott Keeter. 1993. "Measuring Political Knowledge: Putting First Things First." *American Journal of Political Science* 37: 1,179–206.

Delli Carpini, Michael X., Scott Keeter and J. David Kennamer. 1994. "Effects of the News Media Environment on Citizen Knowledge of State Politics and Government." *Journalism & Mass Communication Quarterly* 71: 443–56.

Dilliplane, Susanna, Seth K. Goldman and Diana C. Mutz. 2013. "Televised Exposure to Politics: New Measures for a Fragmented Media Environment." *American Journal of Political Science* 57: 236–48.

Dixon, Jo and Alan J. Lizotte. 1987. "Gun Ownership and the Southern Subculture of Violence." *American Journal of Sociology* 93: 383–405.

Druckman, James N. and Justin W. Holmes. 2004. "Does Presidential Rhetoric Matter? Priming and Presidential Approval." *Presidential Studies Quarterly* 34: 775–8.

Edwards, George C. and Alec Gallup. 1990. *Presidential Approval: A Sourcebook*. Baltimore, MD: Johns Hopkins University Press.

Eshbaugh-Soha, Matthew and Jeffrey S. Peake. 2005. "Presidents and the Economic Agenda." *Political Research Quarterly* 58: 127–38.

Eshbaugh-Soha, Matthew and Jeffrey S. Peake. 2011. *Breaking through the Noise: Presidential Leadership, Public Opinion and the News Media*. Stanford, CA: Stanford University Press.

Evans, Maggie, Helen Stoddart, Louise Condon, Elaine Freeman, Marg Grizzell and Rebecca Mullen. 2001. "Parents' Perspectives on the MMR Immunisation: A Focus Group Study." *British Journal of General Practice* 51: 904–10.

Farnsworth, Stephen J. and S. Robert Lichter. 2011. *The Nightly News Nightmare: Media Coverage of U.S. Presidential Elections, 1988–2008*. Lanham, MD: Rowman & Littlefield.

Fauvelle-Aymara, Christine and Mary Stegmaier. 2013. "The Stock Market and U.S. Presidential Approval." *Electoral Studies* 32: 411–17.

Feldman, Lauren, Edward W. Maibach, Connie Roser-Renouf and Anthony Leiserowitz. 2012. "Climate on Cable: The Nature and Impact of Global Warming Coverage on Fox News, CNN, and MSNBC." *The International Journal of Press/Politics* 17: 3–31.

Finkel, Steven E. 1993. "Reexamining the 'Minimal Effects' Model in Recent Presidential Campaigns." *Journal of Politics* 55: 1–21.

Finkel, Steven E. and John G. Geer. 1998. "A Spot Check: Casting Doubt on the Demobilizing Effect of Attack Advertising." *American Journal of Political Science* 42: 573–95.

Flamm, Michael W. 2005. *Law and Order: Street Crime, Civil Unrest, and the Crisis of Liberalism in the 1960s*. New York: Columbia University Press.

Franklin, Charles H. 1992. "Measurement and the Dynamics of Party Identification." *Political Behavior* 14: 297–309.

Fusarelli, Lance D. 2004. "The Potential Impact of the No Child Left Behind Act on Equity and Diversity in American Education." *Educational Policy* 18: 71–94.

Galston, William A. 2001. "Political Knowledge, Political Engagement, and Civic Education." *Annual Review of Political Science* 4: 216–34.

Garrett, R. Kelly and Natalie Jomini Stroud. 2014. "Partisan Paths to Exposure Diversity: Differences in Pro- and Counterattitudinal News Consumption." *Journal of Communication* 64: 680–701.

Garrett, R. Kelly, Dustin Carnahan and Emily K. Lynch. 2013. "A Turn toward Avoidance? Selective Exposure to Online Political Information, 2004–2008," *Political Behavior* 35: 113–34.

George, John and Laird M. Wilcox. 1996. *American Extremists: Militias, Supremacists, Klansmen, Communists & Others.* Amherst, NY: Prometheus Books.

Gerber, Alan S., Dean S. Karlan and Daniel Bergan. 2009. "Does the Media Matter? A Field Experiment Measuring the Effect of Newspapers on Voting Behavior and Political Opinions." *American Economic Journal: Applied Economics* 1: 35–52.

Gibson, John. 2005. *The War on Christmas: How the Liberal Plot to Ban the Sacred Christian Holiday Is Worse than You Thought.* New York: Sentinel.

Godlee, Fiona, Jane Smith and Harvey Marcovitch. 2011. "Wakefield's Article Linking MMR Vaccine and Autism Was Fraudulent." *BMJ* 342: 64–6.

Goldman, Seth K., Diana C. Mutz and Susanna Dilliplane. 2013. "All Virtue Is Relative: A Response to Prior." *Political Communication* 30: 635–53.

Gorecki, Maciej A. and Michael Marsh. 2012. "Not Just 'Friends and Neighbours': Canvassing, Geographic Proximity and Voter Choice." *European Journal of Political Research* 51: 563–82.

Granger, Clive W. 1980. "Long Memory Relationships and the Aggregation of Dynamic Models." *Journal of Econometrics* 14: 227–38.

Granger, Clive W. 1988a. "Causality, Cointegration, and Control." *Journal of Economic Dynamics and Control* 12: 551–9.

Granger, Clive W. 1988b. "Some Recent Development in a Concept of Causality." *Journal of Econometrics* 39: 199–211.

Green, Donald P. and Bradley Palmquist. 1994. "How Stable Is Party Identification?" *Political Behavior* 16: 437–66.

Groeling, Tim. 2008. "Who's the Fairest of Them All? An Empirical Test for Partisan Bias on ABC, CBS, NBC, and Fox News." *Presidential Studies Quarterly* 38: 628–52.

Gronke, Paul and John Brehm. 2002. "History, Heterogeneity, and Presidential Approval: A Modified Arch Approach." *Electoral Studies* 21: 425–52.

Hasen, Richard L. 2005. "Beyond the Margin of Litigation: Reforming US Election Administration to Avoid Electoral Meltdown." *Washington & Lee Law Review* 62: 937–1,000.

Hess, Frederick M. 2006. "Accountability without Angst? Public Opinion and No Child Left Behind." *Harvard Educational Review* 76: 587–610.

Hillygus, D. Sunshine and Todd G. Shields. 2014. *The Persuadable Voter: Wedge Issues in Presidential Campaigns.* Princeton, NJ: Princeton University Press.

Hofstadter, Richard. 2008/1966. *The Paranoid Style in American Politics.* New York: Vintage.

Hopkins, Daniel J. 2012. "Whose Economy? Perceptions of National Economic Performance During Unequal Growth." *Public Opinion Quarterly* 76: 50–71.

Hursh, David. 2007. "Assessing No Child Left Behind and the Rise of Neoliberal Education Policies." *American Educational Research Journal* 44: 493–518.

Iyengar, Shanto. 2014. "A Typology of Media Effects." In *The Oxford Handbook of Political Communication,* ed. Kate Kenski and Kathleen Hall Jamieson. New York: Oxford University Press. Published online September 2014. DOI: http://dx.doi.org/10.1093/oxfordhb/9780199793471.013.49.

Iyengar, Shanto and Donald R. Kinder. 2010. *News that Matters*. Chicago, IL: University of Chicago Press.

Jacobsen, Rebecca and Andrew Saultz. 2012. "The Polls – Trends: Who Should Control Education?" *Public Opinion Quarterly* 76: 379–90.

Jolley, Daniel and Karen M. Douglas. 2014. "The Effects of Anti-Vaccine Conspiracy Theories on Vaccination Intentions." *PLOS ONE* 9: e89177.

Karabell, Zachary. 2004. *Chester Alan Arthur: The 21st President, 1881–1885. The American Presidents*, vol. 21. New York: Macmillan.

Kata, Anna. 2012. "Anti-Vaccine Activists, Web 2.0, and the Postmodern Paradigm – an Overview of Tactics and Tropes Used Online by the Anti-Vaccination Movement." *Vaccine* 30: 3,778–89.

Katz, Elihu. 1957. "The Two-Step Flow of Communication: An Up-to-Date Report on an Hypothesis." *Public Opinion Quarterly* 21: 61–78.

Katz, Elihu and Paul F. Lazarsfeld. 1955. *Personal Influence*. Glencoe, IL: Free Press.

Kayden, Xandra. 1985. "Effects of the Present System of Campaign Financing on Special Interest Groups." In *Before Nomination: Our Primary Problems*, ed. George Grassmuck, 261–80. Washington, DC: American Enterprise Institute.

Keith, Bruce E., David B. Magleby, Candice J. Nelson, Elizabeth Orr and Mark C. Westlye. 1992. *The Myth of the Independent Voter*. Oakland, CA: University of California Press.

Krosnick, Jon A. 1989. "Attitude Importance and Attitude Accessibility." *Personality and Social Psychology Bulletin* 15: 297–308.

Kruschke, Earl Roger. 1991. *Encyclopedia of Third Parties in the United States*. Santa Barbara, CA: ABC-CLIO.

Kunda, Ziva. 1990. "The Case for Motivated Reasoning." *Psychological Bulletin* 108: 480–98.

Lau, Richard R. and David P. Redlawsk. 2001. "Advantages and Disadvantages of Cognitive Heuristics in Political Decision Making." *American Journal of Political Science* 45: 951–71.

Lau, Richard R. and David P. Redlawsk. 2006. *How Voters Decide: Information Processing in Election Campaigns*. Cambridge: Cambridge University Press.

Lau, Richard R., David J. Andersen and David P. Redlawsk. 2008. "An Exploration of Correct Voting in Recent US Presidential Elections." *American Journal of Political Science* 52: 395–411.

Lazarsfeld, Paul F., Bernard Berelson and Hazel Gaudet. 1948. *The People's Choice: How the Voter Makes Up His Mind in a Presidential Campaign*. New York: Columbia University Press.

Lebo, Matthew and Dan Cassino. 2007. "The Aggregated Consequences of Motivated Reasoning and the Dynamics of Partisan Presidential Approval." *Political Psychology* 28: 719–46.

Leonard, Thomas C. 1986. *The Power of the Press: The Birth of American Political Reporting*. Cambridge: Oxford University Press.

Levendusky, Matthew. 2013. *How Partisan Media Polarize America. Chicago Studies in American Politics*, ed. Benjamin I. Page, Susan Herbst, Lawrence R. Jacobs and Adam Berinsky. Chicago, IL: University of Chicago Press.

Lipsitz, Keena and Costas Panagopoulos. 2011. "Filled Coffers: Campaign Contributions and Contributors in the 2008 Elections." *Journal of Political Marketing* 10: 43–57.

Littlefield, Jon. 2013. "The US Gun Culture Seen through the Lens of Consumer Culture Theory: Self-Sufficiency, Safety, and Privacy." *Research in Consumer Behavior* 15: 25–40.

Lodge, Milton and Charles S. Taber. 2000. "Three Steps toward a Theory of Motivated Political Reasoning." In *Elements of Reason: Cognition, Choice, and the Bounds of Rationality*, ed. Arthur Lupia, Matthew D. McCubbins and Samuel L. Popkin, 183–213. Cambridge: Cambridge University Press.

Lodge, Milton and Charles S. Taber. 2005. "The Automaticity of Affect for Political Leaders, Groups, and Issues: An Experimental Test of the Hot Cognition Hypothesis." *Political Psychology* 26: 455–82.

Lodge, Milton, Kathleen M. McGraw and Patrick Stroh. 1989. "An Impression-Driven Model of Candidate Evaluation." *American Political Science Review* 83: 399–419.

Lupton, Robert N., Shane P. Singh and Judd R. Thornton. 2014. "The Moderating Impact of Social Networks on the Relationships among Core Values, Partisanship, and Candidate Evaluations." *Political Psychology* 36: 399–414.

Lynfield, Ruth and Robert S. Daum. 2014. "The Complexity of the Resurgence of Childhood Vaccine-Preventable Diseases in the United States." *Current Pediatric Reports* 2: 195–203.

MacKuen, Michael B. 1983. "Political Drama, Economic Conditions, and the Dynamics of Presidential Popularity." *American Journal of Political Science* 27: 165–92.

Manna, Paul. 2006. *School's In: Federalism and the National Education Agenda*. Washington, DC: Georgetown University Press.

Marshall, Bryan W. and Brandon C. Prins. 2007. "Strategic Position Taking and Presidential Influence in Congress." *Legislative Studies Quarterly* 32: 257–84.

Mayer, William G. 1996. "Forecasting Presidential Nominations." In *In Pursuit of the White House: How We Select Our Presidential Nominees*, ed. William G. Mayer, 44–71. London: Chatham House.

Mayer, William G. 2000. "The Presidential Nomination Process Reconsidered: The End of Momentum?" *Northeastern University Alumni Magazine* 25.

Mayer, William G. and Andrew E. Busch. 2004. *The Front Loading Problem in Presidential Nominations*. Washington, DC: Brookings Institution Press.

McAvoy, Gregory E. and Peter K. Enns. 2010. "Polls and Elections: Using Approval of the President's Handling of the Economy to Understand Who Polarizes and Why." *Presidential Studies Quarterly* 40: 545–58.

McGowen, Ernest B. and Daniel J. Palazzolo. 2014. "Momentum and Media in the 2012 Republican Presidential Nomination." *Presidential Studies Quarterly* 44: 431–46.

McGraw, Kathleen M., Milton Lodge and Patrick Stroh. 1990. "On-Line Processing in Candidate Evaluation: The Effects of Issue Order, Issue Importance, and Sophistication." *Political Behavior* 12: 41–58.

McKee, Seth C. and Daron R. Shaw. 2003. "Suburban Voting in Presidential Elections." *Presidential Studies Quarterly* 33: 125–44.

Miller, Joanne M. and Jon A. Krosnick. 2000. "News Media Impact on the Ingredients of Presidential Evaluations: Politically Knowledgeable Citizens Are Guided by a Trusted Source." *American Journal of Political Science* 44: 295–309.

Miller, John Chester and Alan M. Dershowitz. 1951. *Crisis in Freedom: The Alien and Sedition Acts*. New York: Little, Brown.

Mooney, Chris. 2012. *The Republican Brain: The Science of Why They Deny Science – and Reality*. New York: Wiley.

Morris, James P., Nancy Squires, Charles S. Taber and Milton Lodge. 2003. "Activation of Political Attitudes: A Psychophysiological Examination of the Hot Cognition Hypothesis." *Political Psychology* 24: 727–45.

Morris, Jonathan S. 2007. "Slanted Objectivity? Perceived Media Bias, Cable News Exposure, and Political Attitudes." *Social Science Quarterly* 88: 707–28.

Muddiman, Ashley, Natalie Jomini Stroud and Maxwell McCombs. 2014. "Media Fragmentation, Attribute Agenda Setting, and Political Opinions about Iraq." *Journal of Broadcasting & Electronic Media* 58: 215–33.

Muhlmann, Géraldine. 2008. *Political History of Journalism.* Washington, DC: Polity Press.

Mulligan, Kenneth, J. Tobin Grant, Stephen T. Mockabee and Joseph Quin Monson. 2003. "Response Latency Methodology for Survey Research: Measurement and Modeling Strategies." *Political Analysis* 11: 289–301.

Mutz, Diana C. 1995a. "Effects of Horse-Race Coverage on Campaign Coffers: Strategic Contributing in Presidential Primaries." *Journal of Politics* 57: 1,015–42.

Mutz, Diana C. 1995b. "Media, Momentum and Money: Horse Race Spin in the 1988 Republican Primaries." In *Polls and the News Media*, ed. Paul J. Lavrakas, Michael J. Traugott and Peter V. Miller, 229–54. Boulder, CO: Westview Press.

Mutz, Diana C. 1997. "Mechanisms of Momentum: Does Thinking Make It So?". *Journal of Politics* 59: 104–25.

Nam, H. Hannah, John T. Jost and Jay J. Van Bavel. 2013. "'Not for All the Tea in China!' Political Ideology and the Avoidance of Dissonance-Arousing Situations." *PLOS ONE* 8: e59837.

Nelson, Thomas E., Rosalee A. Clawson and Zoe M. Oxley. 1997. "Media Framing of a Civil Liberties Conflict and Its Effect on Tolerance." *American Political Science Review* 91: 567–83.

Neundorf, Anja and Richard G. Niemi. 2014. "Beyond Political Socialization: New Approaches to Age, Period, Cohort Analysis." *Electoral Studies* 33: 1–6.

Norrander, Barbara. 2013. "Fighting Off Challengers: The 2012 Nomination of Mitt Romney." In *The American Elections of 2012*, ed. Janet Box-Steffensmeier and Steven S. Schier, 48–72. New York: Routledge.

Norton, Michael I. and Samuel R. Sommers. 2011. "Whites See Racism as a Zero-Sum Game that They Are Now Losing." *Perspectives on Psychological Science* 6: 215–18.

Oliver, J. Eric and Thomas J. Wood. 2014. "Conspiracy Theories and the Paranoid Style(s) of Mass Opinion." *American Journal of Political Science* 58: 952–66.

Panagopoulos, Costas and Jeffrey E. Cohen. 2014. "Assessing the 2012 US Presidential Election." *Presidential Studies Quarterly* 44: 384–8.

Patterson, Thomas E. 1980. *The Mass Media Election.* New York: Praeger.

Patterson, Thomas E. 1993. *Out of Order.* New York: Knopf.

Perlstein, Rick. 2000. *Nixonland: The Rise of a President and the Fracturing of America.* New York: Scribner.

Peterson, Paul E. and Martin R. West, eds. 2003. *No Child Left Behind? The Politics and Practice of School Accountability.* Washington, DC: Brookings Institution Press.

Pew Project for Excellence in Journalism. 2010. "Nielsen Analysis." http://www.stateofthemedia.org/2010/special-reports-economic-attitudes/nielsen-analysis/.

Prins, Brandon C. and Steven A. Shull. 2006. "Enduring Rivals: Presidential Success and Support in the House of Representatives." *Congress & the Presidency* 33: 21–46.

Prior, Markus. 2007. *Post-Broadcast Democracy: How Media Choice Increases Inequality in Political Involvement and Polarizes Elections.* New York: Cambridge University Press.

Prior, Markus. 2009. "Improving Media Effects Research through Better Measurement of News Exposure." *Journal of Politics* 71: 893–908.

Prior, Markus. 2013. "The Challenge of Measuring Media Exposure: Reply to Dilliplane, Goldman, and Mutz." *Political Communication* 30: 620–34.

Redlawsk, David P. 2002. "Hot Cognition or Cool Consideration? Testing the Effects of Motivated Reasoning on Political Decision Making." *Journal of Politics* 64: 1,021–44.

Reeves, Thomas C. 1970. "The Mystery of Chester Alan Arthur's Birthplace." *Vermont History* 38: 291–304.

Rehnquist, William H. 2007. *Centennial Crisis: The Disputed Election of 1876.* New York: Random House.

Ridout, Travis and Michael Franz. 2011. *The Persuasive Power of Campaign Advertising.* Philadelphia, PA: Temple University Press.

Robinson, Michael J. and Margaret Sheehan. 1983. *Over the Wire and on TV: CBS and UPI in Campaign '80.* New York: Russell Sage.

Rosenfeld, Richard. 1997. *American Aurora: The Suppressed History of Our Nation's Beginnings and the Heroic Newspaper that Tried to Report It.* New York: St. Martin's Press.

Scacco, Joshua M. and Cynthia Peacock. 2013. "The Cross-Pressured Citizen in the 2012 Presidential Campaign: Formative Factors and Media Choice Behavior." *American Behavioral Scientist* 58: 1,214–35.

Schroeder, Elizabeth and Daniel F. Stone. 2014. "Fox News and Political Knowledge." *Journal of Public Economics* 126: 52–63.

Schwarz, Norbert and Daphna Oyserman. 2001. "Asking Questions about Behavior: Cognition, Communication, and Questionnaire Construction." *American Journal of Evaluation* 22: 127–60.

Seate, Anita Atwell, Elizabeth L. Cohen, Yuki Fujioka and Cynthia Hoffner. 2012. "Exploring Gun Ownership as a Social Identity to Understanding the Perceived Media Influence of the Virginia Tech News Coverage on Attitudes toward Gun Control Policy." *Communication Research Reports* 29: 130–39.

Shepherd, Steven and Aaron C. Kay. 2012. "On the Perpetuation of Ignorance: System Dependence, System Justification, and the Motivated Avoidance of Sociopolitical Information." *Journal of Personality and Social Psychology* 102: 264–80.

Sherman, Gabriel. 2014. *The Loudest Voice in the Room: How the Brilliant, Bombastic Roger Ailes Built Fox News and Divided a Country.* New York: Random House.

Simon, Dennis M. and Charles W. Ostrom. 1989. "The Impact of Televised Speeches and Foreign Travel on Presidential Approval." *Public Opinion Quarterly* 53: 58–82.

Smith, Charles Anthony and Christopher Shortell. 2007. "The Suits that Counted: The Judicialization of Presidential Elections." *Election Law Journal* 6: 251–65.

Sokhey, Anand Edward and Scott D. McClurg. 2012. "Social Networks and Correct Voting." *Journal of Politics* 74: 751–64.

Steger, Wayne P. 2000. "Do Primary Voters Draw from a Stacked Deck? Presidential Nominations in an Era of Candidate-Centered Campaigns." *Presidential Studies Quarterly* 30: 727–52.

Steger, Wayne P. 2008. "Forecasting the Presidential Primary Vote: Viability, Ideology and Momentum." *International Journal of Forecasting* 24: 193–208.

Steger, Wayne P. 2013. "Two Paradigms of Presidential Nominations." *Presidential Studies Quarterly* 43: 377–87.

Steger, Wayne P., Andrew J. Dowdle and Randall E. Adkins. 2004. "The New Hampshire Effect in Presidential Nominations." *Political Research Quarterly* 57: 375–90.

Stromer-Galley, Jennifer. 2014. *Presidential Campaigning in the Internet Age.* Oxford: Oxford University Press.

Sunstein, Cass. 2007. *Republic.Com 2.0.* Princeton, NJ: Princeton University Press.

Taber, Charles S. and Milton Lodge. 2006. "Motivated Skepticism in the Evaluation of Political Beliefs." *American Journal of Political Science* 50: 755–69.

Turner, Joel. 2007. "The Messenger Overwhelming the Message: Ideological Cues and Perceptions of Bias in Television News." *Political Behavior* 29: 441–64.

TV by the Numbers. 2013. "List of How Many Homes Each Cable Network Is in – Cable Network Coverage Estimates as of August 2013." http://tvbythenumbers. zap2it.com/2013/08/23/list-of-how-many-homes-each-cable-networks-is-in-cable-network-coverage-estimates-as-of-august-2013/199072/.

Vallone, Robert P., Lee Ross and Mark R. Lepper. 1985. "The Hostile Media Phenomenon: Biased Perception and Perceptions of Media Bias in Coverage of the Beirut Massacre." *Journal of Personality and Social Psychology* 49: 577–85.

van Prooijen, Jan-Willem 2012. "Suspicions of Injustice: The Sense-Making Function of Belief in Conspiracy Theories." In *Justice and Conflicts: Theoretical and Empirical Contributions*, ed. Elisabeth Kals and Jürgen Maes, 121–32. Berlin: Springer.

Wattenberg, Martin P. and Craig Leonard Brians. 1999. "Negative Campaign Advertising: Demobilizer or Mobilizer?" *American Political Science Review* 93: 891–9.

INDEX